A Cultural History of
Cuba during the U.S. Occupation,
1898–1902

*A book in the series
Latin America in Translation /
en Traducción / em Tradução*

*Sponsored by the Consortium in
Latin American Studies at the
University of North Carolina
at Chapel Hill and
Duke University*

A Cultural History of Cuba during the U.S. Occupation, 1898–1902

Marial Iglesias Utset

Translated by Russ Davidson

THE UNIVERSITY OF
NORTH CAROLINA PRESS
Chapel Hill

Translation of the books in the series Latin America in Translation / en Traducción / em Tradução, a collaboration between the Consortium in Latin American Studies at the University of North Carolina at Chapel Hill and Duke University and the university presses of the University of North Carolina and Duke, is supported by a grant from the Andrew W. Mellon Foundation.

Originally published in Spanish by Ediciones Unión in Havana, Cuba, as *Las metáforas del cambio en la vida cotidiana: Cuba, 1898–1902,* © 2003 Marial Iglesias Utset and Ediciones Unión.
The paper in this book meets the guidelines for permanence and durability of the Committee on Production Guidelines for Book Longevity of the Council on Library Resources.

The University of North Carolina Press has been a member of the Green Press Initiative since 2003.

Library of Congress Cataloging-in-Publication Data
Iglesias Utset, Marial, 1961–
[Metáforas del cambio en la vida cotidiana. English]
A cultural history of Cuba during the U.S. occupation, 1898-1902 / Marial Iglesias Utset ; translated by Russ Davidson.
p. cm. —
(Latin America in translation / en traducción / em tradução)
Includes bibliographical references and index.
ISBN 978-0-8078-3398-8 (cloth : alk. paper)
ISBN 978-0-8078-7192-8 (pbk : alk. paper)
1. National characteristics, Cuban. 2. Cuba—History—1899-1906.
3. Cuba—Civilization—American influences. I. Title.
F1787.I5613 2011
972.9106'1—dc22   2010045626
cloth 15 14 13 12 11   5 4 3 2 1
paper 15 14 13 12 11   5 4 3 2 1

CONTENTS

A section of illustrations appears after page 86.

TRANSLATOR'S NOTE

Among other things, this book is about how the language of one country—through trade and direct investment, tourism, the inflow of people and cultural artifacts, and outright military occupation and neocolonial practice—invades and takes root in the language of another. Thus in different sections of the text, as part of her description and analysis of the U.S. presence in Cuba, Marial Iglesias Utset cites and discusses the abrupt appearance and use of English-language words, expressions, and figures of speech imported and adopted from the United States. To emphasis how incongruous or jarring these were (at least initially) within the Cuban milieu, she italicizes them. To preserve the effect but also avoid the confusion this practice might cause in the translated text, I have instead put quotation marks around such words and expressions. Elsewhere, on first use in each chapter, Spanish words with no common English equivalents appear in italics. My treatment of the Spanish word *patria* likewise calls for clarification. Since no single term in English adequately conveys its different shades of meaning, I have translated it variously as "country," "motherland," "fatherland," "homeland," and "nation," depending on what best suits the context.

The text and notes also contain several poems. I hope that in freely translating these, I have managed (where called for) to convey their mocking irreverence and playful tone. I have also tried to maintain the stanza form but not the metrical line or rhyming scheme of the originals, since that, in essence, would require that one be a poet himself—something I clearly am not.

ACKNOWLEDGMENTS

A great many people, some of whom came to my aid with their time, books, knowledge, and experience, and others simply with their unconditional caring and devotion, have been key to the completion of this book.

In the first instance, I would like to thank my scholarly adviser, María del Carmen Barcia, for her intellectual generosity and her many valuable suggestions. I am also grateful to Oscar Zanetti, Oscar Loyola, Berta Álvarez, and Olga Portuondo, each of whom read and offered insightful observations on the initial results of my research.

The critical comments made by Jorge Ibarra, Alejandro García, and Gloria García helped me to clarify and sharpen the central themes and topics of this book. Moreover, it was through reading Jorge Ibarra's book that I became particularly interested in studying the interweaving of nationalism and popular culture.

A great many of the ideas which I expound in this work grew out of the exchanges that took place—over a period of years—among the members of a workshop of young historians. The group was organized and overseen by Professor Carmen Almodóvar of the University of Havana, and I am deeply grateful for her enthusiasm and belief in the future and for the confidence that she placed in me. Likewise, Imilcy Balboa, Manuel Barcia, Joel Cordoví, Mercedes García, Latvia Gaspe, Blancamar León, Adrián López, Rolando Misa, and—in particular—Yolanda Díaz, Leida Fernández, Reinaldo Funes, Julio González, Oilda Hevia, Ricardo Quiza, and Pablo Riaño—friends, colleagues, and fellow workshop members—listened with the utmost patience as I addressed the same themes time and time again, offering me not only their intelligent comments, bibliographic suggestions, and references to archival source material, but also the warmth and reassurance of their friendship.

Francisco Pérez Guzmán and Enrique López generously shared with me information and ideas accumulated during many years of historical research. I am grateful for their regard and collaboration, as I am for that of Orlando García, director of the Archivo Histórico Provincial of Cienfuegos, and Fernando Martínez.

I also owe a considerable intellectual debt to a group of historians in the U.S. academic community whose work I have closely followed in recent years.

In large measure, it was the publications of Louis A. Pérez Jr. which led me to concentrate on the complex and fascinating period that I have chosen. His personal efforts and the financial assistance granted me by the American Council of Learned Societies/Social Science Research Council afforded me the opportunity to examine a part of the extensive documentary resources on Cuba held in both the U.S. National Archives and the collections of the Library of Congress. I have learned a great deal from the work done by Rebecca J. Scott, work that is meticulous, painstaking, and yet highly imaginative; I am grateful to her and to Michael Zeuske, professor and research historian at the University of Cologne, Germany, for the support they have given me as well as for the fruitful intellectual exchanges which they arranged, among a "transnational" community of researchers, during the course of meetings and workshops held in Cienfuegos, Havana, Santiago de Cuba, and Cologne.

I owe a special debt of gratitude to Franklin D. Knight, who took time out of a packed schedule to translate an abbreviated version of my work into English. The research conducted by Aline Helg and Ada Ferrer helped shape the approaches I have taken in this study toward the subjects of race and nationalism, and I thank Ada Ferrer, as well as David Sartorius, José Amador, Reinaldo Román, Alejandra Bronfman, and Marikay McCabe not only for sharing texts and ideas but for the concern and affection they have shown me throughout this project, a bond strong enough to overcome any tendency on my part to become isolated or blocked in my work.

It was my reading a little more than seven years ago of the writings of Arcadio Díaz Quiñones on Puerto Rico and Cuba which prompted me to take up the study of the complexities underlying the transition to postcolonial society and to reflect on the symbolic dimension of the changes which occurred as a result of this process. The present work is the direct descendant of that early interest and inquiry. At the same time, the work of Díaz Quiñones's colleague, distinguished Puerto Rican sociologist Ángel G. (Chuco) Quintero, opened my eyes to the rich and multifaceted world of popular culture.

I am particularly indebted to Lillian Guerra, a North American by birth but a Cuban in heart and soul: her moral, intellectual, and material support, extended unconditionally, helped me to overcome numerous obstacles and to stand fast in the midst of difficult moments. Thanks to her willing intercession I was able to carry out research in the Trinidad archive and gain access to documents preserved in the Harvard University Archives, which she kindly reproduced for me. It is both a duty and a privilege to acknowledge, as directly as I can, her extraordinary generosity and spirit of collaboration.

I am also grateful for the assistance given to me by María Dolores Pratt,

Niurys Guerrero, and Lourdes Morales, specialists in the rare book division of the University of Havana's central library, and to Jorge Macle, Julio López, Isabel Mariño, Isabel Oviedo, Julio Vargas (Varguitas), and Olga Pedierro, of Cuba's National Archive, for their generous and able assistance in helping me locate pertinent documents. Marlene Ortega and Patria Cook in particular went to great lengths to pursue specific data for me and to suggest new sources of information. I extend thanks to all of these dedicated archivists and librarians.

In addition, I would like to note the contributions of Lourdes Torres de la Fe, whose attentive professionalism helped improve the readability of the manuscript, of friend and mentor Juan Francisco Fuentes, whose capacity for understanding is inexhaustible, and—especially—of Ramón Ranero, without whose logistical support and unlimited goodwill I could not have written this book. A similar vote of thanks goes to Lourdes Alonso, Grisel Ramírez, and José A. Blanco Ranero, truly "partners" of mine through times both good and bad. Ivette Rodríguez and Ana González watched over my children and my home, compensating for my absence with their warmth and diligent attentiveness. Luis Mariano López made life easier by transporting me on numerous occasions to the very doorstep of the National Archive in Old Havana.

Finally, I wish to thank my family. It was their support through thick and thin that made it possible for me to reach this point. My father, Alfonso Iglesias, my siblings Ana and Alfonso Ricardo Iglesias, my aunts, and ultimately, the entire Iglesias clan are behind every line of this book. Ileana Valmaña, exemplary grandmother that she is, was always there when my children needed her. To my companion, Alexander Canoura, I offer all my gratitude for his love, generosity, and dedication. One person in particular, my aunt, Fe Iglesias, was at my side in this enterprise from the beginning to the end. From her I inherited both the love of old documents and the monastic-like patience which historians need to fulfill their arduous but fascinating task. Step by step she revealed to me the secrets of the archives and encouraged me to persevere whenever I found myself on the point of giving up. In large measure this book belongs to her, as it is does to my children Cristina, Jesús, and José Antonio —who are equally the victims of my passion for history and the source of all my inspiration.

A Cultural History of
Cuba during the U.S. Occupation,
1898–1902

Introduction

Passing through Cuba's cities and towns a little more than a century ago, a traveler would have noticed bright new street signs that bore the names of the country's political and military heroes, for this was a time in Cuba when the *mambises* (Cuban Liberation Army combatants who fought in the nineteenth-century wars against Spain) had yet to be turned into statues in public parks or become characters in comic strips and children's histories but were still persons of flesh and blood, a time when the War of Independence (1895–98) was not simply a tale in a school textbook but a vivid reality, when José Martí's metamorphosis into the "Apostle" had only recently happened, and when General Máximo Gómez still walked bolt upright through the streets of Havana, encountered by its residents as a living man, not just as the figure depicted on a ten-peso note.

It was a time in the country's history when documents were signed with the words "Motherland and Freedom [*Patria y Libertad*]" rather than "Motherland or Death [*Patria o Muerte*]," when the anniversaries of 10 October and 24 February, which mark the beginning of the wars of liberation against Spain, were not just "nonwork" days or days denoted on the calendar, but genuinely popular, festive celebrations, complete with street music and dancing in communities across the island; a time when the "Bayamesa" was a fashionable tune, hummed or whistled in streets and public places; when *décimas* (a form of sung poetry) composed in honor of the Cuban flag filled the pages of popular songbooks, when the Cuban coat of arms was stitched onto the handkerchiefs young men gave their sweethearts, and when belt buckles, or brooches pinned in the hair or on the chest, were decorated with the "single star."

In those days, too, the flag of the United States flew over the fortress of El Morro, and English had replaced Spanish as the official language employed in Cuban government offices. Furthermore, in what seemed like an instantaneous transformation, Havana's *barberías* had become "barber shops," and many of the stores on Obispo—a principal street in the center of the capital—were suddenly filled with U.S. goods and products. The stores also took care to post signs at their entrance, announcing, in large letters, "English Spoken Here." At the same time, high society began to celebrate "teas" and "garden parties"; while young men played "sports," and both women and young ladies liberated from a purely domestic life became known as "new women" and took up jobs "out in the world" as "typists" or "nurses" in offices and hospitals. Seemingly from one day to the next the urban landscape was also transformed, as streetcars and lines for electric lights and telephones rapidly made their appearance. A new element of "comfort" was introduced into Cuban homes with the installation of modern toilets "made in the U.S.A."

The several essays which make up this book attempt to isolate and recapture this unique and complex juncture in the history of Cuba, when the end of the War of Independence against the Spanish metropole and the beginning of the U.S. military occupation set the stage for a time of internal contradiction and confusion. Cuba in this transitional period—the twilight of one century, the dawn of another—was characterized by ambiguity, occupying an indeterminate middle space as neither colony nor sovereign state. While the country had made a definitive break with its colonial past, there was little clarity or agreement about its future shape and direction. Against the background of the symbolic void created by the formal end of more than four hundred years of Spanish colonial rule, a battle broke out among three segments of the Cuban polity: the proponents of a strident nationalism, the advocates of a forceful "Americanization" of Cuban customs and institutions, and the defenders of the Spanish cultural heritage, for whom the greatest threat was the powerful influence of the Anglo-Saxon model of modernization.

The years separating the end of the War of Independence in 1898, facilitated by the U.S. intervention in the conflict, and the proclamation of the Cuban Republic in 1902, thus served as a kind of crossroads between two centuries and—in Louis Pérez's apt phrase—"two empires."[1] The dismantling of Spanish colonial rule went hand in hand with the project of transforming the institutions of Cuban society according to the model of "modernity" and "progress" represented by the United States. Yet the restructuring of institutions and social practices, while deemed a necessary condition for modernizing society —an objective long sought by the Cuban nationalist elites—carried a steep price, since it subjected the country to a process of neocolonial domination by the United States, which by now had taken up the mantle of world imperial power.

At the same time, the sharp clash between values and customs inherited from the colonial period and a new set of political and cultural norms championed by the interventionist authorities led Cubans collectively to question what elements lay at the core of their "national culture." The refashioning of these cultural elements into a new symbolic representation of *cubanía* (the belief in a unique Cuban identity and national consciousness) was accomplished through the creative manipulation of a host of rituals and symbols, along with the elaboration of new historical narratives to explain the country's past. It also involved the adoption of novel practices and conventions, some of which had a formality that was tied to the exercise of citizenship, while others—such as new habits of hygiene or different ways of dressing, eating, and dancing—were more prosaic in nature.

The varying themes entertained in the nationalist discourse, ideas embedded in the Spanish colonial cultural legacy, and viewpoints associated with the U.S. presence were all translated into different systems of signs (images, gestures, inscriptions found in public spaces, rituals, and celebrations). At times, these coexisted and intermixed in a perfectly innocuous or nonantagonistic way. At other times, however, they were arrayed against each other, deployed as weapons in battles that determined the contours of cultural hegemony during this period.

The change that took place in people's ways of thinking and manner of living, a change brimming with contradiction, strongly affected the sphere of everyday life and imbued symbolic practices, even the most ordinary, with new political significance. Under conditions of "normality," daily life is characterized by repetitive cycles of commonplace activities whose meanings are taken for granted. Indeed, their very existence frequently goes unnoticed, since they are not the object of conscious attention. However, during transitional or threshold phases, such as the one under study, the opposite is true—our sensitivities are heightened and apparently banal practices, which in ordinary times seem devoid of any particular ideological importance, suddenly become laden with political meanings. In these situations, two things happen: the strands that weave together life's routines and common spaces, those connections we normally never notice, abruptly stand out, become objectified; and the ensemble of unformulated, implicitly shared conventions which make up what in a vague way we call common sense without warning becomes problematic.

The decentering nature of this experience is intensified when (modernizing) projects and (nationalist) aspirations encompass society in toto. In this way, during Cuba's "between empires" period, day-to-day, seemingly run-of-the-mill decisions, such as whether to go about in the traditional manner on horseback or to eschew that means of travel in favor of the modern but "American" bicycle; whether at parties one should choose to dance the *danzón* or the two-step; whether on Sundays to faithfully attend mass or to play baseball; whether in street processions to march in an orderly way while singing patriotic anthems reminiscent of Europe or to snake to a conga rhythm, accompanied by the beating of drums—all these simple matters rapidly acquired a political coloration, becoming the subject of heated debate and the objects of either praise or censure.

It is precisely this order of sociocultural, quotidian, and small-scale change on which I try to focus in this work. The institutional changes which the watershed of 1898 wrought on Cuba's administrative entities, its form of government, party-political system and associations, and macroeconomy are the superstructure, the "big events" of the time. My interest lies in exploring how such events were translated on a symbolic level and expressed, often in discordant and oppositional ways, in the details and routines of everyday life.

The "grand narratives" that define Cuban history and historiography in this period have been organized around transformative political developments, such as the convention of 1901, whose delegates deliberated and approved both the country's future republican constitution as well as the Platt Amendment, through which the ties of "singular intimacy" that linked the island to the United States not only received legal sanction but were woven into a strict neocolonial fabric. These narratives, however, are complemented by a range of more finely grained, less dramatic stories, which—though the focus of much less attention on the part of historians—are nonetheless of equal relevance to understanding Cuba in this period. Research devoted to this type of activity must concern itself with what is contingent and shifting in human experience, that realm of action and behavior which Michel de Certeau calls the silent practices and operations of everyday life, a realm in which there are neither heroes nor villains but simply plain, anonymous men and women, entangled in a web of ongoing, apparently inconsequential activities, immersed in the muffled clamor of ordinary happenings.[2]

To emphasize how symbolic gestures were translated and incorporated into everyday routines is not, however, to limit or downgrade the subject to the description of local folkways and customs, nor is it to deemphasize or devalue the high politics of Cuba's transition from Spanish colony to neocolonial state. Relationships of power, as expressed in struggles concerning the exercise of political hegemony, the decolonization of the country, and the new imperial presence, as well as in contending viewpoints about the rights and privileges of citizenship and the deeper question of what it means to belong to a national community, continue to figure centrally in my analysis. I simply examine these matters in another dimension, what Michel Foucault might call "the capillary."

The political changes taking place in Cuba were reflected within the physical space of urban landscapes, reified in walls, public squares, and buildings; they were internalized and normalized through the adoption of new mannerisms, fashions, ceremonies, and rites; and were realized within the arena of everyday practice in the form of "meetings" (for the English word was used), processions, fiestas, and graveside burials. In this way, the emblems and more allusive symbols of the Spanish monarchy disappeared not only from the facades of government buildings and the stamped paper used for official documents but from more commonplace objects as well, such as personal letterhead, the illustrations found in calendars and almanacs, and postage stamps. The widespread appearance of consumer merchandise coming "from the north" —clothing and shoes, canned goods, and other domestic items, together with a range of products utilizing the superior technology of the U.S. manufacturing base, like telephones, sewing machines, bicycles, electric lamps and fans (including even certain electrically powered belts which were promised to restore male sexual vigor)—coincided with a major renovation and modernization of public walkways and parks, state buildings, and private residences, self-consciously carried out in line with U.S. architectural styles and patterns of urban development.

Yet at the same time, and as a kind of counterpoint to the growing "Americanization" of Cuban life, the country also witnessed an intensely nationalist "rebranding" of its urban spaces. Cuban flags were flown from houses and business establishments, and plaques, burial mounds, and modest monuments were put up in many places to honor the memory of the wars of 1868–78 and 1895–98 and their human cost. A new set of patriotic place names "effaced" the colonial and monarchical past and inscribed—in quite literal terms—the allegories of "republican" nationalist discourse on the network of streets and public squares in the majority of the island's cities and communities. The past was likewise purged from the almanacs—days set aside to honor Spain and the royal family disappeared, replaced by new Cuban nationalist celebrations, which, in an oddly mixed way, shared space with dates, such as 4 July and 22 August, taken from the U.S. calendar of civic celebrations.

Far from silencing demonstrations of nationalism, the imperialist designs underlying the policy initiatives of the U.S. military occupation (designs that at times were also markedly racist and class-based) actually succeeded in catalyzing them. The island's nationalist sectors also reacted against the moralistic

North American campaign, which formed part of the U.S. "civilizing mission," warmly endorsed by some sectors of Cuban society, to modernize the country. By recourse to a wide variety of written, verbal, and visual forms of communication, Cubans across all parts of the island endeavored to trace, celebrate, and above all display before the eyes of the interventionist authorities the existence of a sense of national identity.

In defense of their right to be treated not as natives or as mere inhabitants of a territory occupied by military force but as future citizens of a national republic, Cubans laid claim to a fundamental principle and characteristic— their spirited and patriotic civic-mindedness, earned at the expense of great "sacrifice and blood" over the thirty years which transpired between the wars of 1868–78 and 1895–98. Thus any number of occasions, such as the birthday or the anniversary of the death of the "martyrs of the Fatherland," but above all the dates marking the beginning of the wars against Spain, became the pretext to hold demonstrations and meetings, at which flags and banners were displayed, anthems sung, fiery nationalist speeches delivered, and the citizenship enjoyed by all reflected in the celebration of community-wide activities. Such occasions, moreover, enabled the indwelling civic-mindedness of Cubans to be put on full public display.

An attempt to acculturate the country to North American values and practices through the device of making English an obligatory part of the Cuban school curriculum also sparked an intense nationalist backlash which, ironically, renewed belief in the Spanish cultural tradition, many elements of which had been cast into doubt. Embodied in words and language, Hispanic culture had to be preserved at all costs as a vital means of resistance against the aggressive spread of Anglo-Saxon culture.

Despite (or perhaps due to) the absence of a Cuban state with the means and power to foster nationalism on a massive, institutional scale, these years were characterized by the participation of an influential elite of political figures and intellectuals who—sometimes in collaboration with the interventionist authorities, sometimes in opposition to them—strove to inculcate in Cubans acceptance of the new idea that they belonged to a national community by promoting public discussion and displays of the same. This effort by the elite unfolded within and was dominated by the process of "inventing tradition," in which, ironically, the same "fluid and interchangeable" repertoire of formulas that framed U.S. nationalism was used to mold Cuban citizens who would be "imbued with a national spirit."

However, in contrast to studies which place undue emphasis on the "artificial" and "constructed" character of nationalism, viewing it as an ideology manufactured for hegemonic purposes by educated elites in the founding of modern national states, my work takes a different approach. It analyzes the development of an extensive corpus of symbols, images, and discourses which—as essential components of the nationalist imagination—are both cause and effect of a political and cultural process of great complexity. If it is true that intellectual and political elites play an important role in this process, it is also true that the participation "from below" of subaltern groups cannot be ignored or diminished.[3]

Benedict Anderson, whose work on nationalism has reached a wide audience in recent decades, stresses the importance of the printed word, the periodical press in particular, in forging the ties of solidarity which constitute "the imagined community of the nation."[4] Yet, in the case of societies like that of late nineteenth-century Cuba, in large measure still agrarian and with a national illiteracy rate above 66 percent, it is necessary to go beyond the study of the circulation and reception of written material in considering the diffusion of what Anderson has called "print-capitalism."

The study of certain phenomena (less textual, more performative in nature), such as the countless fiestas, marches, burials, and other public ceremonies which flowered more or less spontaneously in Cuba's towns and small cities during these years, allows one to document more fully and accurately the span of popular participation in both the efforts made by different sectors and interest groups to validate the existence of the imagined community of the nation and the creation of the symbolic languages through which this entity took shape.

A décima recited or sung, a joke passed from one person to another, or a political argument turned into the refrain of a popular couplet that is not just read but danced to (perhaps to the sound of drums) in street demonstrations, opens up a different type of communication, one which transcends the narrower (and elitist) limits of formal writing. These modes of expression, repeated time and again in popular venues far removed from the political forums and chambers in which official policy was "concocted" or from the scenes of bourgeois social interaction typical of the educated urban elites, give convincing evidence of the participation of many thousands of uneducated individuals, who at this time constituted the majority of the Cuban population, in the formation of political platforms and opinion.

Undoubtedly, the main obstacle to this genre of study is the precariousness and evanescent character of many of the sources. To rescue from the past the little written (or visual) evidence saved out of what was once a vibrant and expansive oral and performative culture, and then—calling on one's imagination—to assemble the surviving shreds of these popular forms of political expression into a coherent narrative line, is a major challenge. To meet it, and clear the obstacle, I have complemented my examination of three principal sources—the central Havana press, the numerous reports and memoirs authored by persons who served in the U.S. government of occupation, and official documents preserved in Cuban and U.S. archives—with the extensive consultation of local source material. The minutes of municipal councils, the far-flung but extraordinarily rich provincial press, and local histories and memoirs, as well as a mass of highly diverse documentation, such as private correspondence, popular poetry, broadsides, commercial advertisements and other printed ephemera, almanacs, and prints and photographs, disclose—if only partially—the existence in this period of a flourishing political culture generated "from below," diffuse and relatively inarticulate, at times antiestablishment in tone and substance, at other times proestablishment or accommodationist, but in all cases overflowing with creativity.

The shaping of ideologies of Cuban nationalism during this period, and the continuation of this process into the twentieth century, was influenced by another critical transformation: Cuban national identity, and its corollary of cubanía, which had been defined in relation and by comparison to the Spanish metropole, now came to be defined against the existence of and distancing from a new "other": U.S. imperialism. This process, however, was anything but linear or unitary, nor was the notion and representation of a national "us" either seamless or homogenous. On the contrary, it was contested and fractured, riven by class tension and by ethnic and racial conflict, which resurfaced sharply after the end of the War of Independence. And the "other," the "foreign" element and presence—increasingly embodied not in Spain but in the occupation government—was at once hated and admired, rejected and imitated. In the eyes of many Cubans at this time, the North Americans represented an alien force which, capped by its intrusive military presence, prevented the nation from "taking shape" and attaining the status of an independent republic. At the same time, however, the people of the United States were also seen in a positive, fraternal light insofar as they embodied the ideal of modernity and social progress sought for the island: the fantasy of a perfect civic order in which equality, the spontaneous expression of the democratic spirit, and the energy of modern progressivism would be harmoniously integrated. Thus, the reformulation of a national "us" was complicated and convoluted; it progressed through an intricate process of compromise and accommodation, a process defined by its malleability and permeable boundaries, in which notions of identity were in constant flux within a larger struggle—both concrete and symbolic—to control the levers of power and the dynamics of political representation. As Louis Pérez has shown, this tense but exceptionally productive relationship with the new "intimate enemy," a relationship that began to be institutionalized in precisely the period under study here, is vitally important in understanding the evolution of Cuba's political and cultural history up to the present day.[5]

To the extent that we leave behind the realm of the purely discursive, that terrain par excellence of the "high dramas" of official ceremony and of the rigid dualities of nationalist historiography, and enter the less rhetorical, more performative world of "the little poetics of everyday interaction," we encounter diverse spaces of intensive production of what Michael Herzfeld has called "cultural intimacy." Within these spaces, iconic social distinctions (a national "us" and a foreign "them," the people and the state, the public and the private, the high-brow and the popular, the elites and the masses) are continually being articulated and recreated. Moreover, the boundaries between them are also called into question, reinterpreted, and challenged as they get creatively reshaped by the ordinary practices of everyday life.[6]

In sum, Cuba's years "between empires" were the scene of the "production" of a raft of symbolic performances in which processes carrying distinct and at times opposed messages—such as the end of Spanish rule and the break with the colonial past on the one hand, and modernization *a la americana* versus the reaffirmation of Cuban nationality through the canonization and institutionalization of the heroic legacy of the revolutions for independence on the other—were unveiled and represented by means of symbols, graphics, spatial transformations, gestures, ceremonies, semiritualized practices, flags, music, new words and lexicons, fashions, labels, polite expressions, and other devices. Within the worldly spaces of daily life, behind the apparent casualness with which "parties" and revolutionary meetings, English-language advertisements and patriotic place names, danzones and two-steps, hairstyling *a la americana* and mambise straw hats, coexisted, there were fierce struggles to assert and command political supremacy. In turn, that power was the power to define the contours of the nation and to set the boundaries of citizenship, as the country moved toward the establishment in 1902 of a republican state.

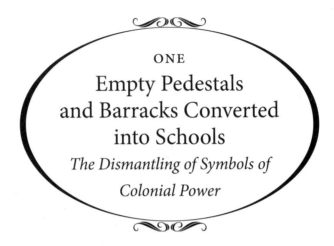

ONE

Empty Pedestals
and Barracks Converted
into Schools
The Dismantling of Symbols of
Colonial Power

Conflicts of Identity

At exactly noon on 1 January 1899, the boom of a cannon rent the air over
the esplanade of El Morro, signaling the official lowering of the flag of Spain.
According to a witness, "The tearing down of the edifice of secular authority
deeply affected both participants and spectators alike."[1] With this move, the
island's long colonial past, more than four centuries of Spanish metropolitan
rule, was formally consigned to the grave.

The flag of the former mother country had been brought down, but in place
of a new nation's flag—Cuba's—there was raised that of "the powerful neighbor who with her potent hand had severed the last colonial ties."[2] The island
thus ceased to be a Spanish colony. Yet, despite the promises contained in
the joint resolution passed by the U.S. Congress, its standing as an independent nation remained no more than an aspiration in the impassioned minds
of nationalist patriots who for the previous three decades had struggled to
achieve political sovereignty.

Neither Spanish colony nor sovereign state, Cuba in the first months of
1899 was an entity without a name. Suspended in a kind of juridical limbo, its
immediate future became the stuff of speculation among little groups huddled
on street corners.

The sense of living through a time of far-reaching and unprecedented
change was reinforced by two simultaneous, transcendent events: the end of

Spanish domination and the end of the century. The powerful symbolism of this unity was unmistakably one of the fundamental components of the "stage setting" before which power was transferred from Spanish to U.S. hands. The dawn of the twentieth century was thus linked, in people's minds, with the founding of a new era, an era marked by two aspirations existing in constant tension: a refashioning and modernization of the old colonial structures, frequently cast in terms of the cultural and institutional "Americanization" of Cuban society, versus the nationalist yearning for a sovereign, independent republic.

The inconsistencies between these two opposing impulses created an inner void, a loss of identity and sense of confusion that was everywhere apparent. In a letter sent to a newspaper first published for the Cuban exile community in New York, one of Havana's residents described the atmosphere of uncertainty that gripped the city in the days between the end of the war and the beginning of the U.S. occupation:

> We are living here in a sort of limbo. Since the blockade was lifted
> we find ourselves like bugs that, having wintered in darkness under a
> stone and then being dazed and disoriented by the light of the sun when
> a worker removes it in the spring, scatter in every direction, running
> into and over each other, and at last disappear into the freshly growing
> grass. That's how we went about, beside ourselves, for a period of days,
> tripping over one another on the streets and in the squares, not knowing
> where we were going, congratulating ourselves for having escaped alive
> from one danger after another, and promising ourselves no end of happiness and good fortune which a looming, bounteous future was going
> to bring us with outstretched hands.[3]

The feelings of uncertainty and disorientation experienced by many during this period were also summed up by Isaac Carrillo y O'Farrill, a contemporary poet and publicist: "On the one hand, the American intervention has yielded numerous benefits, on the other it has produced a series of things so anomalous as to be the source of constant confusion. *All that we want to be, we know; but we are entirely ignorant of what we are.*"[4]

Among the carefully compiled and ostensibly "hard," objective data contained in a census of the island of Cuba, a census planned, carried out, and published by the U.S. government, there are clear indications of the indecisiveness felt by some elements of the Cuban population when asked to specify their nationality. In a table breaking down the composition of the island's population according to "citizenship" and level of education cited by its inhabitants, those who designed the census found themselves obliged to include—next to the headings "Cuban citizens," "Spaniards," and "foreigners," the rather peculiar classification of "citizenship still undeclared," in order to reflect the fact that among those of Spanish origin, 11 percent had yet to decide which citizenship to opt for.[5]

The classic conflicts of identity noted by Clifford Geertz in his studies of the trauma suffered by new states in their transition from colonial to postcolonial status thus played out with particular drama and intensity in Cuba.[6] The former colonists, far from transforming themselves smoothly from "subjects of the mother country" to "citizens of the national state," languished in a state of confusion. Cut loose from the ties that once bound them, and now subject to the dictates of a foreign military power, they found that defining themselves anew had become highly problematic. Observers from the period thus witnessed firsthand the disintegration of the symbolic universe of colonial society, a process fueled by the War of Independence (1895–98) and made far more acute by the circumstances surrounding the shift from one ruling power to another. The critical questioning of long-standing practices together with the disappearance of old associations and forms of social etiquette resulted in a crisis of identity. This crisis sparked a sometimes anguished search for a new ideological roadmap as well as a new symbolic framework that could impose order on the chaotic mélange of images and representations encountered by people.

Achieving a reckoning with the colonial past, purging it from memory, even physically erasing its traces from walls, plazas, and streets, served as a kind of palliative, helping mitigate the uncertainty, the lack of firm, stable definition underlying Cubans' sense of their social, cultural, and political identity. If we are not yet full-blown citizens of a new national state, it was reasoned, we shall at least no longer be subjects of the old colonial power. The crisis of identities was linked not only to the disassociation from the symbolic world of the colonial past but to Cubans' inability to bring a coherent vision of the nation's future into clear focus. Modernity and independence, the fundamental aspirations around which nineteenth-century separatist campaigns had been structured, took on new meanings in the fin de siècle political atmosphere. The two goals were now frequently seen as the embodiment of opposite values and, consequently, as clashing with each other. As I have already noted, a significant part of the imagery through which the idea of "modernity" was conveyed came from the perception that the United States was its leading exemplar. At the same time, however, the U.S. intervention in the affairs of Cuba was viewed as a latent threat to the country's independence and, above all, to the preservation of its distinct cultural identity.

The break with the Hispanic past, modernization styled along North American lines, and nationalist aspirations were each given symbolic expression. The forms these took varied according to where they fell in the spectrum of public life. Conflicts concerning the flying of flags, the replacement of seals, emblems, and coats of arms representative of the old colonial order, statues toppled from their pedestals, or specific sites granted new iconic or honorific status as a reflection of the changed environment—these are all excellent sources for the study of the war of symbols and representations that ensued once the real war was over in 1898.

Dismantling the Emblems and Insignias of Colonial Rule

During the last days of 1898, the most visible signs of Spain's centuries-old presence began to come down in rapid succession. Spanish flags were removed from public buildings, and in less than a month they could only be found, according to Emilio Núñez, "concealed in counter drawers [a clear allusion to the pro-Spanish sentiments of most merchants] or . . . fluttering atop the ships bearing back to Spain the huge army which on this soil met dishonor and defeat."[7] Although the U.S. flag took its place on top of government buildings, the Cuban flag was still widely displayed in private residences and in such "nongovernmental" locations as private clubs, union offices, recreational and educational institutions, and social centers established for veterans of the wars of liberation.

Some months later, bands of loyalists tried to raise the Spanish flag over buildings belonging to private associations, such as the Centro de Dependientes in Havana and the Casino Español in Puerto Príncipe. In the face of these incidents, Havana's mayor issued an order making it illegal to hang or fly the Spanish flag outside any building or any public site, the sole exception to which was the Spanish consulate in the capital.[8]

Insignias and emblems depicting or alluding to the Spanish monarchy likewise disappeared from the facades of government buildings, as they did from monograms, letterhead, and stamps. Some of these objects were treated as the spoils of war and wound up in the hands of U.S. soldiers and public officials; others were bought as souvenirs by U.S. tourists and collectors. The fate awaiting the coat of arms that for decades had decorated the entrance to the governor's palace in Santiago de Cuba is a prime example of such treatment. Only a few days after the beginning of the U.S. occupation, this official symbol of Spanish metropolitan power was detached from the front of the government building and—reflective of its new status—sent off to the capital some months later as a war trophy. Four years later, in July 1902, with the Cuban Republic now established, the itinerant coat of arms was sent back to Santiago, where it was placed in the Museo Bacardí, undergoing yet another transformation, this time from war trophy into a museum object that helped illustrate Cuba's history as a colony.[9]

When sovereignty over Cuba passed into U.S. hands, stamps and fiscal paper bearing the emblems of colonial power obviously lost their validity. Certain documents (now preserved in Cuba's National Archive) with the date 1899, however, contain a revealing mutilation: where Spain's coat of arms should appear there is simply a hole. The hole punched through the sheet not only allowed stamped paper, employed since the previous year in government offices, courts, and other state entities, to continue to be used, it also reinforced—to striking effect—the end of Cubans' institutional dependence on the former mother country. The replacement of Spain's coat of arms with nothing but a blank opening, a hollow space, summed up perfectly the confused political identity and institutional incoherence running through this period.[10]

The town councils, controlled by new municipal authorities installed at times by U.S. officials and at other times by *mambise* authorities, contributed significantly to the creation of a new system of signs and symbols. The town council of Placetas, for example, through a resolution it adopted on 26 October 1898, decreed the elimination of the Spanish emblem from the municipal coat of arms, leaving the latter with nothing in its center for several months. A new insignia for the municipality, featuring the Cuban coat of arms at its center in place of the Spanish, was finally approved by Placetas's town council in April 1899.[11]

In another small community, this time in the area of Matanzas, council members decided—following the official transference of sovereignty—that when the Spanish troops left, they should take with them not only the Spanish flag that had hung from the council building but also the coat of arms and portraits of King Alfonso XII and his consort, which until the last few days had decorated the walls of the council hall, in order that "there be no continuation of any symbol of colonialism on the community's principal government building."[12]

In other instances, such initiatives welled up spontaneously from the townsfolk themselves. In Colón, a group of impassioned patriots tried to square accounts with the long record of Spanish colonization by bringing down the monument in the central plaza, erected to honor the illustrious "discoverer" of America. Their "patriotic" intentions were frustrated by the monument's exceptionally solid construction. As hard as they tried, they were unable to separate the statue of Christopher Columbus from its pedestal. The four lions surrounding it, however, enjoyed no such protection. Stigmatized as emblems of the Spanish monarchy, the lions were deposed violently from their places of honor and relegated to a dark corner of the council building. Sometime later, a more dispassionate interpretation of their symbolic meaning permitted them to be restored to their place at the base of the Columbus monument: the lions, the townsfolk came to understand, "could coexist with the Cubans as a free people, because they were the symbol not of slavery but of valor and strength, qualities which inhered as much in the Cuban as in the Spaniard."[13]

The figurative and emblematic representations of Castile disappeared from more than building fronts, public squares, and the labeled paper used in processing official transactions. On this score, Antonio González Lanuza has described the startling changes made in the illustrations used by some merchants to advertise their products or to decorate their letterhead:

In those days, shop names and labels underwent astonishing changes. There was a man whom I knew, a Catalan . . . , owner of an establishment considered then to be very up and up, who composed his business letters on stationery with a vignette at the top, containing the name of the company accompanied by some specific information about it, the business's telegraph address, the commercial ventures to which it was dedicated, etc. On the left-hand side of the vignette there was a medallion in whose center appeared General Prim, in Castillejos (as I've indicated, the establishment's owner was a Catalan). Well, as of the first of January, General Prim disappeared from the vignette! The new version was the same as its predecessor in every way, except for one difference: the distinguished leader of the "African war," a figure for whom Cubans could have no reason to feel antipathy, had been replaced, on the medallion, by the image of the Statue of Liberty which looms over little Bedloe's island in New York harbor![14]

Barracks Converted into Schools

Some of the old forts and barracks of the Spanish army were demolished while others were remodeled for civilian use. During the war, many towns and cities had quickly been surrounded by wire fencing, which impeded free entry into and exit from them and also facilitated control over the movement of Spain's troops and the activity within its garrisons. Around the city of Santa Clara, one memoirist relates, "there were forts planted at short distances from each other, manned by soldiers, and the only way one could leave was through the guarded and well-secured gates which the Spanish forces had constructed. So, those were veritable corral-cities or prison-cities." It is therefore not surprising that one of the first "liberating" measures taken by local town councils, as soon as Spain's sovereignty was officially ended, was to uproot the odious wire fencing that had turned the cities into prisons and demolish the makeshift forts standing on the outskirts of communities.[15]

One of this period's most representative alterations of physical structures, in whole or in part, for symbolic reasons was the conversion of barracks or other military buildings into schools, a development that repeated itself more than a half century later in the aftermath of the 1959 Revolution. In Havana, the building housing the old military hospital was renovated and converted into a model school, and the barracks of an artillery unit (the former military explosives production unit), to which the land and buildings of the Quinta de los Gobernadores (known to this day as the Quinta de los Molinos), were subsequently added, served as the original nucleus of the future campus of the National University. Similarly, the School of Medicine of the University of Havana was relocated to the former barracks of the Civil Guard. Numerous military installations in Pinar del Río, Güines, Cárdenas, Cienfuegos, Colón, Santa Clara, San Juan de los Yeras, Trinidad, Ciego de Ávila, Puerto Príncipe, Sagua la Grande, San Luis, Santiago de Cuba, Nueva Gerona, and other population centers on the island were retrofitted as primary schools.[16]

In addition to meeting the demand for instructional facilities generated by a massive project, carried out under the auspices of the U.S. military government, to restructure public school education on the island, the transformation of military barracks into schools fulfilled the symbolic purpose of highlighting the differences between the Spanish colonial order and a new order of supposed "civilizing freedoms and virtues." The former was characterized by the words "despotism" and "ignorance" scratched onto the walls of the former colonial power's military forts; the latter were introduced under the aegis of U.S. domination and were represented by the proliferation of classrooms and teachers in place of soldiers and barracks.[17] The spectacle of the conversion of military installations into primary schools, in which swarms of boys and girls replaced the battalions of soldiers, was etched in the memory of those who witnessed it. One contemporary recalled, "I still remember how joyously in those days we gazed at the comings and goings of a troop of teachers, armed with books, that to our pure delight replaced a troop armed with the implements of death. . . . And this was the first and perhaps most radical break made by the colony freed from the customs, practices, and ways of our former mother country."[18]

Other military structures experienced a different fate. After housing U.S. troops for a few months, in place of its regular contingent of Spanish soldiers, the barracks of the Real Fuerza—a structure of some grandeur that since the sixteenth century had protected the entrance to Havana's bay—was converted into the main site and offices of both the Archivo General de la Isla and the public library; the latter became the National Library some years later. The building underwent renovations to make it compatible with its new civil functions. Among other changes, the centuries-old latrines of the colonial castle were turned into modern "water-closets" containing lavatories and sinks imported from the United States.[19]

The crumbling remnants of the capital's seawalls, symbol of another great fortification from colonial times, were demolished as part of a project to clean up and develop Havana's coastal strip. Characterized by the press as "warts" ruining the city's general appearance, the seawalls were subjected to a "surgical operation," razed and the land leveled and graded. Only a few fragments were preserved. The effect of their appearance, as noted architectural historian Carlos Venegas described it, was "to transform the Spanish legacy into a poetic ruin, it was absorbed by the humdrum atmosphere of parks and promenades."[20]

Although these transformations of the built environment put a visible, public face on the break with the colonial past, not all colonial-era government structures were vacated or remodeled with the intent—implied or explicit—of recasting their symbolic significance. Moreover, as the new controlling power, the United States and its agents also used buildings and sites that over the course of long years had been the privileged locus of metropolitan authority. Although the new regimen established under the U.S. occupation was seen to be fundamentally different, "modern," and "civilized," places such as the venerable Palacio de los Capitanes Generales nonetheless maintained their symbolic stature as the sources par excellence of power and authority. Cases like this one, in which the symbolic legacy of Spanish power carried over into the new environment, underscored the strength and centrality of imperial authority, now wielded by a new set of foreign occupiers.

"American-Style" Development of the Capital's Urban Spaces

The North American presence in Havana, where the U.S. military government was based, led to a renaissance of development that noticeably altered the physical face of the city. The urban redevelopment plan included such major projects as the present-day Malecón (seafront promenade), pretentiously dubbed, in those days, the Avenida del Golfo; and the construction of new buildings, such as the Academy of Sciences and the School of Arts and Crafts. Numerous public places acquired a new physical appearance, paralleling their transformation into iconic sites, where the ideology of progress, enunciated as part of the interventionists' "civilizing mission," took on tangible form and became visible to all. As core elements of this modernizing creed, both "hygiene" and "democracy" were integral to the new civic spaces, spaces now designated as "clean," "open," and "public": accessible to everyone—male and female, rich and poor alike.[21]

The renovation of streets and parks within the larger development scheme promoted by the U.S. military government had a significance that went beyond mere urban beautification and the improvement of traffic conditions for pedestrians and carriages. Ramón Meza, a literary personality and historian of the architectural changes made during this period, asserts that the new components defining Havana's organization and streetscape brought with them a range of additional important "civic" attributes. In Meza's opinion, the existence of wider avenues and open-air venues stimulated, above all, "the activities and the free flow of city dwellers, [whose very character as a result of their healthful exercise] becomes [more] honest, decisive, energetic, and purposeful when there is ample space in which to walk, as well as an abundant amount of pure open air with which to nourish the lungs and oxygenate the blood."[22] Colonial Havana, constructed on the model of "narrow," "airless" streets characteristic of the European medieval city, bore out Meza's thinking. If one accepted the contemporary U.S. city as the model urban setting, then Havana acutely needed broad avenues; expansive, tree-filled parks; and public gardens. In its newly "decolonized" public spaces, it needed well-lit, open areas, laid out symmetrically, in which the former subjects of the Spanish king could gain experience in the exercise of citizenship by simply coming together, preferably on foot or by bicycle, to breathe fresh, clean air, in contrast to the anarchic web of narrow, dark streets and the motley collection of alleyways and bazaars which clogged the old colonial center of the city.[23]

Prototypical of this complex of changes were those taking place in the area of the inlet of La Punta, a longtime military battery which had been turned into a garbage dump during the final years of the colony. Frequented during the day only by workers or lower-class immigrants who congregated there to see off the mail boats that left for Spain three times a month, and during the night by criminals and ne'er-do-wells protected by the darkness and desolation of the place, and top heavy with stones and boulders, cast-off timber, and assorted detritus, it was converted—according to one observer—into "a lovely, splendid esplanade, with a terrace affording a prominent view of the entrance to the port, the Castle of El Morro, and the line of blue water extending to the horizon . . . like a charm, [so the observer claimed], the Americans transformed the setting, introducing civilization to that gloomy, outlying spot." The marginal status of the place thus gave way to the "civilizing impulse," and the gloomy, dismal garbage dump was converted into a fashionable retreat, well lit by electric streetlamps, where Havana residents from every social class gathered at sunset.[24]

Similarly—in keeping with the "hygienic" and "democratic" theme and message of the day—both ladies promenading "on foot along the wide sidewalk" and groups of workers or lower-class citizens seeking "to relieve their spirits worn down by poverty and work" turned up on the Malecón. In terms of urban living, the seafront boulevard embodied the ideal of modernity.[25] The proud owners of the latest model cars parked their automobiles on the recently opened roadway, so people could admire them, while the number of boys and young ladies who came to the La Punta park "to practice the 'sport' of bicycle riding" was so great that the city's mayor felt obliged to prohibit the circulation of carriages on the surrounding streets between 4:00 and 11:00 P.M. in order to prevent accidents from taking place.[26]

During the waning days of the U.S. occupation, the final touches were put on the construction of a bandstand situated on a roundabout where the Paseo del Prado runs into the Malecón. This structure, designed by the U.S.-based French architect Charles Brun as "an elegant, harmoniously proportioned temple built along classical lines," was used for the performance of afternoon concerts by the municipal band. Each afternoon, in fidelity to a custom dating from colonial times, residents of Havana would station themselves on the grassy slope around the bandstand to enjoy the open-air concert. Now, however, to mark the break with the colonial past, the band began its concerts by striking up the martial notes of the "Bayamesa," later to be officially proclaimed the national anthem.[27]

Just a few meters from this spot, the remaining part of a section of wall, which formed part of the old, original seawall, had been torn down as part of the construction work taking place along the coastal strip. On the initiative of a group of patriotic-minded citizens, headed by Fermín Valdés Domínguez, a request was made to the U.S. authorities that a fragment of the wall be preserved. According to the testimony presented, a group of medical students had been lined up against this wall and executed by a firing squad on 27 November 1871. The students had been unjustly accused of desecrating the tomb of Gonzalo Castañón, a Spanish journalist who—as the war of 1868–78 got under way—became a martyr for the integralist cause. The piece of wall identified by the group was duly preserved, enclosed, and marked with a plaque describing its historical significance.[28] In this way, the effort to preserve and consecrate historical-patriotic memory was joined to the "modernizing" imprint of the U.S. development initiative. When integrated into its surroundings, the saved monument injected a nationalistic note into the renovation of the wider area.

The impulse to adopt a different style also operated within the orbit of private homes. There, the contrasts between Havana's newly constructed "American-style" houses and those surviving from the colonial period were more and more evident. At the beginning of the century, the once exclusive residential neighborhood of El Cerro, subjected to a process of "vulgarization forced on it by the imperatives of business, traffic, and the city's growth," sank into decline amid its enormous, classically columned houses, with their neglected gardens sporting fountains and somnolent lions, their great balconies and covered verandas, their trellises, semicircular arches, and grillwork with its intricate arabesque flourishes.[29] Serving as a kind of metaphor for colonial society, the neighborhood slowly crumbled and collapsed. In 1902, in one of his articles on urban development, Ramón Meza observed: "Not very long ago, good fortune smiled on many Cuban families living within those spacious halls and rooms, those verandas, little parks, terraces, and gardens; more often than not, it was multiple generations, grandparent down to great-grandchild, that one saw seated at a long table, where—amid the pleasant after-dinner conversation—the aroma of coffee, served on large silver trays by *criollos* of ebony skin color, suffused the gentle breezes wafting in from the garden."[30]

The patriarchal creole class to which Meza alludes was pulled ever closer to ruin under the vicissitudes of the war and the assertion of U.S. power. Alarmed, too, by the steady influx of working-class elements into the district, its denizens moved away from El Cerro—leaving the mansions empty and opening the way to a new set of residents, whose architectural and landscaping preferences were very different:

> Wood as a building material . . . , unplastered balustrades and brick
> walls . . . , fences made out of wire, lighter and airier, which replaced

those with heavy iron grills or some other material which achieved the same barricade-like effect, grass cut low, like a rug, in place of earth-filled paths, all of these clearly denoted the influence of the taste and standards then prevailing in U.S. home construction. The broad wooden veranda and glass windows instead of iron lattices and bars, the planked and polished pinewood floors and painted walls in place of checkered floors of black and white marble and walls covered with ceramic tile, were on a par with the lighter and freer type of construction and like-wise bore the stamp of a different style. These houses and enclosures came across as less screened and protected; their walls and fences were built on a more human scale, and while they fell short of achieving the ultimate objective—to make the focal point not the house but the line of grass and sidewalk that marked the limit of private property next to the public road—they were not as overbearing as the houses and lots in Jesús de Monte, with their cactuses and trestles crowned by glass bottles. Rather, they foretell a later era or display the elements of a more forward-looking sociocultural environment.[31]

Meza admired this more open and "democratic" North American–influenced style of construction, but also longed for the dying aristocratic traditions of the colony. In predicting, however, that the great houses of El Cerro, complete with stables, gardens, and extensive servant quarters, would never again be occupied, he was utterly wrong. Little by little, the once aristocratic neighborhood was overrun by "democratization" of a different sort. In similar fashion to the fate which befell many of the great palaces in the older part of Havana, its large houses were subdivided into *cuarterías* or *ciudadelas*, residential complexes containing smaller units occupied by several families of a lower socioeconomic order who shared the grounds and facilities. This development opened the way in El Cerro to the formation of another subculture, one just as *rellolla* (just as pure in its Cubanness) as that of the patrician colony but of a fundamentally different character, that of the *solar*, or urban tenement complex.

Over the coming years, in step with the country's script for renewal, the descendants of the old creole plantocracy, together with members of the emergent "national" bourgeoisie, would move into new homes. Though not as spacious or imposing as the older mansions, these new houses increasingly boasted other features: a space for automobiles in place of stables and carriage houses, modern lavatories and washrooms, telephones, electric lights, and all the other comforts and advantages of living *a la americana*. Meanwhile, the urban masses, whose numbers were increasing rapidly due in part to a demographic jump following the devastation of the war and a pattern of migration into the city, and in part to a rising tide of immigrants that began at the turn of the century, lived in crowded tenements, the object of constant recrimination and sermonizing about their "unhygienic" living conditions.[32]

The development that served as everyone's ideal, the model par excellence of urban chic, was El Vedado, a residential zone founded in the latter years of the nineteenth century that had tripled in size by 1903. In contrast to the baroque gardens of El Cerro, with their luxuriant, overflowing tropical vegetation, the grounds surrounding El Vedado's new houses were laid out symmetrically, with neat flowerbeds and well-trimmed grass. They bore witness to a change in the organization of space, according to which "order" and "rationality" became the primary virtues. In Meza's words, the district's layout "with its broad, straight, attractive streets shaded by the swaying, neatly draped overhang of slender cottonwood branches; its ample telephone, telegraph, and cable lines, and its rows of white electric streetlamps, revealed from afar its successful rendezvous with the benefits and trappings of modern development."[33]

A "Civilizing" Sanitization

Along with these architectural changes, the inhabitants of Havana, Santiago de Cuba, Matanzas, and other cities, looked on with amazement as an army of street sweepers, utilities personnel, building contractors, and public health workers spilled into the streets and entered houses as the vanguard of a major campaign to improve sanitation. The campaign set out not only to eliminate the trash polluting and tainting both cities and small communities but—with much symbolic fanfare—to sweep away "the assorted blights inherited from the colonial regime." The contrast between "hygiene" and "civilization" as characteristics of the new political order and the "filthy conditions" and "obscurantism" that underlay Spanish colonial rule was once again stressed.

Not many weeks after the start of the U.S. intervention, street cleaning and garbage collection services were reorganized and put into operation in the island's largest cities. Moreover, as a consequence of the war and the ensuing program of resettlement, towns and cities were teeming with populations of the indigent and homeless. A campaign was mounted to round up these people and confine them in hostels, orphanages, and shelters. Even dogs roaming the streets were picked up and put to sleep. Fines were instituted and levied on those animal owners who defied the municipal ordinances requiring them to care for their pets and other animals properly and to keep them outside of public areas.[34]

The "civilizing" cleanup campaign pushed by the U.S. military authorities was not restricted to purely public areas. On the contrary, it crossed over the threshold of people's residences to include even the most private spaces. According to Venegas, the project of cleaning up the cities depended to a great extent on the state of sanitation inside residential housing. Around 1899, only 10 percent of the houses in Havana and Matanzas were equipped with indoor plumbing and toilets. To help meet the challenge of this situation, Major John G. Davis, the top health official in the U.S. army of occupation, heading up a team of 120 doctors, personally visited homes in the capital to instruct people on the use of drainage pipes, the disposal of waste, and other measures promoting improved hygiene.

The practice of better hygiene was considered an essential prerequisite for entering the "modern era." To this end, a large quantity of hardware for improved sanitation was imported from the United States and sold to Havana's residents at a modest price. According to the local press, the enthusiasm with which health inspectors tackled the problem exceeded the boundaries of common sense. For example, more than one resident received a notice to install a water closet and connect its pipes to the existing sewer system when no drainage infrastructure existed for blocks around.[35] In future years, the promotion of bathrooms with lavatories and running water, and their addition to both public buildings and private residences, would be identified with the jettisoning of the "dirty" habits of life under Spanish colonial rule and their replacement by the "sanitizing" customs introduced during the U.S. intervention. The obsession with public and even personal bodily hygiene became another of the tropes in the discourse about the regeneration (physical and moral) of Cuba which accompanied the transition from Spanish rule to U.S. neocolonial domination.

"The North American and the Englishman worship cold water and 'sports,' and that's why they get ahead," exclaimed a Havana columnist, urging Cubans to "North Americanize themselves" in matters relating to the practice of hygiene. "The neglect of the body brings with it a moral wasting away. Communities that are filthy, and almost all those of Latin origin qualify as such, will not lift themselves up as long as they persist in living like pigs. For the Spanish people . . . a lot of cold water, a lot of exercise, fewer priests and soldiers, and more schools."[36] As Anne McClintock has noted, the close connection drawn between the ideology of domestic virtue, on the one hand, and that of imperialism, on the other, is readily apparent in the discourse about "regeneration through hygiene" which equated bodily cleanliness and domestic hygiene with the moral "cleansing" of the "social body." The fetishistic praise of soap and toilets as "vehicles of civilization" was based on a racist association linking the "whiteness" of the colonizers with the cleanliness and purity typical of correct hygienic practice, in stark contrast to the dark skin color of natives who lived amid the filth and pollution characteristic of "backward" societies. There is perhaps no better expression of this association, central to the rhetoric of the North Americans' civilizing mission, than a cartoon that appeared in a U.S. publication depicting the military governor, Leonard Wood, surrounded by cases of soap, bleach, and disinfectant, energetically scrubbing Cuba, represented by a little black boy, sitting in a bathtub and crying forlornly.[37]

Thus, along with the successive waves of U.S. soldiers, government functionaries, businessmen, investors, tourists, and missionaries, the island received new architectural and building styles and standards, industrial machinery, and modern, more advanced means of transportation and communication. Above all, countless U.S.-manufactured articles and wares for household use found their way onto the island. In the popular imagination, these products signaled the attainment of the good life. Sewing machines, typewriters, bicycles, telephones, kitchen and cleaning accessories, lamps with electric light bulbs, phonographs, bathroom fixtures and hardware, patented drugs, shoes, and—still some years away—automobiles, radios, and "frigidaires" all became features of Cubans' daily lives. Moreover, these objects not only became integral to the general corpus of images and representations equated by Cubans with modernity but gave concrete, tangible expression, on the level of everyday life, to the more abstract notion of progress.[38] This process operated throughout the early years of the century.

Modernization on the North American model was not limited, then, to the redesign of public spaces, the introduction of new technologies, or the adoption of new customs and practices. Nor was it devoid of political content. On the contrary, such modernization was a keystone of the "ideology of progress" invoked by the United States to justify and legitimize its presence on the island. As we have seen, "modern life," associated through a whole set of symbols with the period of intervention and epitomized by "hygiene," "a forward-looking mentality," and "civilization," was contrasted, in these years, with the antiquated society of colonial times, defined by its "filthiness" and "backwardness."

Although the items imported from the North were for the most part luxury goods available only to a small segment of the population, the ordinary Cuban nonetheless participated in the experience, if not directly as a consumer, then nominally as a spectator who witnessed this material "enactment" of the "modernizing" creed. In shopwindows and counter displays, or on posters in public establishments, and through photographs and illustrations in the pages of newspaper advertisements, passersby and readers were invited to make themselves into "gentlemen" by purchasing a derby "made in the USA" or into ladies by wearing a "body" corset designed in New York.[39] In addition, a range of products set out in public places, such as lamps with electric bulbs, telephones, fans, and toilets, were displayed as items that heralded a kind of domestic modernity that promised to change everyone's lives within a short span of time. In the heart of the city, seated on the benches in the newly created public spaces along avenues and in parks, the common citizen gazed at the flow of bicycles or the still exotic and noisy automobiles, while electric-powered trams, supplanting the "unhygienic" carts pulled by horses, which left a trail of feces across the city, now reached all the way to neighborhoods on Havana's periphery.

The Empty Pedestal of Queen Isabel II

On the level of metaphorical representations of change as reflected in the urban landscape, there was no more graphic illustration of the divide between the desire to break with the Spanish colonial past and the feelings of uncertainty regarding the shape of things to come than the image—reproduced in all of the contemporary print media—of an empty pedestal where stood Havana's most representative monument to the mother country's power: a statue of Spain's queen, Isabel II.

On 12 March 1899, as those walking past looked on with curiosity, the statue of the queen, for nearly half a century a fixture along the elegant Paseo del Prado, was unceremoniously removed from its base. This was not the first time that Isabel II had been deposed from her pedestal on the capital's central downtown boulevard. In 1868, during Spain's Glorious Revolution, the statue was toppled by "republican" partisans and ignominiously dragged into a municipal ditch, suffering—as it turned out—no more than a lost finger. Two years later, after the restoration of the monarchy in Spain, the statue was placed back on its pedestal, until it was brought down permanently in 1899.[40]

When viewed in terms of the ambiguity surrounding both the present state and the future direction of the country, the direct correlation between the empty pedestal (a rejected past) and the absence of a new signifier (the problematic present and future) is clear. The acute, widespread sense that the long-accepted meanings of things no longer held, a sensation brought on by the unraveling of the apparatus and symbols of Spanish colonial power, was perfectly distilled in a photomontage published in one of Havana's most influential magazines, *El Fígaro*. The image was compelling. In place of the statue, a huge question mark stood atop the empty pedestal.

In an effort to resolve the tension created by this symbolic vacuum, the magazine carried out a survey to determine what object should fill the empty space left on the pedestal. The survey's results, published in the 28 May 1899 issue of *El Fígaro*, serve as a kind of x-ray of the conflicting attitudes at play. Gaining the most votes was a proposed statue of José Martí. In the minds of his countrymen, Martí—just four years after his death—had come to personify the soul and spirit of Cuba and to embody the nationalist aspiration for an independent republic.[41]

The victory of the Martí proposal, however, was razor thin. Only four votes behind was a proposed statue of liberty. Although the survey results did not spell out whether this referred to the famous statue in New York harbor, it can be inferred that behind the suggestion lay the desire to see Cuba emerge from the current vacuum as a modern republic enjoying the fruits of political freedom, a republic built along the lines of the country which, in the eyes of many, was the lodestar of these principles, the United States, in contrast to the monarchical society long symbolized by the statue of the queen. Still other respondents suggested that the empty space be filled with a statue of Christopher Columbus. Although advocated by a smaller number of people, this proposal nonetheless demonstrated that the partisans of traditional Hispanic values and traditions remained a potent force.

These three proposals were followed by seven others, in which votes were cast for statues honoring either men who had figured prominently in the island's own history, such as José de la Luz y Caballero, Carlos Manuel de Céspedes, and Máximo Gómez, or those of a different stripe altogether, such as the U.S. president (shown signing the Declaration of Independence), or a group representing, in an allegorical rendering, Cuba, the United States, and Spain.

Last among the ten proposals receiving the highest number of votes was a proposed statue of Antonio Maceo. With the possible exception of Gómez, Maceo had been the most distinguished military figure of Cuba's wars of liberation, but he had the "defect," fatal for those whose thinking was determined by racial and class interest, of being both black and of humble origin. Such thinking, furthermore, was most strongly represented in precisely those districts in which the survey was conducted.[42]

The slighting of Antonio Maceo by survey respondents is an instance and reminder of the obstacles to Cuban blacks' inclusion into definitions of "us," as formulated by the "upper classes" in their conception of the Cuban nation. *El Fígaro* served as a prime forum for the expression of such exclusivism. In contradistinction to the prominence achieved by black or mulatto leaders and officials such as Maceo, as well as the massive presence of former slaves and their descendants in the ranks of the Liberation Army, the events of the war — no matter how fresh the memory of them—began to be "retouched" in the elite press, during the first months of the U.S. intervention, to create a "white" and "civilized" image of the nation that would neutralize or refute the accusations of "savagery" or "barbarism" indelibly associated with the African presence.[43]

At the same time, the episode involving the statue was the first installment in the appropriation of a mythical José Martí and his official incorporation into the pantheon of national heroes by elements of the Cuban elite. Under the Republic, this elevation of Martí would become one of the cornerstones in the construction of a "national" epic, whereby the "nation's history" is reconstructed (and "whitened") to facilitate its integration into metanarratives about struggles for political control and hegemony. This official history was canonized not only in writing, to be transmitted through school texts, specialized histories, and commemorative volumes, but iconographically as well, in the form of statues put up in parks and along streets, portraits hung in government offices and halls, and images engraved on Cuban postage stamps and currency.[44]

Despite the results of the survey conducted by *El Fígaro*, followed a year later, in February 1900, by the appointment of a commission to initiate work on a monument to Martí, the pedestal was still empty when the U.S. intervention ended in 1902.[45] That May, as part of efforts to ready the site for festivities accompanying the inauguration of the new Republic, a statue of liberty was purchased in the United States. With the great seal of the United States held in its right hand and a torch in its left hand, the statue, which cost two thousand U.S. dollars, smacked suspiciously of its counterpart in New York. Viewed by many Cubans as the visible symbol of a U.S. annexationist agenda underlying the government headed by Tomás Estrada Palma, the statue was torn down and destroyed as part of a "nationalist" protest that erupted in Havana on 10 October 1903, the thirty-fifth anniversary of the *Grito de Yara* (Declaration of Yara, which announced the outbreak of the Ten Years' War).

The drama of the empty pedestal finally came to an end some eighteen months later when, on 24 February 1905, the tenth anniversary of the uprising of Baire, Máximo Gómez presided over the official installation of a statue (by

Cuban sculptor José Vilalta Saavedra) of José Martí. Since then, the Apostle, Martí, has commanded the space occupied first by the monument to the queen of Spain and later by the statue of *yanquí* liberty, in a kind of parodic synthesis of the vicissitudes of Cuba's history.

As I have tried to demonstrate through these accounts of excised emblems and coats of arms, fences and seawalls torn down and demolished, barracks turned into schools and garbage dumps into stylish parks, neighborhoods laid out and developed on the model of the United States, statues removed from their pedestals, and the widespread installation of lavatories, the urban setting itself became a representational scene of struggle, on which a host of images, conveying different signs and meanings, battled for supremacy. The dismantling of the obsolete insignias of colonial authority created a kind of symbolic void at the center of which a series of contradictory processes played out: the "Americanization" of practices and institutions, the deeply felt emotions of a nationalistic patriotism, and the desperate attempts to preserve the Spanish cultural inheritance in the face of a powerful current of modernization bearing an Anglo-Saxon imprint.

Rather than acting as discrete, sharply defined tendencies, however, these processes were at bottom hybrid, random, and interconnected in complex ways. They illuminate the period "between empires" as a time of ambiguity in which, to borrow the description of one who lived through it: "All that was no longer exists" [and] "all that is to be does not yet exist." At the midpoint between two centuries and two ruling powers, Cubans were crossing a confusing terrain of change, a frontier or threshold that "separates the past from the future, that is neither the one nor the other and that seems to be both at the same time, in which with each step taken, one knows not if the ground underneath bears the seeds of the new or the remnants of a process of destruction."[46]

TWO

Policies Governing Celebrations

Catholic, North American, and Patriotic Fiestas

Innovation and Tradition as Glimpsed through Almanacs

Over the course of the nineteenth century, in Cuba as in Latin America generally, almanacs, or calendars as they were also called, marked the rhythms of social life by specifying all of the festivals, holidays, and special occasions of the civil and religious year—an array of days for rejoicing, fasting and mourning, celebrating saints' days and other anniversaries, observing "patriotic" dates of the mother country, and honoring the members of Spain's royal family.[1]

Almanacs formed a multifaceted genre. Compendia of the mundane, they were consulted by travelers, merchants, ranchers, planters, and others for their abundance of useful information—interspersed with tables and illustrations—about commerce, agriculture, politics, mining, geography, and other topics. On a less obvious, less self-conscious level, however, these quaint little books, with their mixture of predictions to be borne out (or not) and precepts to be followed on the basis of accepted, long-established practice, articulated and reconciled representations of the past and ideological constructs regarding the future. By listing natural phenomena (such as the spring and winter equinoxes and other changes affecting the seasons), religious festivals, and civic occasions in the same chronological sequence, the almanacs "placed" events in historical time and made recently created political commemorations seem as ineluctable as changes in the phases of the moon, the approach of an eclipse, or the recurring celebration of a popular religious festival.

Equally the field of the sacred and the worldly, of popular culture and official convention, the calendars grounded both the consolidation of what society records and remembers and the mediation of its ongoing political demands. Similarly, when calendars registered new commemorative occasions or removed old anniversaries and celebrations, they bore witness to the outcome of struggles over the power to organize social life, whether this power was wielded by ecclesiastical authorities, the state, or institutions of civil society.[2]

The almanacs which appeared in the aftermath of the war of 1895–98, during the initial years of the U.S. intervention, reflected—with their amalgam of Catholic, U.S., and nationalist anniversaries—the complicated symbolic interactions characteristic of the period. Three intersecting interests, each complemented by its own set of symbols and associations, competed for ascendancy: the traditions inherited from the colonial past, the problematic representations of an unsettled present marked by a foreign military occupation, and the assertions of a simmering nationalist will, expressed in the desire of Cubans to take their place as an independent nation in the near future.

Some chance observations written on the blank pages of a copy of an 1899 almanac evoke the heady, turbulent atmosphere of the last days of Spain's four hundred years of rule over its island colony. As the almanac's unknown owner traveled by train from Santa Clara to Cienfuegos on 1 January 1899, passing through various communities, he or she recorded the extraordinary events then unfolding:

> 1 January. I've gone on to Cienfuegos, the train carried very few passengers, and of these, fifty were revolutionary soldiers sent as detachments to Esperanza and Ranchuelo, both of which had been evacuated the day before. The train flew several U.S. and Cuban flags, in La Esperanza a huge crowd, holding flags, met us at the station, raising cheers to a free Cuba, independence, and the soldiers of the insurrection. In Ranchuelo the same demonstration . . . ; Cruces y Camarones the same thing, these pueblos are all decked out.[3]

A short distance from its destination, the train stopped to pick up a company of U.S. soldiers marching from their encampment on the outskirts of Cienfuegos into the heart of the city "in order to preside over the raising of the American flag and take possession of the main square for the United States." Even before this event, however, in the cafés and corner groceries of the seaside town, groups of Spanish soldiers shared drinks and traded toasts with their U.S. counterparts, and also exchanged souvenirs, in the form of badges and other items of military issue, while they waited for their ships to embark.

"Lots of houses were decorated with flags and with curtains in the colors of Cuba and the United States and across the city's neighborhoods many little Cuban flags, not being posted very high up, had been torn down by the American soldiers, who used some of them to wipe the dust off their boots and gaiters."[4] "All of these details," the anonymous diarist notes insightfully, "have not gone by unnoticed by Cubans, and while they may not show it, I believe they understand perfectly well that the U.S.'s military occupation is a long-term affair and in the end could, without too much difficulty, turn into something permanent, justified on the grounds of the Monroe Doctrine—'America for Americans.'"[5]

Thus, in addition to the radical social consequences of the revolutionary struggle for independence and the sense of disorientation produced by the abrupt disengagement from the institutional apparatus of colonial rule, Cubans were forced to contend with the U.S. presence on their island, imposed on them in the form of a government of military occupation. This multilayered process of change left a deep mark on Cuban society, altering its familiar rhythms and representations.

The War of Independence that started in 1895 imprinted itself in two powerful ways. On the one hand, it carved a painful course through Cuban life for nearly four years, leaving many lives turned upside down. On the other, it promised the imminent realization of a new order of freedom and justice. The intervention and then victory of the United States in the war, the evacuation of the Spanish army, and the radical break with the past contributed to the dual sensation experienced by many Cubans of witnessing one era die as another was born. They stood on the verge of a new historical era, and the perception of having broken with the colonial past was intensified by the theatrical symbolism of the ceremonies which accompanied the transference of sovereignty from Spain to the United States.

The colonial heritage of more than four centuries of Spanish control and domination was declared a dead letter; in its place a future of vast new horizons—uncharted as yet in any detail—would open for Cubans. This sense of rupture and discontinuity, heightened by the simultaneous end of Spain's rule and final years of the century (a concurrence invested with great symbolic significance by Cubans), is present in the almanacs and calendars. No other source, in fact, reveals as directly the changes in cycles of festivals and celebrations that for decades had defined and governed the social life of the colony.

More particularly, it would be difficult to find a clearer expression of Cubans' belief that one was living through the very moment when an old order gave way to a new than the proposal, published in *El Fígaro*, that the country inaugurate a new calendar, taking 24 February 1895—when the War of Independence began—as the first day of Cuba's Year 1. As part of the proposal, which recalled the French Revolution, the months of the "Cuban year" would be named after patriots "dead on the field of battle or on the honorable platform of the political scaffold."[6]

The proposal was too radical for all but the most fervent nationalists.[7] Nonetheless, even in an almanac as conservative and traditionalist as that published annually by the diocese of Havana, the break with the metropolitan past and the birth of a new order stand out sharply.

For example, in the *Calendario del Obispado de La Habana para el año de 1899* (published at the end of the preceding year), while a day like 2 May—a date of high honor in the Spanish political tradition—was still set aside for festivities, the celebration of saints' days and the birthdays of members of the Spanish royal family, which in colonial times were commemorated lavishly throughout the year with receptions and school processions, disappeared permanently.[8] Other dates previously set aside, such as those which marked the drawings for the *Real Lotería*, denigrated now as one of the "blights" of the old regime, were also eliminated.[9]

In the almanac of the Havana diocese for the following year, 2 May was replaced as a day for celebration by 4 July—the U.S. Independence Day. At the same time, 10 October and 24 February, which mark the beginning of the two wars of liberation against Spain, appear for the first time as Cuban holidays. This 1900 calendar has a distinctly hybrid character, granting space to just-debuted nationalist commemorations, various U.S. celebrations, and festivities and anniversaries marking the traditional Catholic calendar.

The Catholic almanac, with its endless processional days and saints' days, and its emphasis on such anniversaries as 25 July, the day of Saint James the Apostle, or 8 December, in honor of the Blessed Virgin—both patrons of Spain—remained faithful to the memory of Spanish rule.[10]

Yet even the Catholic almanac came to terms, in its own way, with the changed environment. In 1901—the first year of the twentieth century—it utilized a new format to organize its odd assemblage of disparate festivities and contradictory commemorations. In addition to their customary practice of identifying the year's observances chronologically, the editors included a thematic division as part of the almanac's front matter.

From this point on, the civil calendar—regulated by the state according to its official commemorations—was fully differentiated from the festivals and celebrations on the religious calendar, as determined by the Catholic Church. In the future, this distinction would become commonplace in the popular mind. The notion that there were holidays and festivities appropriate to two distinct realms—the civil and the ecclesiastic—announced a new secular era and the separation of church and state decreed by the U.S. authorities.

Alongside the days of celebration officially accepted by the U.S. military government were a number of unofficial celebrations. The latter were separated or subdivided into two groups: the fiestas pertaining to the "Spanish colony" (which included the days honoring Saint James the Apostle and the Blessed Virgin as well as 1 November, All Saints' Day) and the holidays celebrated by the "American colony," specifically, 22 February (George Washington's birthday), 30 May (Decoration Day, known today as Memorial Day, which for uninformed readers the almanac translated as "similar to our Day of the Dead"), the Fourth of July, and Thanksgiving.

Since the nationalist "occasions" were neither officially sanctioned nor considered distinctive to either of the two "colonies," they were omitted from both of the broad categories. Nonetheless, they did appear in the almanac, identified as "Cuban patriotic holidays" on the pages corresponding to the months of February and October.[11]

With its separate categories of festivals and celebrations coexisting together, the 1901 *Almanaque* mirrors the plurality of cultural and ideological standpoints characteristic of the period. In this respect, it is a unique document. The almanacs and calendars published during these years also provide subtle indications of the negotiations among the ecclesiastical powers, interventionist authorities dealing with the state, and (especially nationalist) organizations of civil society struggling for symbolic mastery of the norms of Cuban social life.

The Thinly Veiled Acceptance of U.S. Celebrations

That Cuba's understanding of itself in this period was fragmented and governed by discordant representations is confirmed by a study of its newspapers as well as other documentary sources. In 1899, after several months during which nobody was sure which were the dates to celebrate, the U.S. military government approved a decree stipulating that only Sundays as well as 1 January, Holy Thursday, Good Friday, and 25 December qualified as officially sanctioned holidays.[12] The dates accepted as official were thus limited to certain days of the traditional calendar of festivities, such as Holy Week and Christmas, while any celebration recognizing political interests or anniversaries was excluded.

Several weeks later, however, on 12 November 1899, the *Gaceta de La Habana* printed a proclamation issued to the Cuban people by the U.S. military governor, John R. Brooke:

> The custom exists in the United States of designating one day in the year to give thanks to the Supreme Being, for the many benefactions granted in the past. The designation of this day and the exhortation that people observe it comes from the supreme authority of the government, making its implementation a matter of national, patriotic duty. The Military Government of Cuba, taking into account what is sacred and true, in according recognition in this way to all blessings granted, in giving thanks for them and in imploring for the future divine guidance, direction and assistance; and believing further than no people or country has more reason to be grateful or has greater hopes for the future than the inhabitants of Cuba, thinks it only natural to call their attention to their present state. Taking this into account, it sets Thursday, the thirtieth day of November, as the Day to Give Thanks to God and urges that the cares and labors of life be put aside on that day so that all might gather in their different places of worship and extend to the Supreme Arbiter of our destiny the thanks and praises which are justly due Him.[13]

To judge by the data I have managed to assemble, the majority of Cubans did not lend themselves willingly to the Protestant-inspired exercise urged on them of showing "gratitude." Whereas in Puerto Rico, according to Silvia Álvarez Curbelo, the populace adapted to U.S. holidays with little conflict shortly after the U.S. occupation, I have uncovered no evidence in Cuba that anything comparable happened there, outside of official circles or certain sectors of the elite, whose members were always disposed to view positively any practice coming "from the North."[14]

Despite their inclusion in the almanacs, holiday celebrations originating in the United States do not seem to have gained much traction among the Cuban population as a whole. To the minor degree that they did, this was confined to a range of relatively modest celebrations (organized, in the majority of cases, to curry favor with U.S. officialdom). Tributes appearing in the periodical press may have helped create the false impression of a widespread acceptance of U.S. holidays. With respect to holiday feasts, dressed turkeys never replaced the traditional roast suckling pig eaten on Christmas Eve, and it was not until much later that Santa Claus began to cast a shadow over the Three Kings of Catholic tradition in children's imaginations. In analyzing these questions, moreover, it is important to note that the U.S. military authorities never tried to pressure or coerce Cubans into celebrating U.S. holidays. Rather, their approach was to "suggest," in an amiable, paternalistic way, that Cubans do so.

Other dates linked to the U.S. presence on the island, such as 12 August (commemorating the signing of the armistice between Spain and the United States), Decoration Day, and the birthday of George Washington, were commemorated in Cuba during these years on a sporadic basis and without much conviction.[15]

An incident which occurred in February 1899, in connection with the first observance in Havana of Washington's birthday, illustrates the ambiguous way in which these anniversaries got incorporated as official public celebrations. The city's municipal council decorated the front of its building with banners on which large intertwined acronyms stood out, in allegorical testimony to the fraternal union existing between the republic of the United States and a Cuban republic as yet unborn. As though in competition with this display, however, curtains had been draped on another part of the building, with the names of prominent separatist leaders, heroes of the wars of liberation against Spain, completely visible on them. Within a few hours, both the acronyms and the patriots' names had disappeared from the banners. The government's explanation for this precipitous action cited "aesthetic reasons." Virtually no one believed the official story. Rather, popular opinion attributed the action to the displeasure of the U.S. authorities, who presumably looked askance at the attempt to link the central figures of the Cuban independence movement with the celebration of Washington's birthday.[16]

In some areas, local U.S. administrators, without obtaining the approval of their superiors in Havana, declared U.S. anniversaries as official Cuban holidays. For example, in the city and district of Trinidad, 22 February was declared a day of public celebration: "Wednesday, the 22nd of February 1899, is proclaimed a public holiday in the City and district of Trinidad. Out of all days in the year, this day is dedicated throughout the United States of America to commemorating the birth and life of GEORGE WASHINGTON, who in America was statesman, soldier, patriot, wise soul, reformer, fount of truth and justice, pioneer, guardian of freedom, first founding father of his country and protector of its inhabitants."[17] Through the proclamation, Colonel George Le Roy Brown, the U.S. military governor of the Trinidad district, invited Cubans not only to celebrate Washington's birthday but "to study and discuss the fundamental principles of the government he inaugurated, which today stands as a monument from which his superhuman wisdom shines forth."[18]

Some months later, a Trinidad newspaper, El Telégrafo, published a story describing a dance held by the La Tertulia social club in honor of U.S. Independence Day. The festivities were attended by U.S. officials and their wives, together with "the most select element of Trinidadian society." According to the newspaper's account, the walls of La Tertulia's hall were lined with Cuban and U.S. flags, which "randomly tied together symbolized the feelings of warmth and brotherhood that have come to unite these two peoples." At the edge of the street, between garlands of roses and laurels, a likeness of Washington had been planted, with a border "on which shone both the forty-five stars of the United States and the bright lone star that lit up the lovely sky of Cuba."[19] To the left of Washington, however, enveloped among flowers, one could also see portraits depicting Cuba's revolutionary heroes: Céspedes, Martí, Gómez, and Maceo. Here again the central symbols and personalities defining Cuban and U.S. nationality—the countries' flags and political heroes—were linked together, at least superficially.

Subsequently, on 12 August 1899, Trinidad's municipal council decided to commemorate the first anniversary of the signing of the armistice which brought an end to the war. Yet, far from paying tribute to the army of occupation, the "peace festivities" of 1899 in Trinidad turned the ostensible celebration of the U.S. victory into a very visible celebration of Cuban nationalist aspirations.

With hours to spare, the public began to gather in front of the municipal council building to witness, at noon sharp, the central event of the celebration: "The act of running up, for the first time at Trinidad's town hall, the glorious flag of Cuba which, once hoisted, would give proof that the island does not depend on Spain, that it is already free, with solemn commitments to be independent."[20] Lino Pérez, a general in the Liberation Army and the mayor of Trinidad, together with other Cuban leaders and officials as well as representatives of the U.S. army, presided over the activities at a table covered with a large Cuban flag. The city's schoolchildren recited poems and sang patriotic songs. At the conclusion of this part of the celebration, the mayor, accompanied by members of the municipal council, the commander of the U.S. forces, and other authorities, climbed up to the building's roof terrace with the flag, which was hoisted by Brigadier Bravo and Lieutenant Colonel García, joined by two other officials, all of whom wore special dress. The flag could barely be glimpsed at the top of the roof terrace wall, over the council's main hall, when—so the newspaper story reported—"the crowd let forth with a spontaneous roar, which thundered over the space. The anthem of Bayamo [the "Bayamesa"] was played, and cheers were followed by still more cheers, until all [of the Cuban flag] hung free, facing the flag of the stars and stripes, which had flown there since 3 December."[21]

Traditional Celebrations and Nationalist Innovations

At a different remove, and despite the reiteration—in written, oral, and other modes of communication—of a policy of "wiping the slate clean" with respect to the past, not all colonial practices linked to the Hispanic cultural inheritance were rejected or abandoned. Notwithstanding the recently proclaimed separation of church and state, announced with great fanfare as one of the landmark achievements distinguishing the "new era" at hand, the dates "to observe" from the colonial era, as decreed by the Catholic religion—saints' days, fasting days, processional days, and days for Easter and Christmas services and celebrations—continued to order the passage of time, regulate social convention, and fill most of the space in the almanacs.[22]

Religious processions, some the object of celebration reaching back centuries, formed a key component of the "ecclesiastical year" laid out for the faithful in different almanacs. These processions continued to take place, although they were considerably scaled down and had to share public space with "patriotic parades" and other civic commemorations. Inevitably, however, once the U.S. military authorities decreed the end of the historic union of church and state, the right of the Catholic Church to celebrate religious rites and events publicly was called into question. In September 1899 a resident of Santiago de Cuba made a request to Cuba's secretary of state, demanding that the government intervene swiftly and forcefully to prohibit religious processions and protect the right to religious freedom, which had been won "with the American cannon and the Cuban machete." The protester argued: "With Church and State having been separated by virtue of the American Occupation, there is no longer any official religion, the only thing which should be proclaimed is the absolute freedom of religion, and the Government should not allow Catholic priests to organize processions in the streets nor permit the Municipal Police and the Rural Guard to protect these processions and require that passersby remove their hats in reverence to the idol being carried."[23] The celebration of a community's patron saint, likewise tied closely to the Catholic calendar of feast days, maintained its preponderance as a festival, though it was increasingly stripped of its original religious content. For example, in the middle of 1899, a year after the U.S. military occupation began in Santiago de Cuba, and despite the strong U.S. presence in the city, Demetrio Castillo Duany, the province's civil governor, referred in his correspondence with officials in the Cuban department of state and interior to the popular demand to celebrate the feasts of Saint John, Saint Peter, Saint Cristina, Saint James the Apostle (the city's patron saint), and Saint Anne, "when people don masks."[24] Whether it was still appropriate in the new political circumstances created by the separation of church and state to hold public, community celebrations tied to observances of the Catholic calendar was illustrated in a debate that broke out in Cienfuegos over the celebration of the festival of Saint John in June 1899. Although some months earlier, the city's municipal councilors had on their own account (that is, without bothering to consult the U.S. military authorities) unanimously approved the celebration of the 24 February anniversary of the *Grito de Baire* (Declaration of Baire), which launched the War of Independence (1895–98), the proposal to commemorate the festival of the saint, "supported as a traditional custom which the people have always observed," sparked a heated discussion that brought to light the tension between the loyalty to time-honored festivals and the anticlerical sentiments stirred up by the U.S. occupation. Ultimately, those in favor of respecting long-standing popular tradition prevailed, and the council approved the celebration of the festival—only to regret its decision a few days later. The public disorder that resulted from the excessive partying led to a violent clash between some U.S. troops encamped in the area and several Cuban policemen, almost all former members of the Liberation Army. The incident threatened to undermine the cordial relationship between the Cuban and U.S. authorities in the city.[25]

In 1900, in the coastal community of Mariel, the program of festivities held in honor of Saint Teresa de Jesús, the pueblo's patron saint, reflected a unique symbiosis combining elements of traditional Catholic ceremonial practice, secular entertainments, modern innovations, and nationalism. As the local newspaper reported, the festival began with the usual procession, in which the image of the saint was carried from the church through the streets of the pueblo, a traditional Hail Mary was said, and a mass was celebrated "with a full musical accompaniment." Cuban flags fluttered from houses and a Cuban banner, belonging to the local committee of the National Party, was solemnly blessed by the pueblo's parish priest. The formal events of the occasion were followed by a variety of informal entertainments. The high-pitched whistle of exploding rockets mixed with the music of the *zapateo*, a traditional campesino dance with rhythmic foot stamping. There were sailboat regattas at sea, and on land, in place of the usual horse races, people raced each other on bicycles around a ringed course, while others competed at various games of skill. In the afternoon, the city's residents gathered to watch a balloon launching. At sunset, they were treated to a show of fireworks. The day's festivities were livened up with still more games, "wholesome" in nature, and with dances accompanied by popular music performed by the "renowned orchestra of Felipe Valdés."[26]

Concurrent with the celebration in Mariel, the residents of the nearby pueblo of Guanajay experienced firsthand an innovation, of "Catholic-nationalist" tint, in their local festival calendar. On 4 October, Saint Francis of Assisi was honored. That year—1900—the anniversary was accorded particular importance in Guanajay. However, the celebration in honor of Saint Francis [*San Francisco*] was not organized, as one might expect, by his devotees but instead by the supporters of the pueblo's mayor, Pancho Oberto y Zaldivar, a lieutenant colonel in the Liberation Army, for the simple reason that the colonel's Christian name was also Francisco. Guanajay's municipal council declared the day a "public holiday." On the morning of 4 October, a special entourage, led by the pueblo's police force mounted on horseback, opened the procession. Schoolchildren and the female workforce from the local cigar factories marched behind it through the streets of the town, cheering loudly for the National Party. They were followed by a car bearing the Cuban flag and an open carriage with "indias" and "criollas" sitting on its single row of seats. A musical band and the pueblo's firefighters on their fire truck, which had been decorated with banners and with the name of the mayor affixed in gold letters, brought up the rear of this outré procession.[27]

The celebration of Christmas in 1899 in San Juan de los Remedios, an old town steeped in conventional religiosity but also known for its high-spirited fiestas, provides another instance of the strength behind the "invention of [nationalist] tradition." The town's celebration of these fiestas dates to 1820, when a priest, upset that parishioners were not attending the midnight mass on Christmas Eve, the so-called *misa del gallo* (rooster's mass), had the boys and young men of the town come into the streets and wake up its residents by creating a din with whistles, cans, and *fotutos* (a type of wind instrument), obliging them to turn up at church. On Christmas Eve in 1899, the townsfolk assembled, as was customary, in the former "Isabel II" square, recently renamed the Plaza José Martí. They uncovered their acetylene lights and launched the festivities with the traditional procession of floats. In keeping with the changed circumstances of the time, however, the floats on this occasion displayed Cuban flags and other patriotic-allegorical ornamentation. The lumping together of religious, secular, and nationalist motifs offended María Escobar, a person from the area sympathetic to the patriot cause, who expressed her dismay in a letter to General Máximo Gómez:

> It seems to me that the people around here have gone crazy by confusing
> what is serious with what is playful. On Christmas Eve, amid pieces of
> colored paper, tins, and [scampering] children, they take a bust of Martí,

set it down in the square and later pass it around through the town to the accompaniment of whistling, vivas, and other such doings particular to that night. Very serious, solemn things to be taken so lightly and in times when the ceremony has been drained of its majesty. You didn't escape the hullabaloo: on the day of the 25th they put a bust of you (in your case it had only your name on it) in a carriage with those of Maceo and Martí and drove them through the streets, guarded by girls dressed as mermaids, fairies, and sailors. I am outraged by the desecration and ridiculousness into which we are falling.[28]

Thus, instead of being treated as objects of dignified, reverent homage, the busts of the national heroes were swept into the festive tumult of the Christmas celebration, crassly intermixed with vivas and whistling, colored paper and tins, mermaids and sailors. The lines between the Cuba of the heroic tradition of the wars of liberation, of the martyrology of Martí and Maceo, and the light-hearted, free-spirited Cuba of irreverent partying and mockery were blurred in the course of the popular celebration. Far from being a "desecration," however, the spontaneous homage paid to the "Fathers of the Nation" demonstrated just how widely and deeply popular they were, well before the republican state officially incorporated them into the national pantheon.

As can be seen, then, one of the most notable features of Mariel's celebration of its patron saint, Guanajay's celebration—converted into a public holiday—of its *mambí* mayor's "saint," and the Christmas festivities celebrated in 1899 in San Juan de los Remedios was the interweaving of elements of traditional religious ceremony with elements of an evolving Cuban nationalism. Although relations between the Catholic Church and the secular authorities were characterized by recurrent tension and conflict during this period, so far as the observance of festivals and anniversaries was concerned, there was no radical break with long-established religious traditions. Instead, the pattern was one of accommodation and adjustment between the symbolic codes of a recently created nationalist sentiment and the far older model of Catholic ritual and practice.

The Cuban Fiesta of Our Lady of Charity of El Cobre

An undeniable early manifestation of this symbiotic relationship between the sacred and the political or, specifically in the Cuban case, between a Catholic-based worldview and a belief system organized in part around the core value of nationalism is the ardent devotion to the "mulatta" Virgin of Charity of El Cobre. During the *Guerra de los Diez Años* (Ten Year's War), an image of Our

Lady of Charity presided over the saying of masses and other religious ceremonies that were performed, in improvised fashion, in the fields and jungles, invoked for her powers to come to the aid of the *independentistas* and their cause. A couplet sung in the camps of the insurrectionist forces during the Ten Years' War evokes the intertwining of this mystical saving presence with the political rebellion, the divinely miraculous with the completely worldly:

Our Lady of Charity
The patron saint of Cubans
With machete in hand
We appeal for freedom

In some notes that he had compiled to buttress his study of the El Cobre Virgin of Charity, which he left unpublished, Fernando Ortiz refers to a curious popular legend passed from one person to another during the Ten Years' War. In the legend, the Virgin is described as an "insurrectionist." According to popular tradition, she disappeared now and then, going into the swamps and "appearing afterward, in her sanctuary of El Cobre, stained with mud, her clothes covered with brambles."[29]

Three decades later, during the War of Independence, the soldiers of the Liberation Army continued this tradition by carrying with them medallions engraved with the likeness of the "mambisa" virgin. Supposedly, even Antonio Maceo, known for his affiliation with freemasonry and for military bravery and daring that bordered on the reckless, invariably carried—"just in case," as a special protection—a small medallion of the Virgin of El Cobre fastened to his underwear.[30]

Juxtaposed to the official body of worship sanctioned and promoted by the Catholic Church, an institution characterized by its class-based, racist, and pro-Spanish positions, the veneration of a *criolla* virgin of color by a group of devotees of like color was rooted among the popular sectors of society, part and parcel of the idea of an authentic Cuba found in the country's heartland, a Cuba linked to the image of Martí and the flag, to the full panoply of symbolic representations constituting *cubanía*. Little by little, the Cuban festival of Our Lady of Charity, celebrated on 8 September, gained ground against other Marian celebrations, such as those devoted to the Immaculate Conception (celebrated on 8 December), the Virgin of Covadonga, and Our Lady of Montserrat. These latter cults began to be seen as foreign inasmuch as they symbolized the Spanish presence on the island.[31]

As recorded in the sanctuary's archive, not long after the war was over—on 8 September 1898—the mambí army general Agustín Cebreco visited the temple of Our Lady of Charity in El Cobre, accompanied by his general staff, to pay tribute to the patron saint. Some days later, on 24 September, a large number of liberation troops from different detachments again made their way to El Cobre. Their purpose on this occasion was to have a Cuban flag "baptized." The flag had been presented to Cebreco's regiment by the residents of the coastal town of Cayo Smith. According to a Santiago newspaper that reported on the celebrations accompanying the blessing of the national colors in the sanctuary, "It was a day of rejoicing for the people of El Cobre. The joyous crowd cheered the flag of our sorrows and our glory."[32] The site continued to maintain its central place as a sacred symbol of the independence movement. More than fifteen years hence, with the island now a separate republic, a procession of approximately two thousand former mambise soldiers, led by General Jesús Rabí and Cebreco himself, set off on a pilgrimage from Santiago de Cuba to the sanctuary of El Cobre to request that Our Lady of Charity be officially consecrated as the patron saint of Cuba.[33]

The identification of the image of the Virgin of El Cobre with a tradition of popular patriotism could also be observed through the incorporation of tributes to her in the program of festivities celebrated on the national holiday, 24 February, which commemorated the Grito de Baire.[34] In Marianao, a short distance from Havana and far from the eastern part of the country where the cult originated, the celebrations in 1900 began with a "patriotic" mass in memory of the martyrs of the war; the mass was followed by a fiesta dedicated to the Virgin of Charity.[35] It is thus not surprising that the ecclesiastical authorities, in an effort to win adherents and recover a primacy lost with the end of Spanish rule, the separation of church and state, and the spread of Protestant denominations sponsored by the U.S. authorities, took the initial steps toward recognizing the Virgin of Charity of El Cobre as the island's patron saint. In 1901 the prelates of Santiago de Cuba and Havana asked the Vatican to proclaim its official support for this proposal. Nothing was heard from Rome for fifteen years, but Cuba's patience was finally rewarded. In May 1916 Pope Benedict XV consecrated the Virgin of Charity of El Cobre as the patron saint of the Republic of Cuba.[36]

The Almanacs' Calendar of Saints' Days and Baptismal Congratulations

Although the years of the U.S. intervention saw the introduction of a civil registry, the majority of Cubans still chose, in this period, to have their marriage ceremonies performed "by the Church" and to have their children baptized according to traditional Catholic ritual. Furthermore, the time-honored custom of selecting names for the newly born on the basis of the published lists of saints' days persisted in Cuba, particularly in rural areas, right up to the victory of the Revolution in 1959. Nonetheless, while the overall practice continued, there was an interesting change of emphasis. Consider, for example, the congratulations offered two new parents in 1899, in the social section of a newspaper published in Güines, a town not far from the capital. The couple was congratulated, not for having brought a new Christian into the world (as was traditional) but for having given the homeland a new "citizen," for whom it was wished, in place of the traditional blessings, that he might "occupy one of the best positions in the future Cuban Republic."[37]

The baptism of the child José Belén López Martínez, born in the community of Guanajay on 7 April 1900, engendered a similar reaction. A notice of congratulations printed in a Guanajay newspaper is a classic illustration of the politicization, with clear nationalist overtones, of ancient Catholic practice. In the words of the newspaper: "This little Cuban enters the world during a period of intervention and is baptized during a time of elections. May God make him the citizen of a free, independent, and honored country!"[38]

The leaders and officers of the Liberation Army, who had a high public profile during these years, often were chosen as godparents of these "little citizens" born at the dawn of the twentieth century.[39] In keeping with the patriotic theme injected into these ceremonial customs, many parents chose to send out baptismal cards printed with flags, insignias, or some other allegorical Cuban emblem.[40]

Another congratulatory note, in this case for someone's saint's day, published in the social events section of a Trinidad newspaper on 21 June 1899, illustrates another remarkable feature of daily life in these years—the confluence of dissonant and contradictory images.

Congratulations

The Almanac says that tomorrow the Church commemorates
St. Ciriaco. Our dear friend, the distinguished and esteemed
Sr. Ciriaco García, Lieutenant Colonel in the Cuban Army,
will mark that occasion on his own day.
I wish you many happy returns of the day![41]

The note's final sentence appeared in English.

It would be difficult to find an example more suggestive of the hybrid atmosphere of these years than this simple vignette, which interweaves the survival of religious traditions of earlier times (the celebration of the "saint"), allusions to Cuban patriotism (in the reference to García's participation in the Liberation Army), and the imprint of the U.S. presence, which left contemporary writing and publications littered with American English terms and expressions, as exemplified in the English-language message contained in the congratulatory note.

The Struggle to Have Days Honoring the Fatherland Sanctioned as National Holidays

In addition to the persistence, albeit in modified form, of celebrations marking the ecclesiastical calendar and the outward adoption of anniversaries of significance for the United States, the most salient feature of these years was the swift consolidation—in the very midst of the U.S. intervention—of a nationalist calendar, on which the dates that marked the start of the Ten Years' War and the War of Independence (10 October and 24 February, respectively) were consecrated, unofficially, as *días de la Patria* (national days, or days commemorating the fatherland), incorporated as such in the almanacs, and—we have seen—celebrated throughout the island.

The celebration of these foundational holidays, not by small groups, as was the case during the wars or as happened for other holidays within immigrant communities, but throughout the country, marked an important milestone in the symbolic construction of a separate national identity. National days, commemorated in massive public ceremonies replete with ritual, held at the same time across the island, and covered in both the local and national press, were a core component in the formation of what Benedict Anderson has called the "imagined community of the nation," an essential construct or building block of the future national republic.[42] On the occasion of these celebrations, thousands of Cubans—as they sang the "Bayamesa" in person and in unison, carried portraits and banners in civic processions, recited patriotic *décimas*, waved flags, and dressed in the national colors—manifested in a visible, public way, for the first time since the conclusion of the war, their feelings of belonging to the nation, while also projecting an image of themselves as citizens, albeit of a "virtual," still nonexistent republic. The open, large-scale demonstration of these feelings of cubanía, tolerated by the U.S. authorities, was perceived at the time as a key indicator of the broad popular support enjoyed by those who wanted to make Cuba an independent nation.

Such support notwithstanding, the two days of national celebration did not get inscribed into the almanacs without considerable effort. The history of the official sanctioning of both dates as national holidays, resulting both from popular pressure and discussion and from complicated negotiations with the U.S. military government, can be reconstructed—at least in part—from documents which have survived down to the present.

In October 1898 there were efforts made in Santiago de Cuba, then occupied militarily by detachments of the U.S. Army, to organize the first large-scale festivities to commemorate the uprising of La Demajagua (the plantation, outside of Bayamo, where the Ten Years' War erupted). The effort failed because the U.S. military authorities prohibited the celebrations. Despite the prohibition, ten thousand residents of the city gathered on the anniversary day and marched in pilgrimage to the gravesite, in Santa Ifigenia, of Carlos Manuel de Céspedes, to pay tribute to "the Father of the Nation," in what was probably the first instance of a massive public tribute to a martyr of the independence movement.[43]

In similar fashion, the date of 24 February was commemorated for the first time throughout the island in 1899, barely two months after sovereignty had been officially transferred from Spain to the United States. The anniversary of the uprising that sparked the recently concluded war was also chosen as the day on which General Máximo Gómez, the most popular nationalist military leader, would enter the capital. To mark the occasion, celebrations and tributes were organized in almost all of the city's neighborhoods. Streets were garlanded with triumphal arches and houses decorated with Cuban flags, while the sound of patriotic music was heard across the city.

The festivities commemorating the fourth anniversary of the Grito de Baire closed with an open-air concert in the Parque Central, accompanied by popular dancing and music for the mass of city dwellers, along with an exclusive formal ball held in the Tacón Theater. A mambí soldier who attended the celebrations paints a picture in his memoirs of an enormous throng which, as it wound its way through the streets adjacent to the Parque Central and the Paseo del Prado, vented its happy patriotic mood to the rhythm of the conga, cracking off-color jokes, singing earthy songs, "dancing to the lively beat of the drums and whirling about." Cuban offices remained closed on this day, and even the customhouse and the stock exchange halted their operations in observance of the holiday.[44]

Paralleling events in Havana, the celebration of 24 February in Cienfuegos was accompanied by the entrance into the city of the forces of the Cienfuegos Brigade, under the command of Major General Higinio Esquerra. The festivities on the program included mambise reveilles played by the Cuban army band, an open-air mass held in the Plaza de Armas, a military procession, a parade which included cyclists carrying flags, "young ladies wearing dresses with symbolic and allegorical meanings," and evening activities and patriotic functions in theaters and social clubs. The large working-class population of the city also made the celebration its own. Stevedores, railway workers, cobblers, carpenters, coopers, bakers, barbers, tobacco workers, and typographers took part in the festive patriotic parade, each marching group representing its own union. The members of the Lucumí Council, proudly carrying "banners with allegorical depictions," likewise marched in the parade, along with representatives of other associations of color.[45]

In nearby Trinidad, the day was celebrated with carriage races, fireworks, and people promenading on horseback. In Trinidad, however, the U.S. military forces stationed in the area interjected a new element. The military chief of the district, Colonel Brown, joined the town's mayor in declaring 24 February a holiday. "By this measure, [the local newspaper wrote] both authorities have earned the gratitude of Cubans. . . . they have . . . solemnized a day which henceforth will be immortal in our hearts and whose memory will last forever in our souls." On the day before the anniversary, as if it were nothing out of the ordinary, it was the Tennessee Regiment's military band that entertained the crowd with an outdoor concert in the recently christened Plaza Carrillo.[46]

In Guantánamo, in contrast, the city's mayor, Major General Pedro ("Periquito") Pérez did not bother to request authorization from Leonard Wood (at that time the U.S. military governor of Oriente province) to celebrate the anniversary. In a letter still preserved in the Archivo Histórico Provincial in Santiago de Cuba, the mambí official notes curtly that he is "observing a courtesy" by informing Wood that "on the day of the 24th and the two days following there will be celebrations in this town in honor of that glorious day of the Cuban nation, soon to see fulfilled its enduring and legitimate and most noble aspiration: that of absolute independence." Only then did Pérez add, more diplomatically, that this would be achieved "with the efficacious assistance of the great nation of liberty and justice."[47]

Months later, toward the end of 1899, the general headquarters of the U.S. Army as well as the offices of the secretary of state and interior began to receive dozens of telegrams and letters from municipal councils across Cuba requesting that 10 October and 24 February, the "most noteworthy dates of a redeemed Cuba," be officially proclaimed and sanctioned as public holidays.[48]

Precisely how and under whose leadership this massive campaign to make both dates days of national celebration got started remains a mystery. The most probable explanation is that it began inside the network of a nationalist organization, the Centers for Veterans of Independence. The organization had branches throughout the country and maintained close ties to the municipal authorities in virtually every community. Whatever the ultimate source, what is certain is that over these months there was scarcely a municipality in the country, no matter how small, that did not put into writing the determination of its inhabitants to see both days consecrated as "national days."

The wave of requests did not abate until the first days of January 1900, when the U.S. military governor announced publicly that no decision on the matter would be reached until municipal elections had taken place.[49] Nevertheless, despite this unwillingness to recognize the Días de la Patria as official holidays, on 24 February 1900 the military government did make a partial accommodation, authorizing the suspension of work in the customhouse, the stock exchange, and state offices. "The look of the city could not be more charming or festive," reported *La Lucha*, one of Havana's more widely read dailies, "every street has its banners with the colors of the Cuban flag. The flag has been run up on all of the houses and public buildings." Amazingly, even the governor's palace, headquarters for U.S. military authorities, was decorated for the occasion, with red streamers hanging from its balconies and four Cuban flags placed on the facade of each corner of the building. A massive "meeting" was celebrated in the Albizu Theater, located in the capital's downtown district, where the Cuban National Party's most eloquent orators pleaded publicly for Cuba's rapid attainment of independence. According to a newspaper account, the display of a huge banner with the picture of José Martí on it was "met with an ovation bordering on the delirious." And while the Albizu Theater hosted its political meeting, in the nearby Havana neighborhood of Matadero, likewise decorated with "palm fronds and Cuban flags," two orchestras—which had been playing since the night before—took turns "livening up" the celebration with "*guarachas*, rumbas, *puntos guayaberos*, and *tanguitos criollos*."[50]

All of these manifestations of support for making the two anniversaries official holidays were noteworthy, but the participation that year of the island's schools provided perhaps the most interesting gloss of all on this "invention of [a revolutionary] tradition" under the direct gaze of the U.S. military occupation. In a public school system reorganized on the basis of the U.S. educational model and overseen by a U.S. superintendent, Cuban patriotic anniversaries were not officially recognized as public holidays. Nonetheless, the Havana Board of Education directed that teachers in the city's schools dedicate 24 February to explaining to their students "the meaning of the grand patriotic occasion and to awakening in them a heartfelt devotion to the cause of our independence." "In the event," a journalist for the newspaper *Patria* wrote, "there was not a single school in Havana that did not decorate the facade of its building with the national colors and hold a rally to celebrate the meaning and triumph of the Cuban Revolution."[51] A custom was started in the classrooms that would be institutionalized some years later, with the advent of the Republic: the students sang patriotic anthems, "above all, the anthems of Bayamo and of the Invasion"; and they listened to explanations about the origin of the Cuban flag and coat of arms, as well as to "brief but substantial evocations in praise of the most stellar figures and heroes of our Revolution." At the conclusion of these scholastic ceremonies, the children received Cuban insignias and pictures of the heroes of the independence struggles.[52]

Tensions between the advocates of a patriotic calendar of nationalist anniversaries and partisans of the traditional calendar of religious celebrations closely linked to memories of the colonial past flared into the open in 1900, when the recently named bishop of the Catholic Church in Cuba, the Italian Monsignor Donato Sbarretti, chose 24 February as the date for his arrival in Havana. The offensiveness of this decision is readily apparent if one considers, first, that a year earlier, Máximo Gómez had made his entrance into the capital on the same day and, second, that among the most nationalist elements, the Vatican's naming of the new bishop was tainted. In their eyes, with the end of Spanish domination, it was Cubans themselves who should fill the highest ecclesiastical offices, not foreign dignitaries.[53]

In a flyer, signed by several leaders of the revolution, that was circulated in the city, the bishop's intended course of action was branded an act of profanation and an "out-and-out mocking of our ideals," influenced by all "those who, in their inexhaustible hatred for this land, want, by striking this black note, to efface the jubilation with which our people are going to commemorate the anniversary of the glorious day on which the Revolution began, and whose end has been the triumph of our freedoms." The manifesto ends by calling on Governor-General Leonard Wood to "block the consummation of this outrage" and on the people to gather in front of the pier at El Templete to repudiate the foreign bishop.[54] Thus, the reception to be accorded a new bishop, an event which in colonial times would have been the occasion for public festivities and an outpouring of respect, became a source of friction between the ecclesiastical authorities and the revolutionary vanguard. It also furnished an opportunity for the open expression of nationalist sentiments.

Later in the year, in October 1900, the Cuban Department of State and Interior, which functioned as a mediator among the U.S. military authorities, the nationalist organizations, and the country's body of municipal officials, sent a telegram to the civil governors of the different provinces authorizing the extraofficial celebration of the anniversary of the Revolution of Yara.[55]

As a consequence, toward the end of year, and in violation of military order

176, even the University of Havana, an official institution little inclined to infringe the order, saw fit to adopt the new patriotic calendar as its own. The university suspended classes and other activities not just on 24 February and 10 October but on 27 November as well, to honor the anniversary of the execution by firing squad, in 1871, of a group of medical students who became the first student martyrs of the independence struggle.[56]

In January 1901, the mayors of Sagua, Abreus, Bahía Honda, Santa Isabel de las Lajas, Mariel, Sabanilla, Holguín, Santiago de Cuba, Cruces, Manzanillo, San Juan de las Yeras, Colón, San Diego de los Baños, Bejucal, Bolondrón, Managua, Cárdenas, Cabezas, Guanabacoa, Puerto Príncipe, and many other communities reengaged the issue, repeating their earlier tactic of petitioning to have both anniversaries officially sanctioned as national public holidays. Once the municipal elections had taken place and local power was in the hands of officials elected by popular vote, the time had come—as the mayor of Los Palacios pointed out and as the letters to the U.S. military governor sent by all the other mayors insisted—"to fulfill the clear wishes of the Cuban people that the memory of the heroic and glorious sacrifices made for our independence be honored on these days."[57]

Diego Tamayo, then serving as secretary of state and interior, inserted himself into the matter by writing a letter in January 1902 to Leonard Wood, in which he summarized the popular demand: "Over the course of the last two years since Spanish sovereignty came to an end on this island, the country has celebrated these days, even though they are not considered holidays in official circles, and they will surely continue to be celebrated with the same enthusiasm with which the sons of America commemorate the anniversaries of their respective declarations of independence. The decision to break from Spain cost Cuba too many sacrifices for her to face the prospect that the two days on which she proved her intentions to the world are not, today, occasions for official celebration."[58]

Thus, in a new effort to obtain legal sanction from the military government for the celebration of Cuba's "national days," the department proposed that a fresh order be issued, through which the dates in question would be given the same legal effect as those noted in military order 176, which dealt with the regulation of public holidays and, as we have seen, embraced only a subset of the older, traditional holidays, while excluding any commemoration with political implications.

Once again, however, the U.S. military authorities managed to deflect the issue, this time by using the excuse of the impending adoption of a constitution for the Cuban Republic. In a terse though courteous note sent to the

Cuban Department of State, the U.S. military governor explained that, while he appreciated the popular desire to have the two anniversaries made into public holidays, he did not feel at liberty to declare them as such given that a constitution for the government of Cuba was still being drafted. Only the Cuban state itself, he believed, would have the legal authority—in the near future—to designate permanent official celebrations. Nevertheless, in a concession to the two years of insistent pressures and demands, the military government yielded temporarily, announcing that the national celebrations would have legal status in 1900 and authorizing the suspension of all public business on the two days.[59]

Consequently, in towns and rural communities across the country, the municipal councils declared the national days as days of celebration. Various commemorative activities were organized. The streets were decorated, and schools, offices, and businesses closed their doors. In the pueblo of Batabanó, for example, it was announced that a grand patriotic dance would be held in the Liceo Martí to celebrate 10 October. The board of the Liceo dramatized the occasion by debuting the club's new electric lighting, which with its gleaming "chandelier of fine cut glass" cast light over a wide area "to startling and dazzling effect."[60] On the next holiday, 24 February 1901, the residents of Batabanó awakened to the sound of "spirited reveilles and to the burst of rockets and firecrackers shattering the air." According to the local newspaper, when the fog lifted that morning, "the Cuban flag could be seen on all of the pueblo's towers and flagpoles." The streets, which had been decorated for the celebration, were filled from early in the day with crowds of schoolchildren who marched along happily, "holding their little tricolor flags and singing the national anthem." The day ended with a dance in the Liceo, where, to everyone's satisfaction, the local orchestra played a great many "delightful" Cuban popular dance pieces.[61]

Batabanó's festive spirit of celebration was repeated in communities across the island. The program of festivities organized by the municipal authorities in Consolación del Sur for 24 February 1901 included a public rally, schoolchildren parading with banners, a reception and banquet in the municipal building, bicycle races, an open-air concert in the main plaza, fireworks, and—as the closing event—the launching of a large balloon. "All of these entertainments," the local newspaper announced, "will be enlivened by a band which will play the Anthem of Bayamo."[62]

Cockfighting and Patriotism

Patriotic anniversaries were celebrated by the populace in a variety of ways, some of which were belittled and condemned by the authorities and the educated classes. In contrast to the newer celebrations, with their bicycle races, hot-air balloons, and electric lighting, the custom in many towns and communities—dating back to the colonial period—was to celebrate holidays and feast days with cockfights, a practice which now came to be criticized as "uncivilized." Indeed, it was declared illegal in military order 165, issued in 1899 by the general headquarters of the military government.[63]

Traditionally, in the western and central parts of the country, cockfights, accompanied by gambling, took place during the month of February—the time of both the sugar harvest, when money flowed freely in the countryside, and carnival. The pastime of cockfighting was extremely popular. Because the 24 February festivities coincided with the celebration of carnival, the "time for cockfighting" on the calendar of popular celebrations now overlapped with the newly inaugurated "time of national patriotic celebration." This coincidence gave rise to friction between the numerous aficionados of cockfighting and the local authorities, who had to decide between allowing cockfights to go on in the midst of the new festivities and suppressing them by enforcing the occupation government's unpopular decree.

A case in point arose on 24 February 1901 in the community of San Juan y Martínez, located in the province of Pinar del Río, when a person acting on behalf of a large contingent of residents requested permission to celebrate the occasion with a cockfight. After the rejection of its request by the local municipal official, the disaffected group went off into the woods on the outskirts of the pueblo in defiance of the prohibition. On their return from their escapade, "with the roosters in their hands and their clothes stained with blood," as the charge against them read, the violators were arrested by the Rural Guard and put on trial.[64]

The incident clearly demonstrates just how differently one group of Cubans, in contrast to another, viewed (and celebrated) the idea that it belonged to an entity called the nation. Although considered a mark of identity by broad sectors of the popular classes, cockfights had nonetheless been declared illegal. As a result, they were excluded from a national program of festivities designed, purportedly, to commemorate the nation's patriotic origins and give public expression to feelings of cubanía in the face of the U.S. presence on the island.

Contrary to the commonly held view, the most fervent champions of the prohibition against cockfighting were not the U.S. authorities but representatives of a sector of the Cuban nationalist elite, who—even as they ardently opposed the tradition of cockfighting—strove to make the two anniversary days into national public holidays.[65]

José Miguel Gómez, the civil governor of Santa Clara (one of the areas of the island most disposed to cockfighting) personified these contradictory impulses. An enthusiastic supporter of the campaign to win official status for the national holidays, Gómez also headed up the list of signatories of a petition sent to John Brooke, asking that the U.S. authorities ban cockfights. In a letter submitted in April 1899, signed "in the name of the majority of the honorable population," the Santa Clara political leader requested the proscription of cockfights "as forms of entertainment contrary to the more cultivated ways of the people."[66] Diego Tamayo, then serving as secretary of state and interior—and, during the drive to win approval for the new national holidays, the foremost mediator between the interests of Cubans at large and the U.S. military government—was also one of the staunchest advocates of a total prohibition of cockfights.[67] In his opinion, all "barbarous" or "uncivilized" traits, however deeply rooted they might be, had to be totally purged from national life or, failing that, carefully "wiped away" or concealed, in order to show the occupying power that Cubans were not roughneck "natives" with ignorant and backward habits but cultured "citizens" with a modern outlook, and therefore deserving of their own government.

The general perception of cockfighting was that of a custom closely linked to a tradition of cubanía with deep popular roots. A very different image of cockfighting, however, emerges quite clearly in various documents dealing with this topic which are preserved in the archives of the U.S. military government. In January 1901, just as the campaign waged by the municipal councils to gain official recognition for the anniversaries of the declarations of Yara and Baire reached its apogee, an anonymous circular was distributed in the rural areas of the country. The circular not only exhorted campesinos to participate in a demonstration organized to demand the abrogation of military order 165 but also made clear that those unwilling to participate would be seen as "bad Cubans." Emilio Acosta, the self-proclaimed "president of Cuba's campesinos," together with two officers of the Liberation Army, Florentino Navarrete and Pedro Delgado, tried to convince the military authorities of the need to revoke the prohibition on cockfighting. In a letter of 30 January 1901 sent to the military government, the three leaders asserted that "80 percent of Cuba's campesinos can't do without cockfights." The U.S. government, they continued, came to Cuba "to grant us liberty, not to deprive us of legal entertainments, grounded in the customs and traditions of this country." Thus, the letter went on to state, "out of respect for the opinion of the majority," the law should be abrogated and the celebration of cockfighting authorized once again.[68]

From this perspective, the alliance formed between the most nationalist sectors of the Cuban elite and the popular classes against the interests of the U.S. occupation, an alliance which flowered most noticeably in the campaign to win legal recognition for celebrating the two revolutionary anniversaries, was not as monolithic as it might have seemed. The cultural and class-based differences among the nationalist groups become fully apparent when one moves from the consensus over the validity of celebrating these "national days" to the debate over the preferred ways—"modern" or "traditional," "refined" or "popular," "civilized" or "atavistic"—to celebrate them. In this sense, the patriotic celebrations held in these years should be examined as more than just strategic vehicles for strengthening and solidifying a broad social consensus underlying Cuban aspirations for independence, conceived both as a break with the colonial past and as opposition to the U.S. imperial presence. Just as the backdrop to the festivities served as a kind of tapestry in which nationalist feelings were woven together and expressed "as coming from one community," so it also served as the complex ground of confrontation and negotiation, where the differences between the celebratory practices of popular culture and an elitist understanding of the "appropriate" way to celebrate holidays were clearly exposed.

Behind the debates over the suitability of marching, according to modern fashion, in the style of U.S. civic parades, over whether to prefer the traditional form of the classic religious procession or the irreverent, high-spirited procession which followed the rhythm of "carnival conga drumming," whether to celebrate the typical horse races or replace these with bicycle competitions, whether or not to include such *yanquí* games as *base-ball* in a program devoted to a nationalist celebration, and whether to tolerate or suppress activities (such as cockfights) considered "atavistic" and declared illegal—behind all these and other such tensions lay important political and cultural differences.

Patriotic Celebrations as the Polemical Expression of Internal Social Cleavages

Thus, under the surface harmony of popular patriotic celebrations, the deliberations and the give-and-take over seemingly trivial issues—who ought to march in a parade and in what order, who should preside over a committee, what type of music should be played, what style of dance was appropriate and with whom should one dance, through what symbolic and allegorical lens a program of festivities should be seen—revealed distinctions grounded in social class, ideology, and gender as well as in ethnic and racial tensions.

The festivities held in the pueblo of Guanajay in 1900 to commemorate the

10 October anniversary offer a telling example of this dynamic. The pueblo's celebration, organized by the veterans' center and characterized by the local newspaper as "magnificent," followed a familiar script: in the morning, the celebration of a mass, a procession through the streets, complete with banners and a priest walking "with the cross and candlesticks," and the blessing by the parish priest of the cornerstone of a clubhouse for local workers; in the afternoon, a baseball game and a bicycle race; and in the evening, in the pueblo's cultural center, a program of patriotic anthems and poems, followed by the customary dance, featuring an orchestra playing popular Cuban music.[69]

Despite the "magnificent" atmosphere surrounding the celebration, a closer reading of the reports appearing in Guanajay's newspaper in the days after the event reveals compromises and disagreements. The pueblo's mayor, who held the rank of lieutenant colonel in the Liberation Army and, according to the paper, had personally fought in both wars of liberation, bypassed the evening program because he felt slighted by the members of the local veterans' association.

Tension existed between some members of the "educated" civil elite of Guanajay, led by the president of the "Progressive Center" (a recreational and educational club) and veterans of the Liberation Army, who congregated in the veterans' center and were led by their president, a black colonel, José Gálvez. The two men and their respective coteries were fighting for local political control. The antagonism between the two camps resulted in a heated dispute between the two presidents over who should have the right to preside at the main table during the evening festivities.

Other reported complaints broadened the picture of socioeconomic tension and resentments within the community. In the newspaper's original coverage, the female workers from the tobacco factory who had been selected to march in the procession were represented as happy and eager to do so. Later, however, these workers vented their displeasure, because the closing of business for the celebration had caused them to lose their daily wage. On a similar note, spokesmen for the pueblo's commercial interests, largely in the hands of Spaniards, complained about the arbitrary way in which they were obliged to close their businesses for the day, an obligation all the more galling for those who (for obvious reasons) did not entertain the same patriotic emotions about the occasion. Finally, the pueblo's newspaper lamented the fact that another paper, with national distribution, had wrongly reported that Guanajay's celebration had taken place entirely on the initiative of its mayor, when in fact the funds supporting the festivities had been collected, penny by penny, in homes and work places by members of the veterans' center, which organized the popular financing of the event.

What is more, some days prior to 10 October, racial and gender divisions among Guanajay's "patriots" had flared into the open when, during another commemoration (honoring the mayor and nationalist "saint" Pancho Oberto) taking place in the town hall, only the white women in attendance were invited to sit down; the black women present were obliged to remain standing, despite their *obertista* loyalties, which they displayed through enthusiastic participation in the celebration.[70]

This small "sampling," taken from a local source but reflective of a wider phenomenon, confirms the existence of a dual reality (the display of a nationalist consensus in the face of the foreign imperial presence alongside the multifaceted expression of social distinctions internal to the country) to the celebration of patriotic festivities. Despite the inclusiveness of popular celebrations, in many pueblos—above all in western Cuba, where racial prejudice was more pronounced—blacks and whites who had shared "as one community" the political side of the celebration, were called on, once the dance began, to stay at a "proper distance" from each other. Close physical proximity at a community event like a dance showed a lack of "respect" for the maintenance of social distinctions. Once the parades and rallies were over, it was incumbent on each "race" to demonstrate its "patriotic feelings" apart from the other, in accordance with practices rooted in the colonial past.

Anthems, *Danzones*, and Drum Beating

The music played to enliven celebrations was also the subject of disagreement and debate during this period. Although the inclusion of anthems (especially the "Bayamesa," by now the unofficial national anthem) was universally endorsed, because it demonstrated that the country had adapted to modern practice and because it showed a desire for independence and the fruits of citizenship, no such agreement existed regarding other ways of expressing the culture of popular music. The differences between an elite culture that defended and celebrated the virtues of a "civilized" Cuba (formed in the image of the nations of the West) and the idea of cultural identity, and of how it manifested itself, held by the masses, were abundantly clear during these years. This was a time in which Cubans found themselves compelled to try to "pass" a kind of civility "test" before the "tribunal" set up by the U.S. interventionists.

As I noted in discussing cockfighting, a segment of the nationalist group believed it imperative to eradicate, or—if that proved impossible—to at least conceal from the eyes of the North Americans popular forms of cultural expression (such as certain types of African-influenced music and dance) which it considered "barbaric," "backward," and "unworthy of modern times."

Even in earlier times, during the colonial period, the more fanatical "modernizers" and "moralizers" had done battle, through the periodical press and by influencing legislation, to control the apparent creole desire to dance everywhere and at all hours. Dancing and idleness, cockfights and the lottery, were key ingredients in the discourse about a set of resolutely *orientalist* qualities which the elite proposed as the nub of the "deeply rooted" characteristics of the "masses," or of the racially mixed person "found in the population of the tropics." This discourse also had a blatantly racist aspect and was laden with sexist stereotypes, the aim of which was to trace a line separating the "correct" and "hygienic" practices and social etiquette of those "above" from the "barbaric" and "uncontrolled" ways in which the masses comported themselves. Such a line between the upper and lower classes would block or at least regulate excessive contact and mixing which encounters like those on the dance floor or in the cockfighting pit furnished. The distinguished Puerto Rican sociologist Ángel Quintero has described "the threshold between the public and the private [that] constituted the field of interpersonal relations."

> To avoid the democratization which this threshold threatened to
> bring, the modalities had to be made *somatic*, their codification—or
> etiquette—needed to be constructed with constant reference to the body
> and to physical movements. . . . Confronted by the rhythmic vitality of
> the threatening *otherness* of the "subaltern" Afro-popular world, it is not
> surprising that the principal concern of the landowning plantocracy,
> with regard to pleasures, morals, and etiquette . . . focused on the public
> act par excellence of physical movement and proximity: couples danc-
> ing. In the Caribbean, it would be at dances, more than at the table, that
> refinement, *cultivated ways*, and *civilization* would be put to the test.[71]

The *danzón*, which had achieved remarkable popularity by the 1880s even among people considered to be part of the "better classes," thus became the focus of a heated argument in these years between those who stigmatized it as "degenerate" and "base," a clear expression of the lasciviousness and sexual promiscuity "characteristic" of African culture, and those who saw in it a sign or mark of cubanía.[72]

In the words of a fashion reporter for one of the country's elite magazines, "the danzón, very nice, very amenable to our climate and all of that, is not however an acceptable or proper dance for a modern soirée. The [U.S.] intervention will bring us a free and stable government and will give us new dances and customs."[73]

The effort by the elite press to dictate and control styles of dancing as part of its larger campaign to gentrify and "whiten" social customs was perceived as a threat to national identity by a majority of popular opinion. Far from aping a North American style of fashionable dance, the Cuban lower class redoubled its affection for its own way of dancing, even inventing a new kind of dance—the "patriotic dance"—in which the danzón became a symbol of protest against the "civilizing" pretensions of a forced acculturation.

As a result, every popular celebration held in these years had its corresponding orchestra complete with a full repertoire of Cuban danzones. Dancing the danzón on the occasion of national celebrations, rather than the two-step, the North American dance then in vogue among high society, was thus seen as a way to reaffirm cubanía. It was a premeditated way of resisting the foreign penetration and subversion of authentic Cuban culture. Outside the milieu of official political life, at social gatherings, and in cockfighting pits and gambling dens, in dance halls and cafés, the "masses" resisted the prompting to remake themselves; they were determined to live by their own lights, persistently denying the call to reform their customs and habits according to the puritanical blueprint shared by the Cuban elite and the U.S. interventionist authorities.[74]

Both the era's poetry and its popular theater (which has survived to the present day) illustrate how authorities' attempts to regulate "undulations of the waist" were mocked by the populace. People danced not only at patriotic celebrations. Weddings, baptisms, birthdays, "saints' days," and *bailes de pensión* (private or home parties) provided an excuse to "let down one's hair" by enjoying in a small space the slow, loose embrace of a gratifying danzón. Although the courts imposed fines on people for "infringing on morality" when they danced the danzón "up against each other," nonetheless, "as native to the soil, by its own measure . . . it kept its standing as the national dance."[75]

The association in the popular mind of the danzón with an authentic Cuban identity, and the recognized threat to the integrity of native culture underlying the seemingly innocuous campaign to "civilize" customs, were readily apparent in the rejection of the two-step, a rejection found in such expressions of popular culture as reveilles, *guarachas* (another type of popular Cuban music and dance), and the comic theater. In Ignacio Sarachaga's *sainete* (one-act musical play), *¡Arriba con el Himno!*, the duel between the danzón and the two-step is clearly settled in favor of the first:

That flighty dance,
—as everyone knows—
is more worthy of a wake
than of a worldly hall.
Why, it's not just a horror,
it offends our patriotism:
so dance it, interventionists,
if that's what you want!
Because the Cuban who manages
to see our future,
need only choose
our Cuban dance!
As long as the danzón exists
and our orchestras wail
Not a sole will saddle us
with the weight of annexation!
Out with the American dance!
And long live our danzón![76]

Some lines published in the press, appearing at the end of 1898, offer another instance of the powerful identification between the danzón as a musical expression of cubanía and the mambí political slogan: "Patria y Libertad!— Does it not seem to you, citizens, that these two words sound sweeter than a danzón played by Raimundo Valenzuela's orchestra? We all but want to dance to their beat."[77]

In this way, on the strength of its great popularity, the danzón began to be recognized as the country's "typical" dance, which had to be performed on any occasion that called for a demonstration of cubanía. Moreover, its reputation was gained at the expense of the zapateo and against the "moralizing" interests of the most Americanized sectors of the elite. This victory was clearly an important development in a wider sociocultural battle, under way since the last decades of the nineteenth century, over the desirability and acceptability of weaving African-based rhythms into the fabric of Cuban social life.

Despite the efforts exerted against "any and all music that sounded black or mulatto," a stylized version of the danzón "with pauses, flourishes with a fan on the woman's part, and a modest embrace made at a prudent distance," had come to seem natural even in the dance halls of "good society."[78] Around 1900, one of the effects of the U.S. presence in Cuba, which had introduced new modes and practices seen as "strange," was to instill a fuller acceptance of the danzón (and, implicitly, its African rhythmic component as well) in the nascent design and formulation of a Cuban national identity.

A still more vivid expression of the undercurrent of African culture running through Cuban society was the custom of "drum beating" maintained by the descendants of slaves as part of ritual holiday celebrations. Under the colony, the public celebrations organized by town councils had been circumscribed by a decree, approved in 1884, legally inscribing a prohibition against the celebration of the *Día de Reyes* (Three Kings' Day) holiday, which included performances by musical groups and other exuberant street activity.

Once Spanish rule had come to an end, many councils and associations composed of "people of color" assumed that they would be fully free, in the new era, to revive the celebration of their own cultural traditions. As it happened, nothing was further from the truth. In 1900 the Havana municipal council totally prohibited the "use of drums of African origin in every kind of meeting and gathering, whether they take place in a public venue or in the interior of buildings." The ban also applied to the passage through city streets of "associations or musical groups, known by the name of *Tangos*, *Cabildos*, and *Claves*, and any others which utilize symbols, allegories, and objects that run counter to the culture and sober nature of the inhabitants of this country."[79]

Steps taken by the municipal council of the southern coastal city of Cienfuegos mimicked those of its Havana counterpart. The council prohibited "tangos and drum beating" not just outdoors but inside buildings, and it urged members of black and mulatto associations to modify their current practices to conform with the strict letter of the law.[80] A year earlier, members of the Lucumí African Cabildo had participated enthusiastically in the program of festivities for the 24 February celebrations. One can easily imagine their feelings as they were denied the right to observe cultural and religious traditions tolerated even during the bleakest periods of Spanish rule.[81]

To pass a decree was one thing, to change ingrained custom was another. In 1900, for example, at the time of the 10 October celebrations, several Havana residents wrote to a local paper angrily protesting that, despite the explicit prohibition against drum beating, "an immoral, antisocial, and uncivilized form of entertainment, there have been three days of street drumming in different neighborhoods of this capital," without any attempt by authorities to enforce the law.[82]

Similarly, music played with percussive instruments of African origin and the public participation of *comparsas*, the conga-playing musical troupes accompanied by street dancing, were noticeable features of the 1899 and 1900 carnival festivities. A witness to the events described how the black comparsas paraded and danced their way through the neighborhoods of the capital, cos-tumed—for parodic effect—in the uniforms of the detested Corps of Volun-teers and Public Order Battalions of the colonial period.[83] Later, in 1902, when the state restored the official celebration of carnival, the comparsas formed by different religious associations were granted the right to march in public. Inspired by that development, a number of *coros de guaguancó* demanded the right, in 1902, to participate in the carnival festivities. These were choral soci-eties, composed largely of black men, who accompanied their singing with drum and other percussion music. A phenomenon of the capital's poorest neighborhoods, such as Jesús María, they had an eclectic repertoire of songs that celebrated patriotic devotion, glorified the participation of blacks and mulattos in the War of Independence, and recounted the great deeds of heroes like Antonio Maceo and Quintín Banderas.[84]

Thus, the partial acceptance of elements of Afro-Cuban culture, implicit in the contagious rhythm of the kettledrum and the swaying (and, for those times, erotic) movements of the hips characteristic of the danzón, contrasts with the draconian prohibition against "the beating of drums," viewed by its critics as a sign of "backwardness" and "barbarism," and considered incom-patible with the "finer customs" and "modern ways" which the elites hoped to cultivate among those who aspired to become "citizens" of the future Cuban Republic.[85] This tension between elitist prejudice against any form of cultural expression of African origin, on the one hand, and the persistent attraction for the force and creativity of Afro-Cuban music, on the other, runs through the subcultures of music and dance through all the years of the Republic. The controversy over whether to accept or reject the danzón was repeated later with the *son* and the rumba, both of which were initially denigrated as "blacks' music," only to be embraced later as icons of the "national culture," albeit in their more insipid and commercial versions.[86]

The "civilizing" obsession, centered on the attempts to control and reform sociocultural practices and channeled during this period through legislation and the press, did not focus solely on the danzón and the playing of drums. In May 1900, just a month after the publication of the decree prohibiting the beating of drums and the appearance of comparsas in the city's streets and public venues, a third element of the popular cultural mosaic, the "Bayamesa," also became—for the first time—the object of municipal regulation. As I noted earlier, this anthem, composed by Perucho Figueredo, was a fixture of the cel-ebrations carried out on the two national days. Played at different tempos and containing varying lyrics, the "Bayamesa" had become an extremely popular tune by the first years of the twentieth century, heard not only on occasions of official celebration but at all sorts of festivities and affairs that might have nationalist connotations.

Attesting to the anthem's great popularity, in February 1900 a young woman wrote to the Havana publication *Patria* to promote her campaign, supported by several other "nice young ladies," "to hear the Anthem of Bayamo played in the Churches, after the sung mass." Those who allege, she stated, that the pope has prohibited national anthems in churches forget that "not long ago our ears were offended by Weyler's March (or better, the Royal March) following the high mass." The young woman ended by writing: "How blessed, sir, to hear this tender music, which makes us delirious with joy, under the holy vaults of the temple! . . . God, it seems to us, will remember the Cubans as that heavenly melody echoes before the altar."[87]

Motivated by the desire to put an end to this "anarchy," the Havana municipal council approved a measure in early 1900 prohibiting the commonplace use of the anthem in "theaters, cafés, processions, demonstrations, etc.," and reserving its use for "serious functions only." The mayor of Pinar del Río was even more explicit. He had an order published spelling out in detail the reasons for the prohibition:

> In all refined communities, anthems and coats of arms are the most sacred symbols of patriotism, for which reason they are accorded profound veneration and great respect.
>
> Eruptions of patriotic sentiments, for so long bottled up and held in check in Cuba, have given the National Anthem, like other such popular scores, such commonality as to hear it played at every kind of celebration and entertainment, some of them of little moment, with the result that the expression "long live the anthem" has come into use recently, constituting another kind of mocking abuse.
>
> For these reasons the mayor's office of Pinar del Río issues the following order:
>
> 1. From this date, the National Anthem, that is, that of Bayamo, may not be publicly played in any place within the city limits other than at official ceremonies, patriotic functions and events, public open-air concerts, and affairs of a genuine political nature.
> 2. Orchestra directors who infringe this order and those prompted to disobey it will incur a fine of ten U.S. dollars, or its equivalent.[88]

These efforts to regulate the "indiscriminate" playing of the "Bayamesa" were severely criticized in *La Nación*, a nationalist political daily published by

General Enrique Collazo. Collazo rose to the defense of the popular appro-priation of the anthem. "The bayamés Anthem," his paper asserted, "resides in the Cuban people and in our judgment, the people have the right to hum it, whistle it, play it, and sing it as the desire comes upon them, where they will and how they will. Because that is to make it popular, not to profane it."[89]

La Nación was riding a popular tide, and the various measures adopted by municipal councils to control the use of the anthem were largely unsuccessful. For example, a press account from December 1900 describes how, at a wed-ding ceremony celebrated in El Mariel, the sound of the "Bayamesa" could be heard inside the church as the bride and groom entered. A few weeks later, the same newspaper printed a story about a meeting of the National Party in the municipality of Caimito. According to the paper's coverage, a large crowd marched to the site of the meeting accompanied by a brass brand joyfully play-ing the notes of the National Anthem.[90] The reality is that the "Bayamesa" continued to be used, willy-nilly, right up to the issuance of decree 154 by the Republic of Cuba on 28 April 1906, which spelled out exactly how and under what circumstances the anthem, coat of arms, flag, and stamps of the nation were to be officially used.[91]

In ways large and small, then, the thinking and orientation of an elite sector, for whom the "proper" form in which to express one's nationality was to sing anthems resonant of Europe in civic parades that were disciplined and orderly, clashed with a mass culture which found a pretext on every festive occasion to abandon itself to the wild and undulating sensuality of popular dance.

Represented as antithetical opposites in the elite discourse of the period, these images of "citizens" who paraded with restraint and composure versus an unruly mass of bodies gyrating to the pounding of a drum are clearly ste-reotypes taken to the extreme. The true picture of nationalist celebrations dur-ing these years is more nuanced. As we have seen, in many cities and smaller communities, patriotic marches and popular dances, solemn revolutionary anthems and lighted-hearted danzones, perhaps even in some cases, despite the prohibitions, cockfights and conga drumming, were successfully woven into the full program of "national day" celebrations.

The dates of 10 February and 10 October were finally approved as official national holidays in 1902, when the United States ended the military occupa-tion and the Cuban Republic was formally inaugurated. Nevertheless, when Tomás Estrada Palma, Cuba's first president, signed the decrees which made the two anniversaries days of national celebration, he was merely putting the stamp of formal state approval on the observance of celebrations which had already been fully integrated into a traditional popular calendar of festivities.

During the years of the U.S. military occupation, the anniversaries commemorating the start of the wars of liberation were the subject of inspiring speeches and newspaper articles and were celebrated in cities and communities across the country with flags, rallies, parades, and a tide of patriotic song and dance. In their totality, these festivities represented the upwelling of a nationalist sentiment that ran through and, on one level, unified all sectors of society.

As Eric Hobsbawm's work has shown, political elites since the mid-nineteenth century have been very successful in elaborating and instituting a schema of symbols and rituals, in which anthems, flags, coats of arms, and— not least—commemorative celebrations dictated by an annual calendar of patriotic festivities assumed a privileged place. The importance of such "invented traditions" in the "production" of citizens and the exercise of social control is incontestable. However, as Hobsbawm himself recognizes, popular participation plays a vital role in the adoption or, better put, the appropriation of these symbolic elements.[92]

Cuba's consecration of a patriotic calendar, during the years of the first U.S. intervention, grew out of a web of factors. First, the commemoration of the country's revolutionary beginnings had a dual cast or character; it both signified and solemnized the break with the colonial past and represented a clear challenge to the imposition of U.S. imperial authority. Second, the sanctioning of the official national holidays resulted from initiatives taken by popular elements combined with the active but controversial mediation of a nationalist-minded elite committed to the creation of an independent state. This latter group, through its involved dealings with U.S. military government authorities, helped to clear the way for the large-scale, public expression of Cubans' collective sense that they were members of a single nation.

The role played by local-level institutions, such as municipal councils, party committees, patriotic clubs, and veterans' associations in this process of constructing a Cuban national identity and its complement of symbols and representations merits deeper study. The images furnished by histories written on the basis of "official" documents generated in the capital, where the U.S. presence was overwhelming, reflect a side of Cuban society which had been thoroughly Americanized or humiliated under the boot of the military occupation. This history and its imagery can and should be contrasted with the picture obtained through other sources, including those generated by local and provincial bodies.

In Cuba's smallest communities, where often not a single North American was to be found for miles around, municipal power was frequently wielded by former members of the Liberation Army or their civilian allies. This situation created the setting for vivid public displays of cubanía, as expressed in parades, banquets, dances, and functions for celebrating the placing of plaques and monuments. In turn, all of these events and ceremonies revealed the exceptional dynamism and creativity of popular political culture. Underlying them as well, however, were complex negotiations between the local elite and the lower classes, between a popular tradition of celebration and an elitist mentality, over the "proper" way to commemorate patriotic occasions. These ritualized, nationalist-inspired activities, freighted with symbolism, were crucial antecedents to the future consolidation, under the Republic, of the "imagined community" of the Cuban nation.

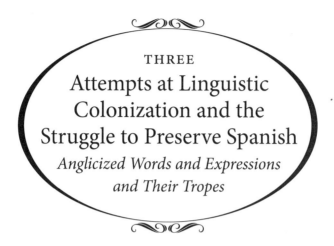

THREE

Attempts at Linguistic Colonization and the Struggle to Preserve Spanish

Anglicized Words and Expressions and Their Tropes

The notions of modernization filtering into Cuba from the United States carried with them a small universe of neologisms, whose function was both practical and symbolic: they gave names to experiences for which the old lexicon of colonial Cuba seemed to lack words.[1] Overnight, in urban areas, *barberías* became "barber shops," *bodegas* turned into "groceries," and many merchants put up notices announcing, "English Spoken Here."[2]

At the appointed time or season, high society (or the "smart set") celebrated "teas" and "garden parties" and spent its summer holidays idling at yacht clubs. The social columns of fashionable magazines and periodicals were often laced with sentences in English, at the expense of French, which had previously been considered the chic language par excellence. While young men enthusiastically enjoyed the activity of different "sports"; "emancipated" women and young ladies, now known as "new women," took up employment "outside the house" as "typists" in offices or "nurses" in hospitals. The political issues of the day were expounded on at "meetings" held on street corners or in "interviews" (conducted by "reporters") published in the press. The *alcaldes* of pueblos were now given the title "mayor" and—to quote a popular play—went about "these worlds, previously of God, now of the Interventionist," not on horseback as had been the custom but, in tune with the new times, on bicycles.[3]

The use of words and phrases in English began to extend beyond middle- or upper-class circles. In this respect, baseball jargon functioned as a precursor. Alluding to the remarkable popularity which baseball had already attained in

Cuba during colonial times, a reporter for *El Fígaro* noted: "'base-ball' it seems has been the precursor to the intervention; we were so familiar, for so many years, with 'bats,' 'pitchers,' and 'balls' that when uttered by the government, the English terms 'deputy collector,' 'chief of police' really don't sound very discordant to our ears."[4]

As the year 1898 got underway, even a devoted partisan of independence like Máximo Gómez became interested in learning English. In a letter to José L. Rodríguez, editor of a book titled *El inglés sin maestros* (*English without Instructors*), Gómez commented on the need for a "simple and practical formula," accessible to everyone, for studying the language.[5] Approximately a year later, inexpensive language texts, such as *El inglés al alcance de todos* (*English for Everyone*) or *El inglés sin maestros en veinte lecciones* (*English without Instructors in Twenty Lessons*), were on sale everywhere.[6] The practice of dropping elementary English-language words and phrases into ordinary speech was not restricted to teachers and students or to office workers and people in the business world. Indeed, a reporter for the *New York Times* commented that in Havana even the shoeblacks in the streets began to solicit customers in choppy English, while the beggars, determined to extract some benefit from the U.S. presence, learned to implore, in broken English, "Please give me a cent."[7]

The language of the newly arrived Anglo-Americans soon became familiar to the average Cuban through the proliferation of signs and notices as well as the advertisements which appeared for a seemingly endless supply of consumer products imported from the "North." In the wake of a gathering stream of thousands of North American tourists, soldiers, businessmen, merchants, journalists, workers, and fortune seekers, Havana filled up with signs and advertisements written in English. "On Obispo Street," writer and journalist Enrique Hernández Millares attested, "even before the Spanish troops had been evacuated, one would read 'Shirt Store,' 'American Shoes,' as if the merchants had calculated ahead of time that the change would be drastic and definitive, and that English was going to be spoken from the very first day after the flags were changed at El Morro."[8]

Some advertisements were bilingual, directed equally at Cuban and Anglo audiences; others used an odd mixture of words and phrases from both languages. A good example of this type of "hybrid" advertisement appeared in the Havana daily *El Reconcentrado*. In June 1899 the paper carried a notice by Crusellas' Store announcing the opening of a *salón de descanso* (lounge) for "ladies" in its establishment, "where all flavors of 'ice cream' would be sold by pretty young ladies."[9]

The hospitality industry burgeoned to accommodate the influx of Anglo-Americans. Between 1899 and 1900, numerous hotels, restaurants, bars, and cafés—many of them operated by North Americans—were opened in response to this new market. In Havana during these months, one new hotel seemed to open on the heels of another—the Thrower Hotel on O'Reilly Street, the New York, Columbia House, and Bay State House guesthouses, and the stylish International Hotel in the district of El Vedado—creating something of a sense of bafflement among the local population. Older hotels, such as the centrally located Hotel Pasaje, were renovated to suit the new clientele. In 1899, in addition to featuring a new electric-powered elevator, the Pasaje was expanded to include forty additional rooms, all "furnished in American style."[10] In the capital, a great many establishments, having names like Yankee Bar, New England Bar, Manhattan Bar, American Tea Room, Gay Broadway Café, Hail Columbia Restaurant, Greater New York Café, and the American Soda Shop provided service *a la americana* during 1899 and 1900.[11]

The flawed translations into Spanish of official U.S. military government documents, which circulated in printed form or were reproduced in the newspapers, also helped implant a bureaucratic lexicon replete with anglicized words and phrases, many of which are still used today. As the end of the U.S. intervention approached, social critic Rafael M. Merchán was moved to observe: "One no longer says *inspector* but *supervisor*; *obstruccionar* has replaced *obstruir*; *reportar, precinto, recesar, aduanal, auditor, vetar*, and its participle *vetado*, have all come to seem natural."[12]

The rampant spread of anglicized words and expressions was not limited to the country's capital. For example, *El Occidente*, a modest newspaper published fortnightly in Guanajay, reported in its sports section how a group of young men, "sportmen," who had won a local bicycle competition were awarded bands, reading "champion," by pretty "ladies," to the great satisfaction of the aficionados of the "sport."[13] In 1901, writing in another small provincial newspaper, a columnist decried the "uncontrolled invasion of words, crassly 'incorporated' as it's said nowadays, stemming from English, thanks to the truly monkey-like, incessant mania for imitation which has been stirred up here since the first day of the North American intervention. . . . what need is there," he wondered, "to say *endoso* for *traslado, supervisión* for *inspección, precinto* for *distrito, forma* for *estado, reportar* for *informar* and numerous other words which have been introduced recently into our language?"[14]

Thus, through a range of sources, such as technical, bureaucratic, or baseball-related jargon, textbooks and inexpensive editions of manuals and pocket dictionaries, and announcements, labels, and posters advertising products, the average Cuban gradually familiarized himself with the "strange" language of the occupier. All the same, notices in English were not always well received.

In one case, the Café Washington—one of the many businesses with an English-language name which opened in Havana during the first months of the U.S. intervention—was shut down in the middle of February 1899 for refusing service to persons "of color." The North American owners were unwilling to serve a black patron who entered the café. The man happened to be a distinguished general from the War of Independence (1895–98), and he protested vehemently. The incident, covered by the nationalist press, turned into a public scandal, obliging the city's governor to order the closing of the café.

The owners, though, were not prepared to concede the fight. They protested the order and obtained permission from the governor to reopen, under the condition that they "observe the country's laws and serve the public without distinctions or differences." On reopening the café, however, the owners chose to defy the Cuban authorities by placing signs in the front window reading: "We carter [sic] to white people only." Their insistence on denying service to nonwhites, as evidenced in the English-language message printed on the signs, resulted in the definitive closing of the establishment and the owners' being prosecuted. They were each sentenced by the Havana court to two months in jail and ordered to pay a fine of 325 pesetas, plus two-thirds of the court costs.

The North Americans filed an appeal, based on a crude literal translation into Spanish of the sign's message ("Nosotros *carreteros* a gente blanca solamente"), alleging that the posted notice did not explicitly say that service would be denied to people "of color." Since the law did not penalize the simple placement of English-language signs in storefront windows, the sentence—they argued—should be revoked. The consideration of the appeal by the Supreme Court led to a lengthy discussion regarding the literalness of the translation as well as the real meaning intended by the message, with its blatantly racist connotations. Ultimately, the court rejected the owners' appeal for annulment and upheld the original sentence.[15]

On the one hand, the Café Washington incident was a reminder that the service provided in hotels, bars, restaurants, and cafés frequently brought with it the racial discrimination openly practiced at that time in the segregated United States. Needless to say, such practice clashed with the advertisements and announcements which sought to create an image of the new "American-style service" as representing the pinnacle of the "modern" and "civilized." On the other hand, the closing of the café and the penalty imposed on its owners for having window signs upholding discrimination clearly demonstrates that even under the difficult conditions of occupation, there was opportunity in

Cuba to assert nationalist and antiracist positions, a prime example of which was the ruling of the country's highest judicial authority, making such actions as those taken by the owners of the Café Washington punishable by law.

The "Americanization" of Teaching

The appearance of English-language notices and advertisements in magazines, newspapers, and businesses, as well as the anglicized words and phrases that began to creep into the spoken Spanish of everyday life, were the external and superficial signs of a wider process—the essentially spontaneous assimilation of elements of Anglo-American social and material culture. The more serious and menacing attempt at linguistic acculturation, however, occurred as part of a project, championed by the U.S. military government, to reform education. In contrast to other initiatives (which in general were limited to the capital and major urban areas, and, within these, to those sectors of society that tended to come into direct contact with U.S. government officials, investors, or military officers), the projected overhaul of public education, and primary education in particular, would affect thousands of schoolchildren of both sexes and of all classes and races, across the length and breadth of the country.[16]

U.S. "Nongovernmental" Organizations and the Learning of English

In September 1898, H. K. Harroun, a U.S. educator, founded an organization whose declared purpose was "to stamp the American educational system upon Cuban ignorance and laxity."[17] Harroun's Cuban Educational Association (CEA) proposed to bring college-age Cubans to study in U.S. universities and centers of higher education and to provide the students with scholarships covering the cost of books, tuition, and other academic fees. The students' families were expected to provide the funds needed to pay their campus living expenses (food, clothing, pocket money, and other incidentals), which were calculated to run between two hundred and three hundred dollars annually. Although this sum is miniscule in today's dollars, it was nonetheless totally out of reach for the majority of people in a country still mired in the ruins of a devastating war. Thus, virtually all the scholarships ultimately went to students whose families were either middle or upper class.

This project, conceived and implemented by a "nongovernmental" organization, more than met its objective, as more than three hundred universities, spread across all forty-five states, agreed to participate in the program. Through the efforts of the CEA, scores of Cuban and Puerto Rican students left home to study on U.S. campuses, having promised to return to their country on graduation. The CEA initiative, like so many others introduced during this complex transitional period, was motivated by contradictory impulses. It reflected the sense of solidarity and altruism felt by certain sectors of the U.S. population, coexisting with an unbridled will to exercise imperial domination. At the same time as it appealed to a fraternal spirit exhibited by the public as well as by state and private institutions (the universities offered books and tutors and modified their admission policies, the railroad companies transported students free of charge, families housed them either gratis or at very low cost, and Anglo-American students at these universities volunteered to help them learn the language and overcome difficulties in the classroom), the CEA's leadership did not conceal the element of cultural colonization embedded in the project.

In an article published in the *American Monthly Review of Reviews*, Harroun described the benefits of bringing Cuban and Puerto Rican young adults to study at U.S. universities, "educating them and liberating them from the harmful influence of militarism, instilling into their youthful hearts the doctrines of peace, order, love of work which sustain our people and our government."[18] The idea was that these students, imbued with a knowledge not only of the language but also of the distinctive "American" spirit and approach to the world, would then return to the island to take up positions critical to directing the affairs of their country.

Harroun's article, written in the grandiloquent style typically employed by exponents of the white man's "civilizing mission," was full of the racist stereotypes and clichéd sentiments about the "Latin races" shared by many North Americans of the time: "In forwarding the educational interests of these young Latins the American educator finds himself obliged to be somewhat patient. Of all the race compounds with which our country has had to deal, these young men are found to be the greatest novelty. Their ideas of liberty are incongruous; they have been reared to live in their imagination, each family being a sort of clan and possessing its own idol, whose sympathy can be relied upon in all family emergencies."

Despite these defects, Harroun concluded, the students were docile and pliable; their bad habits could be easily corrected once they acquired knowledge of English and a certain familiarity with the "American way of life." This large-scale pedagogical experiment was expected to have important consequences over the long term: "Bringing . . . 2,500 of these worthy, malleable young men . . . and tutoring them among the 16,000,000 of our own bright American school boys and girls and then returning them to their homes cannot but produce a stage of human development that will glimmer as a beacon light in aiding to create a stable pacific government in the Antilles."[19]

A second "nongovernmental" U.S. organization, the Cuban-American League, also expressed a desire to collaborate on the project. Its wish to do so was conveyed in a letter written by the league's president, William McDowell, to Joseph Wheeler, CEA vice president, in which the former underscored his organization's support for the plan to provide free education in the United States to Cuban students.[20] Francisco Figueras, the league's vice president and a well-known member of the annexationist lobby, added his own thoughts to Wheeler's letter about the outcome that might be achieved through the combined efforts of the two associations: "If General Wheeler's plan of providing free education in American colleges, could be carried out in accord with the League, it would prove of such value to us that I do not doubt that all obstacles in our way would vanish and adhesion and converts to the cause of union with the United States would flock in hundreds and thousands."[21]

Figueras was not only an enthusiastic proponent of the plan but also proposed enlarging its scope so that in addition to young men whose families could afford the cost of food, clothing, and the like, it would include the "orphans of the revolution," that is, the hundreds of young men—many the sons of soldiers and officers in the Liberation Army—whom the war had left without families. "This I consider indispensable," wrote Figueras, "to install American sentiment among the Cuban[s] and, at the same time the desire for annexation."[22] This part of the project does not appear to have been adopted. Nevertheless, on a purely individual basis, some sons of *mambise* leaders and martyrs did manage to benefit from the program. Among others, the only son of Antonio Maceo, one of Calixto García's sons, and the eldest son of Juan Gualberto Gómez pursued their university studies in the United States, under the partial sponsorship of the CEA.[23]

Learning English was clearly a keystone of these projects. Harroun's efforts are a case in point. Not content simply to implement the CEA's scholarship program, he tried to influence the redesign of the Cuban educational system, focusing in particular on university-level teaching priorities. In a report that he prepared aimed at sketching out new guidelines to follow for restructuring university teaching in Havana, Harroun suggested that the study of English be made obligatory. In his view, English should come to occupy the preeminent place once assigned to Latin in the school curriculum.[24]

Expanding on this theme, Harroun's counterpart and fellow enthusiast from the Cuban American League, McDowell, maintained that the teaching of English in Cuba would ultimately lead to the annexation of the island.[25] Around the same time, in Matanzas, the U.S. military governor, James H. Wilson, wrote to the wealthy philanthropist Andrew Carnegie, appealing for funds with which to purchase books in English, since the people in that region "are anxious to learn English and read and study American books." "Unquestionably," Wilson added, "our literature will promote their knowledge, improve their morals and give this people a new and better trend of thought."[26]

Unsurprisingly, the "moral improvement" of the "natives" and their acquisition of these "new and better" ways of thinking through the study of the English language and North American texts were not to be entrusted to volunteers and philanthropists. Quite soon, under the terms of a new law governing the schools, the teaching of English would be required at the primary level.

The English Language in the System of Primary School Teaching

Twelve months after the U.S. intervention was launched in Santiago de Cuba, the *New York Tribune* reported that, starting with the new school year in September 1899, English would be taught in all public school grades, "for the purpose of its Americanizing effect."[27] The need for early instruction in English was spelled out in the *Manual para maestros* (*Teacher's Manual*), a text written by the newly appointed superintendent of public schools in Cuba, Alexis Frye, which set down standardized techniques for teaching the language and provided a curriculum guide for the English-language program in the country's primary schools. In Frye's words: "In light of both the important commercial relations and ties of friendship that exist between Cuba and the United States as well as the important role which Cuba is destined to play in relations between the Great Republic of the North and the Hispano-American Republics to the South, it is vitally important that Cuban children learn to speak and read the English language."[28]

Books as well as other scholastic material used in the program were imported from the United States and distributed uniformly and free of charge throughout the country. The provision of these materials was a boon to U.S. publishing houses—such as Appleton, Ginn, and Company; the American Book Company; and Silver Burdett and Company—who received purchase orders from the U.S. government for large quantities of manuals, notebooks, wall charts, and other items.

On this score, Leonard Reibold, a representative of the American Book Company, confided in January 1899 to Harroun: "We are supplying a good many of our American school books to Cuba through the booksellers at Havana, Santiago, and other places on the Island, and have also had a very large order from the Military Governor of Puerto Rico." He also informed Harroun that the island would soon have a superintendent (Alexis Frye), who would contract the services of the best teachers in the United States. The latter would travel to Cuba to "instruct Cuban teachers how to teach." As part of the educational project, children in the country's schools would be given a daily lesson in English so that they could begin to acquire the language in a gradual, methodical way.[29]

In line with the overarching interest in bringing the fruits of Anglo-American life to Cuba, and reaping the economic benefits of doing so, Sam W. Small, an agent for the Silver Burdett publishing company, wrote in 1900 to the well-known Cuban writer Raimundo Cabrera, requesting his cooperation in a project to translate and adapt U.S. history texts, in particular *First Steps in the History of Our Country* and *The Rescue of Cuba*, so they could be used in Cuba's schools. The first book was used in the lower grades, to introduce students to the study of history. It contained a section with biographical profiles of the founding fathers and other important figures in the history of the United States. Burdett proposed that it be adapted for Cuban children by adding biographical sketches of major figures in Cuban history to this section. With respect to *The Rescue of Cuba*, a book dealing with the "Spanish-American" war, he observed: "In the absence of any distinctively Cuban history of the late revolt and its successful issue, we are of the opinion that this book will serve a most useful purpose in acquainting Cuban children with all the details of the deliverance of their Island."[30]

Translations and adaptations of U.S. textbooks were rushed into print. Some, like the bilingual edition of *McGuffey's Revised First Reader*, were a travesty of translation. Indeed the translation of *McGuffey's*, a manual for learning English widely used in U.S. elementary schools, was criticized so severely for its butchering of Spanish grammar and syntax that it was quickly removed from the list of texts designated for use in Cuban schools. A representative of the publisher that produced *McGuffey's* tried to rationalize this failure by explaining that the text was originally adapted for use in the schools of New Mexico, and so had been translated not into Spanish but into the "patois" that was spoken along the frontier between the United States and Mexico. All of the translated texts, even the better ones, used images and described objects and scenes—apples, pears, and peaches, for example, or houses with chimneys and toboggans on snowy slopes, that made no sense to children living in the tropics.[31]

Not even the very youngest children were exempt from the plan directed at linguistic "Americanization." To some extent, in fact, the success achieved in teaching a new language was inversely related to the age of those being taught. As Marie Keil, the director of kindergarten instruction on the island, realistically pointed out in her first annual report, children at that level—three to six years of age—were more readily able to learn English.[32]

The emphasis, then, which U.S. government authorities placed on teaching English was anything but incidental. Louis Pérez Jr. has clearly shown that the U.S. educational project was conceived as a mechanism through which Cuban society could be drawn into the Anglo-American cultural mainstream. It would accomplish, in a short period of time, what the U.S. military governor Leonard Wood called "annexation by acclimation."

In Pérez's words: "At a more fundamental level, education functioned as the cultural component of the larger annexationist design. The classroom was transformed into an agent for the transfusion of cultural values and the transfiguration of political attitudes. Indeed, education provided the means of penetrating Cuban society . . . for the purpose of arresting the development of an autonomous and potentially rival national culture."[33]

To the bureaucratic mind, the plan may have seemed unassailable. Yet, as experience often demonstrates, the results achieved through a particular course of action or policy initiative may differ from the outcome originally intended by those devising it. Pérez's analysis is based on exclusively North American sources and thus ignores the multiple strategies which Cubans employed to confront and, in my judgment, frustrate Anglo-Americans' expectations regarding the cultural assimilation of Cubans through the agency of the schools. As Pérez himself has pointed out in a much more recent work, Cubans rapidly mastered the art of "metabolizing" U.S. cultural influences by honing a fine-grained capacity to absorb and accommodate, into their own culture, "modernizing" elements from the North without surrendering their own identity in the process.[34] With respect to the Americanization-through-language project promoted by the U.S. government authorities, a project pushed at times very directly and at other times more subtly, the Cubans managed to obstruct the introduction of any full-scale program of teaching English in the schools without—as we shall see—flatly rejecting the most progressive principles and elements of the U.S. educational system.

The lack of primary school teachers with the requisite knowledge of English was one of the main reasons why the ambitious plan to teach the language to more than 150,000 school-age children could not be immediately implemented. Near the end of 1901, out of a national enrollment of 159,267 elementary-school children, only 6,267 had received instruction in English.[35] The government planned to address this problem by increasing the salaries paid to language instructors.[36] The earlier idea of introducing bilingual education in the schools by bringing U.S. teachers to Cuba had been quickly discarded. The possibility that teachers from the United States would be hired to fill positions otherwise occupied by Cubans was unanimously opposed from the start.

A contemporary educational journal put the issue as follows: "It must be Cubans, then, who teach our children in the schools, because they are the ones, not others, who know our children's language, their particular way of being, their virtues, their aptitudes, and their own drawbacks."[37] The most distinguished figures in Cuban arts and letters, men such as Enrique José Varona, Manuel Sanguily, Rafael Montoro, Vidal Morales, Juan Gualberto Gómez, Carlos de la Torre, and Esteban Borrero, who on other matters hewed to their own point of view, pooled their efforts to select and compose manuals and curricula that would replace, as soon as possible, those imported from the United States.[38]

Harvard's Summer Program for Cuba's Teachers

If the plan to hire North Americans to teach in Cuban schools had met with open, direct opposition from the outset, the same could not be said for the controversial education project itself. The more muted reaction to the latter enabled a project to go forward in 1900, under which almost half of the island's primary school teachers, some 1,273 individuals, were invited to spend part of that year's summer at Harvard University.[39] The visit was in large measure the brainchild of Alexis Frye, himself a graduate of Harvard. After consulting with Leonard Wood, Frye wrote to Harvard's president, Charles W. Eliot, at the beginning of February 1900 laying out his proposal: "You will easily understand the enormous benefit which would accrue to Cuba with those thousand souls spread out over the entire Island after receiving such learned instruction. The benefits will certainly outweigh their cost. Could not the university arrange a free course of study? . . . My wish is that the teachers acquire the culture which such travel brings and that afterwards they introduce it in Cuban homes and schools. We need them to know our country and our people."[40]

Harvard's response was positive, and April 1900 found Frye in Washington and Boston drumming up the support from the federal government and Harvard that would permit the project to go forward. He organized a public meeting in Boston to mobilize the community behind the project, and in less than four months (between April and August) he received pledges totaling more than seventy thousand dollars to defray the students' travel costs.[41]

In Cuba, however, the sailing was far from smooth. Criticism of the proposed project came from different quarters. Several articles appeared in the press assailing the project on nationalist grounds. A portion of public opinion focused on the fact that young women who scarcely left the house unchaperoned in their own country would be making a long trip to a strange land without the accompaniment of any family members and under circumstances that would bring them into close contact with unknown men, a situation which could threaten their moral virtue. For its part, the Catholic Church expressed reservations about a program that would potentially expose half of Cuba's teachers to the "pernicious" influences of Anglo-Saxon Protestantism.

Despite these objections, however, hundreds of male and female teachers from all parts of Cuba responded to the call, and in less than a month, the 1,273 teachers (more than half of whom were women) who would travel for the summer course at Harvard had been chosen. The enormous difficulties in bringing together and equipping such a large and heterogeneous mix of people in such a short time (the teachers were selected from almost all the country's municipalities in barely one month) were overcome thanks to efforts of municipal and provincial school committees and the personal charisma of Frye, who quickly won the affection and confidence of the Cuban teachers. With the logistics of the trip handled by the U.S. Army, the teachers departed Cuba on military ships from five port cities (Gibara, Matanzas, Cienfuegos, Sagua, and Nuevitas) between 25 and 29 June 1900.[42] Although by this point public opinion had generally turned in favor of the project, a minority of the country continued to view it as destructive of Cuban national identity. On the eve of their departure, the teachers selected from Havana were invited by the Asociación de Maestros, Maestras y Amantes de la Niñez Cubana (Association of Teachers and Supporters of Cuban Children—an organization similar to the U.S. Parent Teacher Association) to attend a talk given by Manuel Sanguily. Invoking the memory of José de la Luz y Caballero, known as the father of Cuban pedagogy, Sanguily urged the teachers not to forget, under the pressure of foreign influence, the values and tradition of *cubanía*, repository of "our language, our honor, and our nationality."[43]

Arriving in Boston shortly before the Fourth of July, the Cuban teachers were taken to Cambridge on streetcars, a source of wonderment for the many among them who knew no other form of transportation than the horse-drawn carriage. The male teachers were housed in Harvard dormitories, whose regular residents gave them up temporarily, and the women stayed with Boston families, who—as part of the public support for the project—lodged them free of charge. Anglo-American lady "chaperones" were also assigned to each of these private residences to assure that the female teachers were properly taken care of and protected. To accompany the Cubans on trips and excursions out of Cambridge, a group of guides, translators, and assistants was recruited from the Harvard student body.

Over the course of six weeks, from Monday to Saturday, the teachers received instruction in various subjects, including education, geography, psychology, Spanish-American history, U.S. history, and—twice daily—English. The program also incorporated excursions to schools, factories, and industrial plants, as well as places of historical and geographic interest. Time also was made for dances, receptions, and other social gatherings.

For the Cuban teachers, however, the heart of the summer program, and its greatest challenge, lay in the attempt to learn English. As one observer noted, "The Cubans take great interest in the study of English, and avail themselves of every opportunity that offers, to learn new words and expressions."[44] Some especially enterprising teachers managed to improve their skills in the language by exchanging conversation lessons with Harvard students who wanted to learn Spanish. For every program participant, though, the language component was paramount. As one of the North Americans who wrote about the Cubans' Cambridge experience put it: "All seem to feel that, now that the study of English in the Cuban schools has been made compulsory, those of them who do not possess a good knowledge of this language will be left behind in the race."[45]

Shortly before the program was completed, Elena Cancio—one of the Cuban teachers—assessed the progress that her colleagues had made in assimilating the new language: "There were but few of the teachers who were able to speak any English when they arrived here in June." Now, the *New York Herald* reported her as claiming, "everyone has managed to absorb a good number of words and wishes to continue learning." "In a few years," Cancio concluded (the *Herald*, it should be emphasized, had a penchant for hyperbole), "nothing but English will be spoken in Cuba."[46]

In an article submitted in slightly awkward English to a local newspaper, another teacher in the group, Julia Martínez, applauded the Anglo-Americans' use of English-language classics in their schools while at the same time rejecting the Spanish cultural tradition: "Perhaps some day we may take up the Spanish classics as you do your English authors; but now, Don Quixote? Ah, no! it is Spanish! And too much have we had of that."[47] While Martínez may have repudiated the legacy of Hispanic ways and customs and professed admiration for the sophisticated state of U.S. education, she quite pointedly did not reject her own language: "We are studying English but we are keeping our own language, our accent; for outside of old Castile we hold that nowhere do you hear our language spoken with more perfection."[48]

Beyond the matter of language per se, the piece written by this young Cuban teacher betrays a clear tension between, on the one hand, admiration for the U.S. model and appreciation for the hospitality extended by the local community, and, on the other, the patriotic ideal of national freedom to which generations of Cubans had aspired: "We Cubans feel grateful to Americans . . . for all that they have done for us, but *Cuba Libre* has been the watchword now, not for a year, nor a decade, but for generations. It is the ideal for which we have prayed, and fought, and starved when need be, handing it down as a heritage from father to son, from mother to daughter. Such an ideal is not to be treated lightly, as you will well understand, it must be kept in mind when any plan is made for us by others."[49]

Martínez's divided outlook was true for the group as a whole. To read what she wrote, or what any of the other teachers wrote that survives today, about that singular Harvard summer, is to recognize the ambivalence coloring their reactions and attitudes. The reality of that ambivalence makes it difficult, if not impossible, to fit the Cubans' experience into a convenient, preconceived scheme of rigid binary relations operating between the colonizer and the colonized.

The teachers' visit was unquestionably part of a larger design to exert indirect control over a people and their territory by means of educational and in particular linguistic acculturation. The magnitude of the project (almost half of Cuba's teachers participated) provides the measure of the effect it could potentially have had—should the attempt at acculturation have succeeded— on the formation of new generations of Cubans.

At the same time, however, the visit was an expression of the warmth of feeling toward and ties of friendship with Cuba which existed in U.S. society at that time. Quite apart from the imperialist designs, whether explicit or disguised, entertained by the key figures in the U.S. establishment who directed and supported the project—Leonard Wood (Cuba's military governor), Elihu Root (the U.S. secretary of state), and Charles Eliot (the president of Harvard University)—the people in Cambridge and Boston who collected the funds to defray the costs of the trip opened their doors to take in the teachers, decorated the facades of their houses with Cuban flags, and applauded the teachers on their walks through the streets and public squares. Harvard students raised funds and gave up their rooms or used their summer vacation time to work as guides or interpreters. Theirs was simply the admiration and solidarity felt for a small land in its intrepid struggle against a powerful colonial overlord.

The case of the U.S. superintendent of public schools, Alexis Frye, deserves to be analyzed separately. Far from replicating the pattern of action which defined the typical colonial administrator, Frye genuinely worked to advance education in Cuba. He rallied strongly to the side of the country's teachers, so strongly in fact that he found himself in direct disagreement with Leonard Wood, leading him eventually to resign his position. The Harvard summer program changed Frye's life fundamentally. Six months after its conclusion, he married a young Cuban teacher whom he met during the students' journey to Cambridge. It was on that trip, too, that he made the acquaintance of many Cuban teachers with whom he formed close and lasting friendships.

The Harvard experience had a jolting effect on some of the Cuban participants. They were bedazzled by the specter of a society much more technologically and culturally advanced than their own. One teacher wrote from Harvard:

> Everything here is impressive, it's all done by machines, with electricity. ... There are seven hundred trains a day and eighty thousand to one hundred thousand passengers travel on them. We visited a watch factory where three thousand workers are employed, half of them women, educated and elegantly dressed. A huge soap factory doing business in the millions, enormous printing presses, tall hotels, etc., a collar and cuff factory representing hundreds of thousands of pesos! The public library has more than 1.3 million volumes and its building, which covers two acres, cost 2.5 million. Hundreds of streetcars, always full of people, go in every direction and a multitude of ships, filling the large and beautiful bay, are loaded with cargo and people heading off to different beaches and really beautiful towns.[50]

The teacher's admiration for all the eye-catching technological achievements is preceded by his idealization of the U.S. social order: "Everything is so admirable, customs almost innocent, pure on the whole; women, unencumbered, live on their own. ... There's no fear of walking anywhere in the dark at night: the flower bouquets and many display cases, and the apples and the pears are just left there; nobody touches anything, everything is respected. There are few police and they are unarmed. Houses, clothing, furniture, garments, and foodstuffs, all cheap; that accounts for all classes living and getting on well, satisfied and always happy and mixing together."[51] Almost spellbound by the picture of a society that he imagines to be perfect, the teacher not surprisingly ends his letter by writing: "The sky is not our blue sky, the vegetation not lush like ours, nor is the food like ours; on the other hand, everything is healthful, hygienic, private and public life morally upright in their ways and means. My friend: I am not an annexationist, I can't be an annexationist, but I am charmed: Who might be able to impart some of this to our homeland!"[52]

This same admiration, compounded by feelings of gratitude for all the considerations that he received during the visit, prompted another Cuban teacher to propose—in all seriousness—that the lines of the national anthem, the "Bayamesa," be replaced with these new lyrics:

Affectionate respect do we owe
To the nation of the magnificent Lincoln
Thus did it generously come to our aid
To lend us effective assistance.
Comrades: love and labor!
Long live, long live America our sister!
Long live a happy Cuba, sovereign,
noble and worthy of liberty![53]

In many of the teachers, perhaps even in the great majority, the separation from their homeland engendered an opposite reaction, arousing more intensified nationalist feelings. This phenomenon did not pass unnoticed by the North Americans: Writing in *Donahue's Magazine*, Joseph Roger Williams described the Cubans' reaction as follows: "Great and admirable as they think America is, there is no land so dear to them as their own. . . . Their patriotism is the growth of years of suffering and persecution. They are most hearty in their praise of the United States, most sincere in their gratitude to our government for having finally broken Spain's power in the West, but they are people intensely national."[54]

Williams's contention was corroborated by Ralph Waldo Gifford, who taught English to a group of Cuban teachers in the summer program: "The thought of their independence is naturally uppermost in the minds of all the Cubans. Among the teachers there is practically no desire for annexation. Though the Cubans are grateful to the Americans for freeing them from the Spanish domination, there is not the slightest desire among them to be an integral part of the United States. The many years of warfare for Cuban independence have made the idea of nationality supreme to them."[55]

The Cubans' strong nationalist feelings were evident in the testimonials which they wrote in an autograph book presented to the university (and still conserved in the Harvard University Archives) prior to their departure. Along with statements of gratitude and appreciation for the fellowship and hospitality extended by the public and the university community, they express—in

ATTEMPTS AT LINGUISTIC COLONIZATION

clear, sharp language—the desire to see full freedom and independence for their country. For example, Pedro Aragonés, a teacher from Cienfuegos, wrote that he "wishes for his beloved homeland a Free Republic, sovereign and independent, as is that of the United States of America." Echoing Aragonés's sentiments are those of Enrique Rodríguez Batista, a teacher from Punta Brava, who aspired "to see the flag with the lone star fly as soon as possible from Havana's El Morro." In a similar vein, "The independence of a sovereign Cuba is the deepest desire of Antonio Gutiérrez Ávila, a teacher in the municipal boy's school in Holguín"; and, muses a teacher from public school 7 in the rural town of Güira de Macuriges, in the province of Matanzas, "A people under a protectorate and a colonized people are equally enslaved, their true freedom lies in independence of thought and action."[56]

Not all of the testimonials were as simple and straightforward as these. Some of them manifest the contradiction between the storyline produced by the U.S. Revolutionary War, in which the United States is represented as the pinnacle of freedom and democracy, and the country's latent imperialist desires, which are seen as a threat to Cuba's attainment of independence. As one teacher declared, "Here where one breathes the pure air of liberty, where order and respect are the foundation of society, I can't believe that for my native country, virgin Cuba, each American harbors in his heart any idea but that of the absolute independence for which so many heroes and martyrs have shed their blood." Another teacher, Rafael Sentmanat, from the municipality of Rancho Veloz, in the province of Las Villas, left the following testimonial: "A transient in this great Republic, indisputable empire of greatness, morality, and civilization, I pay sincere tribute to its traditional virtues and hope that it seals its universal good name by creating now, without delay, a Cuban Republic, absolutely independent and sovereign, and letting the heroic Filipinos enjoy in the sanctuary of their homeland the holy liberty for which they fight."[57]

As the teachers' testimonials make evident, their visit to the United States generated admiration, respect, and gratitude. Yet they also reveal that such feelings were not extended unconditionally. In addition to the manifold technological progress achieved by their "neighbor to the North," the Cubans admired the democratic and libertarian tradition spawned by its revolution, a tradition which—joined to that of the French—had served throughout the nineteenth century as one of the pillars of inspiration for their own struggles to achieve independence. At the same time, however, they forcefully rejected the imperialist and expansionist designs of the U.S. government, which hung threateningly over the island.

In the course of various excursions and trips organized for them during their stay, the teachers participated in Fourth of July celebrations and the observance of Washington's birthday in Cambridge, and they also visited the tomb of Ulysses S. Grant in New York and Independence Hall in Philadelphia. These submersions of the Cuban teachers in classic U.S. patriotic events and sites can be "read" in different ways. In a narrow sense, the Cubans' participation in these foreign rituals of celebration can be seen as one more attempt—conscious or unconscious—at "Americanization," with its consequent threat to undermine their sense of themselves as a separate people. A more penetrating interpretation, however, leads to the conclusion that they were not passive victims of a program of indoctrination, but rather that they actively appropriated certain elements of their experience on behalf of a politicized *cubanía*. The act of listening to the singing of the U.S. national anthem, respectfully saluting the "Stars and Stripes," paying tribute in parades and "processions" to the "great nation's" political heroes and visiting the monuments and sites which enshrined their memory gave the Cuban teachers valuable exposure to the unifying power of a vibrant spirit of nationalism. Far from embracing the cause of annexation, many of the teachers returned to their pueblos and cities convinced that Cuba needed to become a sovereign nation and were prepared, through the use of these same patriotic rituals, to mold their students into "citizens" who possessed the respect and affection for country without which no nation-building project could succeed.

In sum, the teachers' Harvard experience was rich and complex, weaving together a series of plotlines, each with its own set of signs and signals: the imperialist designs to "Americanize" the teachers through a process of acculturation built around the outwardly laudable aim of learning English; the racist stereotypes common to this period, representing Anglo-Saxons as superior and the Latin "races" as inferior; the feelings of solidarity with Cuba held by a substantial segment of the U.S. population; the desire on the part of the Cuban teachers to modernize their island's outmoded public education system by appropriating and applying the more advanced pedagogy of the United States; the open, unaffected admiration for the powerful engine of U.S. capitalism and its technological sophistication, and—as a kind of check on the seductions of that system—the awareness shared by many of the teachers of the threat which the muscular expansionist spirit of the United States posed to the sovereignty of their island.

To know in any full and definitive sense what ramifications the summer project truly had for Cuba would require a depth of research that goes beyond the scope of this study. What can be said, however, is that those who were eager to see a society Americanized down to its core, who were prepared even to renounce their native language in order to embrace "modernization" patterned on the Anglo-Saxon model, saw their aspirations frustrated. If it is true that U.S. culture strongly influenced Cuba in these years, it is also true that such influence was curbed by Cuba's own deeply rooted cultural inheritance and potent nationalist tradition. Above all, Cuba exhibited a strong, enduring capacity for negotiation and adaptation, a capacity characteristic of "hybrid" societies formed through the in-migration of different ethnic groups. Cuba's historical experience of accepting and absorbing immigrant groups allowed it successfully to incorporate and "recycle" foreign elements into its own cultural framework.

In Defense of the Spanish Language

The effort overseen by the U.S. authorities to redesign the Cuban school system by importing U.S. texts and educational doctrines as well as teachers trained in the United States represented an attempt at cultural conquest that was not only noticed but firmly denounced by the nationalist press. Sergio Cuevas Zequeira, a professor at the University of Havana and an active National Party speaker, lent his voice to the protest:

> The arbitrary application of American teaching methods and procedures, the learning of English in our schools, and the use of official texts published in the United States, texts badly translated and sometimes poorly written, are the symptoms of things gone awry, a malady unglimpsed at first, of which the myopic and indifferent will become aware only when the coffin has been nailed shut. . . . There's something more serious than imprisoning the body and that is to suppress the soul, more vile than inhibiting freedom of action and that is to deform thought. This is being done in Cuba with impunity. Luz y Caballero came out of a Spanish school and Cubanized Cuba. Likewise out of the schools, however our reformers go about designing them, will come sensible and serious-minded men, sufficiently straight-thinking to withstand all manner of oppression.[58]

The threat posed to the survival of the Spanish language produced widespread alarm even among sectors of the Cuban elite, who were frequently more disposed to mimic and assimilate North American styles of social conduct and had, as well, accepted the newer methods of U.S. pedagogy as unquestionably superior to the antiquated teaching approaches handed down through the island's colonial-era public school system. *El Fígaro*, which often published articles celebrating the "civilizing virtues" of the "American way of life" and the institutions buttressing it, published an impassioned piece in defense of Spanish:

> In our simplistic willingness to believe that the virtues and wonders of the interventionists' country will lead us to a greater glory, we are endorsing and opening ourselves up to orientations, laws, codes, institutions, practices, and ways of governing that, if you will, are superior to our own but corrosive and dissolvent of a pure, untainted Cuban essence. This poses a very grave danger to Cuba's own unique character. ... Men and communities that cherish profound hopes of a different, distinct life, do not put the core of their true selves at risk in exchange for adding a few more layers of radiance or beauty to their adornments. What, everywhere, is the primary, most spontaneous, most vigorous expression of the national spirit? What is the soul of a people? Its language, its native tongue.
>
> Take care! Everyday, on the summits, on the flatlands, right through to the crossroads of this society, more conjurers abound every day who, uttering and getting us to repeat their incantations in English, try to pry away our soul. ... The adoption of a new language is not possible without visiting enormous change on the essential character of the people who adopt it. The country that embraces a strange language gets swallowed up in the other country. Knowing, as I do, that it would go badly for Don Quixote, I will not bring up any of his numerous misadventures. Rather, I recommend that Sancho be the one who is imitated, since these days his pragmatism has pride of place. In a humorous interchange, which comes before the La Mancha hidalgo's third departure, Don Quixote begins to intone to Sancho: *quando caput dolet* ... And the squire who carries his shield immediately parries the Latin phrase with this reply: "I understand no language but my own." Behold in this what all of us should do. Though we may take the language of the interventionists as a sign of the well born, who wants to be prodded with a: *English Spoken?* Our answer should be: I do not understand any language but my own. Because, where our language is lost to us, oblivion looms.[59]

In short order, a line was drawn between the dismantling of colonial political institutions, an undertaking viewed as commendable, and the wholesale scuttling of the Hispanic cultural tradition. The latter—embedded in the Spanish language—had to be preserved at all costs as a vital bulwark against the strong, penetrating influence of Anglo-Saxon culture.

The campaign to preserve the Spanish language, now seen as something inextricably linked to the Cuban "national soul," ranks as another of the many paradoxes of this period. Cubans were pulled in different directions, unable to unite ends and means. As an article of faith, they believed that political and cultural modernization demanded a process of "de-Hispanicization." Yet they also believed that the modernizing project had to be anchored in the familiar terrain of their cultural inheritance with its deep Hispanic roots. Some decades before, in an effort to draw sharper distinctions between themselves and the Spanish metropole, the anticolonial, nationalist elite had invented a kind of "American race," in virtue of which Cubans—despite the obvious cultural and linguistic differences—belonged with their northern neighbors to a community founded upon the existence of a New World promised land, "modern" and "progressive" by its very nature and thus opposed to the encrusted, reactionary ways of old Europe.[60] That narrative no longer served, and so the elite increasingly appealed to the existence of a "Cuban essence" which, paradoxically, was defined as "pure." Those Americans who lived to the north and their European forbears fell within the conglomeration of the "Anglo-Saxon race," which confronted the "Latinos" on both sides of the Atlantic in a dynamic conflict of "civilizations." According to this new discourse, the events of 1898 were but the surface manifestation of this greater conflict.

"Within the social and political admixture of the intervention, destiny imposes tremendous tests on us," warned poet and writer Esteban Borrero in reference to the "Americanization" of Cuba's system of teaching. In his opinion, the question was not one of mere institutional change. Rather, "the survival of the country's soul, the soul of the race," was at stake. In his estimation, Cubans were witnesses, whether clearly conscious of the fact or not, "to a tragic spectacle being enacted at the scene of the nation's social struggle for its soul in conflict with the soul of another country which, though perhaps not wanting to, threatens it with extinction." "Look at it however you like," Borrero declared with dramatic emphasis, "the intervention is a conflict between two peoples, between two different civilizations."[61]

In this manner, then, the Cuban-American alliance—so lauded during the final episodes of the war in 1898 and the first months of the military government—started to unravel, as many Cubans began to see the North Americans differently. No longer were the latter the perfect embodiment of the ideal of modernity and social progress which Cubans yearned to superimpose on their island; rather, they were a disquieting presence that tried to force an alien language and culture on them while also thwarting their hopes of achieving the independence for which they had struggled for more than thirty years. The arrogant, domineering, and racist attitudes of many U.S. military government bureaucrats, or of the investors and fortune seekers who arrived with them, helped accentuate the divide.

Against this backdrop, the differences between Cubans and Spaniards, though still a source of tension and friction, became less pronounced, and it was not unusual in this period to hear appeals that the dispute be forgotten, in the interests of forming a common anti–North American front.[62]

Thus, suspended between two poles, or (as I have said earlier) two sources of external domination; wanting to be "modern" and "democratic" (equated, in this period, with being "like the Americans") while simultaneously possessing their own identity (closely allied to a Spanish cultural tradition and the Spanish language), Cubans found themselves at cross-purposes, parties to an internal conflict of recognition-rejection. This tension, which played out in both relationships—Cuba's to the cultural inheritance bequeathed by Spain, and Cuba's to the powerful influence of U.S. culture—was stressful but also supremely rich and productive, and it would underpin the construction of a republican-based national culture in the years to come.

The ceremonial changing of flags taking place at Havana's El Morro castle, 20 May 1902.
Source: *Journal of Decorative and Propaganda Arts*, no. 22 (1996): 100

Spanish troops marching to the Havana waterfront on 1 January 1899, the day that had been set for their final departure from Cuba. Source: Emilio Roig de Leuchsenring, *El libro de Cuba: Obra de propaganda nacional* (Havana: n.p., 1925), 164

View of the Malecón in Havana, showing the bandstand and roundabout designed by Charles Brun, as well as an electric-powered streetcar running on the recently inaugurated line. Source: *Journal of Decorative and Propaganda Arts*, no. 22 (1996): 101

View of the La Punta promontory, which juts out on one side of the entrance to Havana bay, and its seafront, with two streetcars running past it. Source: *Cuba y América* 5, no. 107, (December 1901): 94

Curious onlookers watch as the statue of Spain's Queen Isabel II is removed and lowered from its pedestal in Havana's Parque Central on 12 March 1899. Source: *El Fígaro*, no. 12, 26 March 1899, 74

A view of some of the crowds that gathered along the streets of Havana to witness and celebrate General Máximo Gómez's entrance into the capital on 24 February 1899. The general and his entourage are making their way on horseback down Calle Obispo, one of the capital's main commercial streets. Source: *El Fígaro*, nos. 9–11, 19 March 1899, 55

Women and children lead a procession by members of the Cuban National Party's San Felipe Committee as they take part in a patriotic march with their new banner held aloft. Source: *El Fígaro*, no. 28, 24 July 1900, 346

A children's chorus, from the Liceo de Camajuaní. As part of the festivities held in 1900 to commemorate the still unofficial national holiday of 10 October, the children sang the hymn "Patria." Source: *El Fígaro*, no. 43, 18 November 1900, 326

— Señorita, ¿ quiere *uté* rendí cuto á *Tesicore* bailando *ete amonioso dansón* ?
— Oll raigh, pero el caballero ha de *cumplí* las honesta diposiciones de Miter Nuñez.

Cumpliendo el Bando.

— Me parese que ete negrito se va pa el antiguo régimen.

Illustration by the caricaturist Torriente satirizing the prohibition authorities tried to enforce against couples' holding each other in a tight embrace while performing the *danzón*. Source: *El Fígaro*, no. 13, 10 April 1900, 149

A view in 1899 of the front of the Crusellas shop on Calle Obispo in Havana, with its name advertised in English. Source: *El Fígaro*, no. 23, 11 June 1899, 192

A gathering of Cuban teachers on 3 July 1900, during their summer at Harvard. The group is standing at the foot of Boston's "Washington Tree," at which they placed a laurel wreath. Source: *El Fígaro*, no. 30, 12 August 1900, 366

A young woman in Matanzas displaying the "single star" in her hair and on the bodice of her dress. Source: *Cuba y América*, 11, no. 9, 28 June 1903, 485

Children seated in the classroom of their school in Havana, in 1900.
Two Cuban flags hanging near the top of the front wall frame a picture of José Martí.
Source: *El Fígaro*, no. 37, 7 October 1900, 451

The anthropologist Carlos de la Torre, flanked by his colleagues Luis Montané and José Montalvo, during their examination of Antonio Maceo's skull, following the 17 September 1899 exhumation of his remains. Source: *El Fígaro*, no. 36, 24 September 1899, 358

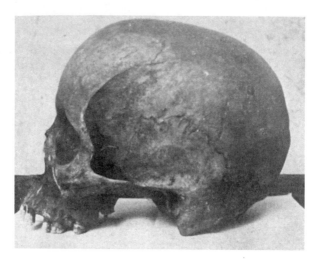

A civic procession of 28 January 1899 in Havana, held to commemorate the forty-sixth anniversary of the birth of José Martí (1853–95). At its front, two women carry the Cuban and U.S. flags, respectively. Source: *El Fígaro*, nos. 9–11, 19 March 1899, 50

The coffin holding the body of General Calixto García 9 February 1899 as it was placed on a gun carriage, prior to the general's burial and after the vigil held over his remains in Havana's town hall. Source: *El Fígaro*, nos. 9–11, 19 March 1899, 57

Havana's El Morro castle, where the Cuban national flag was raised and flew for the first time on the day Tomás Estrada Palma arrived in the city to assume the presidency of the Republic of Cuba. Source: Emilio Roig de Leuchsenring, *El libro de Cuba: Obra de propaganda nacional* (Havana: n.p., 1925), 186

Havana's seafront, swelled with crowds on 20 May 1902. Across the bay is El Morro castle and its nineteenth-century lighthouse. Source: Emilio Roig de Leuchsenring, *El libro de Cuba: Obra de propaganda nacional* (Havana: n.p., 1925), 255

One of the arches installed on Havana's streets as the city readied itself to celebrate the inauguration of the Cuban Republic. This arch, filled with allegorical and figurative depictions, was on Calle Obispo. Source: *Journal of Decorative and Propaganda Arts*, no. 22 (1996): 102

The same occasion saw this arch erected at the intersection of Havana's Calle Muralla and Calle Bernaza. Source: *Journal of Decorative and Propaganda Arts*, no. 22 (1996): 103

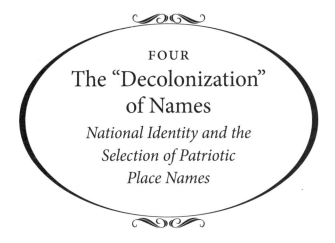

FOUR

The "Decolonization" of Names

*National Identity and the
Selection of Patriotic
Place Names*

Devising New Place Names

As if they were palimpsests stretched over immense distances, countries that once were colonial territories still carry with them—like a second layer of skin—signs and traces of names from earlier epochs. During the initial years of conquest, the "virgin lands" of Spanish America were relieved of their aboriginal names and rebaptized. Across what became Spain's New World empire, the physical features of the land and places of habitation were renamed to mirror the system of political and religious beliefs of its latest occupants.

Even today, centuries later, the numerous "Santiagos," "San Juanes," "Santas Cruces," and "Trinidades," the "Córdobas," "Valencias," and "Geronas," evoke memories of Spanish colonization. Just as with colonial censuses, the maps on which these places appear are not and never were innocuous and "objective" descriptions, devoid of ideological and political content and purpose. On the contrary, such cartographic and demographic formulations aided the colonizer's task in several respects: they helped spearhead and legitimize territorial conquest; they represented a way of controlling the physical, environmental, and human context they denoted, and they were an inseparable element of the "technology" of imperial domination.[1]

The (symbolic) appropriation of a territory or expanse of land through the simple expedient of "naming it" differently has not, however, been exclusively the property of the colonizing power. The reverse process, decolonization, has often been accompanied by a wave of toponymic redescription, with the intention of fulfilling two interconnected purposes; first, "blotting out" all memory embedded in the former names and, second, endowing the landscape and built environment with new "marks of identity." As the antithesis of their corresponding marks in the colonial system—the new set of names would convey, in semiotic terms, a sense of "the national," or of "what is native to us."

During the last days of 1898 (hence prior to the official lowering of the Spanish flag and transfer of power at El Morro on 1 January 1899) and the first months of 1899, a singular, dramatic process of assigning new place names got under way across Cuba. One by one, the emblems of colonial authority were removed: raising the Spanish flag in public was prohibited by official decree; the statue in downtown Havana of Queen Isabel II was detached from its pedestal; and shields and coats of arms associated with the Spanish monarchy disappeared from building facades and from seals, dies, postage stamps, and official paper. Streets, plazas, and avenues were renamed. Old signs and plaques were pried off walls and barricades and replaced with vivid inscriptions denoting the new order.

The act of renaming public spaces symbolized, in a visible way, the break with colonial history and the past. At the end of the nineteenth century and beginning of the twentieth, struggles in Cuba for political control got hammered out and resolved not only in social and intellectual spheres, through the exchange of ideas in meetings and assemblies, and in newspapers, manifestos, and other printed ephemera, but also in the physical sphere, where municipal streets and buildings, and the fixtures on them, became a medium of partisan dispute and confrontation. In communities across the island, a flag seen atop a building, a cross or an inscription on a tombstone, or a plaque bearing the name of a street or plaza—things which might have remained in those places for decades without drawing much if any notice—soon became the focus of attention and controversy.

Two things were broadcast through the process of toponymic "redesignation": the dawning of a new era and the institution of a new authority with the power to "name." Contrary to what might be surmised, however, it was not the U.S. authorities who, by virtue of their new imperial power, arrogated to themselves the right to toponymically "mark" their recently acquired territory. Although the U.S. military occupied a majority of the country's towns and population centers, streets, parks, and plazas with traditional names linked to persons, events, or dates in colonial history or to the Catholic calendar of saints' days were rechristened with the names of heroes and martyrs of the wars of liberation or given patriotic or allegorical names reflecting the new "republican" order.[2]

Old Streets, New Names:
Patriotic Place Names for the Island's Cities

A handbill from December 1898 titled "Viva Cuba Libre" and signed with the *mambise* slogan, *Patria y Libertad*, proudly announces that on the basis of the peacefully expressed sovereign will of its inhabitants, the pueblo of Alquízar has agreed to change the names of its streets. The handbill declares that those names "which remind the pueblo of so many horrors and disastrous times" are to be changed in their entirety "to the names of the heroic defenders of our independence."[3] A parallel event occurred in the community of Güines, where during the last days of 1898 a debate ensued about how to replace old street names with new ones, more suitable to the temper of the times. "Today," stated F. Calcagno in a letter he sent to the local paper, *La Luz del Hogar*, "we have heroes' names to burn, because Cuba, today, has its own history, and it is our inescapable duty to honor the memory of those who gave their lives in order to give us a Country." Consequently, Calcagno proposed that Calle Reina be renamed "Arango y Parreño," and that Calle Real, "since we no longer have kings," be changed without delay to República.[4]

It is noteworthy that this street-renaming campaign, which occurred on a massive scale during the first months of 1899, does not seem to have resulted from any centralized initiative. To judge from contemporary reports and memoirs, the decisions were made by the municipal council or mayor's office of each pueblo, or—as in the case of Alquízar—spontaneously agreed to in the course of a popular political rally, without regard to any decision taken by the U.S. military government or, for that matter, by any national revolutionary organization.

In contrast to the situation in the capital, where the overbearing presence of U.S. Army troops and officials of the military government prevented representatives of the Cuban revolutionary forces from directly exercising power, local control in many pueblos and cities in the interior of the country was in the hands of former Mambí Army officers or their civilian allies.[5] As a result, though they acted in accord with the broad directive of the central government, the local municipal councils enjoyed considerable independence, permitting them to take measures, such as those involving the changing of street and place names, which reflected strong nationalist sentiments.

Several months later, in September 1899, the U.S. military government tried to gain control of the situation by issuing a decree requiring that local councils submit requested name changes to the island's U.S. military governor, who would have the final authority to approve them or not.[6] The government's attempt to establish and enforce a uniform policy in this area, however, came too late. By this time, changed street names were a fait accompli. "Tacón," "Concha," and "Cánovas" had been changed to "Martí," "Maceo," and "Gómez," and streets which had previously honored the Spanish monarchy, with the names Real or Reina, now carried names that lionized republicanism. Some localities, such as the municipal district of Macuriges, restored their original native names—four centuries after the Spanish had cast them aside.[7]

The change and replacement of street and place names in Cuba's cities and pueblos happened so rapidly that the postal services found it difficult to cope and people got lost in the streets. A columnist for El Fígaro poked fun at the situation by asking, in one of his articles, "How far is it from 'José Martí' to 'General Bentancourt'? It's impossible to answer you without remembering that 'José Martí' is Corral Falso and 'General Betancourt,' Ceiba Mocha."[8]

A serious study of the changes in street and place names would undoubtedly open a window onto the deeper forces affecting Cuban society in this period. The break with colonial traditions and the past, the sensation of passing over a threshold into a new era, the tensions produced by the conflict between religious and secular symbolism, the imprint of "modernizing" or "civilizing" influences, the articulation of local authority versus the hand of central power, and, above all, the firm decision to transform a colonial territory into an independent nation through a deliberate search for the signifiers of a higher, unitary Cuban identity were all demonstrated in the headlong rush to implant a new lexicon of place names.

The municipal council of San Juan de los Remedios, an old community in the central part of the island, held a meeting on 18 January 1899—just a few days after the formal transfer of sovereignty—and agreed to change the city's street and place names. Henceforth, Calle San José would be called "Máximo Gómez," and Calle "Fortún" would be known as "General Carrillo" (both generals were camping on the outskirts of the city as the decision was being made). A plaque was placed on the street named after General Gómez to commemorate the spot where the Liberation Army entered the city once the Spanish troops had evacuated it. The most central place in San Juan de los Remedios, its Plaza de Armas, also called Plaza Isabel II, was renamed Plaza "José Martí," and Santiago (the patron saint of Spain) and Amargura streets were changed, respectively, to "León Albernas" and "Alejandro del Río," in honor of two local heroes who had fallen in the wars of liberation. Streets with religious names were "secularized": Calle Jesús de Nazareno became "Antonio Maceo," San Francisco Javier was changed to "Calixto García," and San Juan de Dios was renamed "Calle de la Independencia." The Calzada del Cementerio, which led to the city's graveyard, was given the name Paseo de los Mártires.

The renaming of San Juan's streets continued into the following month. Soledad, Mercaderes, and Santo Cristo streets were renamed "Adolfo Ruiz," "José A. Peña," and "Hermanos García," while Jesús del Monte became "General Zayas." Several days later, at the behest of some of San Juan's residents, rather than on the initiative of its town council, the Calle de Ánimas was renamed "Calle Pedro Díaz," in honor of a black general of the War of Independence (1895–98).[9]

To the west of San Juan de los Remedios, along the north-central coast of Cuba, the city of Sagua presented a similar pattern in early 1899. Calle [Antonio] Cánovas del Castillo (which bore the name of a leading Spanish statesman) was renamed "Calle Martí;" Calle Tacón became "Calle Carlos Manuel de Céspedes"; Calle Intendente Ramírez became "Calle Solís"; Calle Esperanza was given the name "Calle Luz y Caballero"; and Calle Cruz was changed to "Calle Padre Varela." "Calle Antonio Maceo" and "Calle Carmen Ribalta" replaced Calle Estrella and Calle Amistad. Sagua's public squares and parks were similarly renamed to honor nationalist military and political figures or to celebrate the country's emergence from colonial rule and its independence from Spain. "Parque González Osma," which had been named in honor of a prominent benefactor of the city, became known as Parque de la Libertad; the Plaza de la Cárcel and Plaza de las Pailas were grandly renamed "Plaza del General Robau" and "Plaza del General Peraza," for two leaders of the Mambí Army. The city departed from this otherwise unvarying pattern by renaming one of its old colonial streets, the Calle del Progreso, after the pioneering U.S. nurse and humanitarian Clara Barton, who had traveled through Cuba in 1898, caring for wounded survivors of the war.[10]

It is hardly surprising that the wholesale changing of street and place names carried great symbolic meaning for Cubans, whether they had been directly immersed in the independence struggles or not. Take the example of an old, traditional town like San Juan de los Remedios. For peaceable residents who had lived all their lives on, say, Calle Jesús de Nazareno and worked every day on Calle Ánimas, to find themselves suddenly living on Calle Maceo and working on Calle Pedro Díaz must have been disorienting, especially since Maceo had all along been represented, by the Spanish press, as the incarnation of Lucifer, and Díaz had been branded a "seditious" black whose head was called for on posters pasted on street corners, only to be transformed into a decorated general honored for his deeds by having a street named after him.

The secularization of street and place names is undoubtedly a factor to consider when evaluating whether the religious practices inherited from colonial times persisted as before or lost some of their force. Although it would be premature to hazard any firm conclusions, it is clear—at least with respect to place names—that religious martyrs gave way to a pantheon of secular martyrs.

The street-renaming campaign had still another interesting politico-cultural dimension—that of the local versus the national, of heroes known exclusively or largely within their own region versus figures whose fame or reputation extended across the country. To investigate name changes from this perspective, along a regional axis, is to see how the balance of political power played out between local or regional authorities and those with national recognition. Céspedes and Ignacio Agramonte are the names most frequently encountered among the pool of national heroes from 1868, while there is practically no pueblo in Cuba which does not have a street or public square named after José Martí, Máximo Gómez, and Antonio Maceo. At least in the central part of the island, one is struck by the marked presence of a group of heroes tied specifically to the region, as well as the glorification of military caudillos, such as generals Carrillo, Peraza, and Robau, who were not only still alive but central figures in the current political affairs of the country.

Despite the absence of a detailed, carefully researched analysis, one can make the broad claim that in Oriente and Camagüey, or in the central part of the island, the pattern in name changes, via the placement of plaques and other types of signage, reflected a strong bias toward consecrating the memory of local figures and events. This orientation had its origin in the country's recent political history. Each of these areas had figured directly in both wars of liberation, and a significant percentage of their inhabitants were veterans of military conflict. They were the groundswell and bearers of a living revolutionary tradition, with its own set of heroes and memories of valiant feats. To the west, however, the pattern was different. The wars had never reached many of the towns and communities in that part of the island; for them, the experience of these conflicts was reduced to stock or even mythical accounts of heroic acts performed by unknown mambise revolutionaries, or this history was identified with a few representative figures. As a result, a restricted, uniform scheme of name changes generally took hold in these localities, with their central streets renamed "Martí," "Maceo," and "Gómez," others "Calixto García," "Céspedes," or "Agramonte," and still others given names of symbolic or allegorical import, such as República, Libertad, Mártires, and Independencia. In many pueblos, too, streets were named after important figures in Cuban political and intellectual history, such as "Luz y Caballero," "Varela," and "Arango y Parreño," who were not military heroes or otherwise known for their exploits during the wars of liberation. This practice demonstrates that another strand of *cubanía*—one woven into a tradition of enlightened public service—also entered into the dynamic of changing street and place names.

The comparatively small number of streets named after women or after black heroes of the wars of liberation is clearly a sign of gender and race prejudice. Agreeing with estimates made by Louis Pérez and Jorge Ibarra, Ada Ferrer posits that at least 60 percent of the Liberation Army was composed of blacks or mulattos. She further asserts that this multiracial force did not consist of a great mass of black soldiers commanded by a handful of white officers. On the contrary, many black soldiers rose to rank of captain, colonel, and even general, with a substantial number of white men under their authority. Near the end of the war of 1895–98, some 40 percent of officer slots in the Mambí Army were held by men "of color."[11] If these data are valid, there is nothing approaching an equilibrium between the contributions made in the war by black mambises and the recognition of these same contributions, once the war was over, in memoirs, tributes, emblems, and statues.

Despite the important role played by the female figure in the iconographic representation of the nation (for example, the classic image of the homeland which incorporated the Phrygian cap and the robes of a Greek woman), very few streets in this period were named after women. While the direct participation by men in war and military conflict was considered a source of glory and honor, worthy of being memorialized in the form of street signs and monuments; in the case of women, it was viewed as a kind of debasement of their chastity and honor, any vestige of which should be erased. The identities of the hundreds of women who, in one way or another, found themselves caught up in military conflict are thus suppressed in the interests of honoring an abstract representation, stripped of first or last names, in which the heroic figure of the *mambisa* combatant is supplanted by the image of the suffering mother, passive victim of the violence wrought by war and its forced resettlement of people. Thus, the feminine figure widely honored (as earlier noted) in busts and plaques in the region of La Villa was not exactly a mambisa heroine, but Marta Abreu, a wealthy landowner who—from her refuge in Paris during the war years—donated, using a male pseudonym, more than one hundred thousand pesos to the coffers of the Cuban Revolutionary Party. A local benefactress of great generosity, Abreu matched the image of the discreet, asexual "wife-mother" perfectly. Self-abnegating, devoted to charitable causes and to

the protection of the destitute while equally a dedicated and generous patriot
—this role and personality posed less of a threat to masculine hegemony than
the figure of the mambisa soldier.[12]

Thus, hand in hand with the expression of a strong unitary nationalist spirit,
as embodied in the statues and signs put up in local parks and along streets,
class tensions and contradictions continued to make themselves felt in Cuba,
as did race conflict and discrimination, which reappeared with renewed force
after the conclusion of the war against Spain.

The War over Signs in the Capital

If the names given to streets and plazas, and signage in the interior of the
country, reflected a commonly shared outpouring of patriotic sentiment, the
pattern in Havana was noticeably different. There, posters and other material
with a nationalist slant that were put up on the facades of businesses juggled
incongruously for space with notices in English and with the traditional signs
of Spanish commercial establishments, with their religious imagery or their
allusive references to Spain or the "mother country." With respect to streets
and avenues, while some names were changed—for example, Calle Obispo,
which had been ignominiously renamed "Valeriano Weyler" in 1896, regained
its old name in 1898, and two streets associated with "derelict, disreputable
living" known as La Bomba and La Samaritana were given the more "correct"
names of Progreso and Porvenir (the future)[13]—it was not until after the inauguration of the Republic in 1902 that many of Havana's most important streets
were rechristened with patriotic names.[14]

Although the names of many shops, groceries, department stores, and cafés
in Havana did change between the last months of 1898 and the first months
of 1899, the process was much more confused and disorganized than in the
rest of the country, since in the capital such changes were not a function of
municipal decrees but of decisions made independently by business owners.
As González Lanuza put it, in referring to a kind of "opportunistic" mindset
underlying the changes made to business signs in Havana, "Because choosing
names, most of which are typically whimsical and picturesque, is a matter of
local custom, our business establishments have been like a barometer, consis-
tently registering with considerable precision the higher or lower pressure, in
one sense or another, of our political atmosphere."[15]

During the last days of the colonial regime, when—even though the armistice had been signed—the capital remained under the control of Spanish
authorities, the first nationalist signs began to appear on the front of certain

commercial establishments. The advertisements placed by businesses in the pages of *La Estrella Cubana, La Guásima, El Machete, Cuba Independiente,* and *El Grito de Baire*—ephemeral, underground newspapers, edited and sold clandestinely in Havana between November and December 1898—left no doubt about the political loyalties of their owners. Groceries and modest restaurants with names like Mi Patria, El Cubanito, El Campamento Cubano, El Sol Cubano, El Jardín Cubano, Cuba Libre, Cuba Es Mi Patria, La Bandera Cubana, and La Estrella de Baire, played up Cuban patriotism in contrast to the Hispanic tilt and tone that frequently characterized the notices and signs displayed by businesses in Havana.[16] Still other merchants made early preparations for the future influx of North Americans by posting a notice saying "English Spoken" next to the name of their establishment, or—like the owners of The Cuban Star and the Cuban Grocery Company—simply advertised their wares or services in English.[17]

Some merchants, like the owners of a grocery on Monte and San Joaquín, paid dearly for trying to get ahead of the game. This business was founded in 1898 by two Cubans, who named it La América. In keeping with the sign advertising their establishment, they displayed both Cuban and U.S. flags in the shop's windows. On the night of 8 December 1898, the day set aside by the Catholic calendar to honor the Immaculate Conception of Mary, a patron saint of Spain, a group of hotheads, commanded by a Spanish army lieutenant, attacked the business, breaking the windows and ordering the owners to remove the flags from the front of the building.[18]

Another case that compels interest, through its attempt to appeal to all interests and parties, was that of a restaurant called La Flor de Galicia, located—in late 1898—on Calle Habana between Teniente Rey and Amargura. Rather than alter the name of their restaurant to suit the new scheme of things, the owners opted for a different strategy—keeping the name of the establishment while broadening its menu to encompass "all tastes and preferences," so that none of the contending parties should feel excluded. The business's advertising announced:

> Cubans, Spaniards, Americans: We have a colossal selection to satisfy all tastes. For Spaniards from all provinces. For Cubans and Americans in general. For honored Cubans and Yankees. For the most honorable Cuban workers and Cubans from the countryside. For Cubans from the Revolution who worked so notably for the peace and reconstruction of the country. . . . all tastes and preferences are catered to in this establishment; a rich *agiaco* [*sic*], *picadillo*, Basque and Catalan *bacalao*, meat

stew in tomato and roasted pepper sauce, Galician broth, bean stew, roastbeef, beefsteak Chauteabriand [*sic*], and a thousand and one other offerings at incredible prices.[19]

It would difficult to find a better example of the shifting, hybrid conditions of the period than the menu of this restaurant, where criollo dishes such as *ajiaco* and *chilindrón* (mutton or goat stew) were happily prepared and served alongside bean stew, Galician broth, Basque-style *bacalao*, "roast-beef," and "beef-steak."

An anecdote related by González Lanuza provides still another telling example of the complex give-and-take, playing contradictory marks and identities off each other, which characterized the symbolic sphere of everyday life in Cuba:

> Going back many years, there was a shop called Las Glorias de Pelayo that stood on the El Monte road. The owner of this establishment, which operated until a short while ago, undoubtedly thought it was dangerous in those days, right after Spanish sovereignty had ended, to go under the name of the first king of the Reconquista. You interject that you can't see why! But the fact is that he put into practice what his fears suggested and changed the name of his business, keeping its same form, altering only the name of the person to whom the "glories" referred; yet warning of this change at the end, in order to leave a clear echo of the former title, maintain his status as a commercial entity, and not lose either the credit he had extended or his steady customers; and in light of all of these things, the shop came to be called, for a certain period of time, by the most extraordinary name: "Las Glorias de Maceo, antiguas de [formerly of] Pelayo!!!"[20]

Beyond the story's comic aspect, the symbolism of the transmutation of the Iberian king, Pelayo, into the *mambí* hero, Maceo, is noteworthy. All the same, the fact that on a shop sign a Spanish sovereign was dethroned by a Cuban mulatto does not mean that the same thing was happening in society at large. Just as the name change affected nothing more than the sign, leaving the shop to operate as before, so in Havana society itself the exaggerated emphasis placed on symbolic change, as evidenced in labels, signs, announcements, and official protocol, tended to obscure the survival—through and after the War of Independence—of oppressive structures and exploitative and discriminatory practices. In this sense, Maceo's racial brethren, many of whom shared the glory of his military triumphs, soon perceived that in the new Cuba, far from gaining social recognition or mobility, they were frequently shunted aside or kept out of sight, considered an embarrassment, and instructed to "civilize themselves" as the price of their integration into society.[21]

Popular businesses, such as small shops, family restaurants, and corner groceries, were not the only ones to change their names. The pricier and more elegant establishments frequented by Havana's high society responded in similar fashion to the patriotic demands of the day.

Illustrating this fact is a promotion that appeared in *Cuba y América*, a magazine that had been founded in New York in 1895, during the war, as an outlet for members of the creole aristocracy living there in exile. On resuming publication in Havana in 1899, it maintained its self-appointed role as mouthpiece for the social elite and invited its readers to patronize a café called El Guajiro. Despite its name, El Guajiro (a term for a Cuban peasant) was an "elegant establishment, offering fruits, pastries, ice cream, and soda fountain drinks, served by refined, pretty, and well-educated young ladies." This place, it was predicted, would absolutely be the "rendezvous favored by Havana's most distinguished families." With its sign conveying populist and patriotic overtones, El Guajiro exemplified the conjunction of the modern and the national, the cosmopolitan and the homespun, characteristic of the period. It combined an upper-class clientele, a folksy design to its menu, sign, and other advertising, and a distinctly modern style of service (the employment of ladies to attend to customers, rather than the male attendants traditionally employed by colonial-era businesses, was a recent innovation and was considered a sign of women's emancipation in these "new times").[22]

There was a world of difference between the elegant production of *Cuba y América*, with its high-gloss paper and lavish spread of photos and illustrations, and the primitive graphics of *El Ciudadano*, a newspaper published in 1900 in San Antonio de los Baños, a small pueblo near Havana. The magazine's self-conscious admiration of things "American" also contrasted with the resolutely patriotic tilt of the rural paper. In one respect, however, the two publications were alike—*El Ciudadano*, no less than *Cuba y América*, recognized the changes being made in street and place names. Fortunately, the announcements placed in the newspaper's advertising section enable one to reconstruct the range of political leanings prevalent in the locale: the advertisements placed by La Estrella, a Cuban chocolate manufacturer, competed for attention against those placed by La Española, owned by Rubine e Hijos, a chocolate company based in La Coruña (Galicia). The tobacconist La Mina de Oro also sold "fantasy art cards with Cuban flags and insignias on them" and was located on Martí and General Gispert streets. El Cubano Libre, a shop stocked with "national and foreign provisions," was situated on Maceo, at the corner of República, while the Salón Martí, which advertised itself as a "great café, restaurant, 'lunch,' and sweet shop," was located on Calle Martí, where it crossed Gonzalo de Quesada. The barber shop El Ariguanabo (the indigenous name of a local river) was also distinguished for its combination of nationalist names. Its owner was Francisco Díaz, known in the pueblo by the altogether Cuban nickname of Guayaba, and it, too, was situated—as if it were all in the time-honored course of things—on Calle Martí, at the corner of Maceo.

In contrast to the wholly Cuban character of these examples, the Purísima Concepción pharmacy was characterized by its toponymic ambiguity or fuzziness. The business, with a traditional Catholic name distinctive of colonial times, was located at the intersection of Martí and McKinley, two streets whose names symbolized diametrically opposed political orientations and ideologies. The juncture of these two names, purely a matter of happenstance, evokes the image of a Cuba that, while intent on leaving the colonial past behind, nonetheless vacillates between taking Martí, which leads toward the realization of national sovereignty, or McKinley, which points in the direction of a "modern" yet dependent future.[23]

In general, despite a few servile examples to the contrary, such as giving the name "Leonard Wood" to a street in Santiago de Cuba, or the separate case of expressing a measure of genuine gratitude toward the United States by naming streets after such people as Clara Barton or Theodore Roosevelt (mythologized as the hero of San Juan Hill), the trend in the renaming of streets and public places, with its emphasis on repeatedly using the names of heroes and martyrs of the wars against Spain, was predominately nationalist.[24] It reflected the firm will to form and mold a Cuban nationality, founded on the legacy of the anticolonial struggle and the patriotic memory of the revolutions for independence. At the same time, however, this legacy was never an island of consensus, nor was Cubans' patriotic memory a source of unimpeachable authority.[25]

The experiences of those who took up the revolutionary cause were varying and complex. The experiences of slaves or their descendants, who fought not just for independence from Spain but also for their own emancipation and dignity as human beings, or of the thousands of peasants and menial day laborers who joined the ranks of the Mambí Army in quest of a new order of equality and social justice, were far removed from those of the landowning minority, former slave owners, who through the war sought to free themselves from the metropolitan yoke without losing either their privileged class status or their leadership of the nation-building enterprise.

This dynamic helps to explain why, in the immediate aftermath of the war against Spain, the fragile coalitions that made up the anticolonial front disintegrated so quickly, giving way to a complicated phase in which attempts at consolidating a new national consensus in order to confront the U.S. imperial threat foundered under the renewal of alliances that were based on more solid group identity, such as that formed by common regional, class, racial, or ethnic interests.

To define the nature and substance of *cubanía* in this transformed environment thus entailed an intense battle of competing narratives, in which the educated elite tried to impose on the nation a hegemonic discourse in constant tension with promises of democracy and freedom made to subaltern groups during the anticolonial campaign and with the even more radical projects fomented, from below, by these same groups.

The appropriation and interpretation of historical memory, as Peter Burke has written, is a complex process that turns, in large measure, on the place one happens to occupy socially and culturally. As such, there is no single, monolithic memory harmoniously subscribed to by all but rather alternative memories, often in conflict, which are formed and nurtured in diverse ways by different social groups.[26]

Thus, the symbolic recollection of memories of the wars of liberation against Spain and the creation of a national pantheon of martyrs and heroes, while central to the process of constructing Cuban culture and national identity, was also fraught with difficulty; it was a process of inclusions and exclusions, of recalling and forgetting, beset with compromises and conflicts.

The ambiguous, often tentative, or superficial, appropriation of a nationalist system of symbols in the capital, fully evidenced in its signs and plaques, contrasted vividly with the sincere, impassioned nationalism conveyed in the pattern of names found in pueblos across the interior of the country. Yet even on a local level, in small communities and cities, the discussions that took place over the names for streets or public places, or the persons to be honored on emblems or in a painting or sculpture, or the question of who should march in a parade or public procession and in what order, involved complex negotiations, negotiations that ultimately determined whose memory would be preserved on street signs, set in stone or in bronze, published in histories, or reproduced in photographs and prints, just as they determined whose achievements would be forgotten, classified as unworthy of being commemorated or inscribed in the "annals of history."

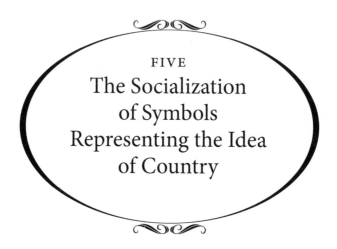

FIVE

The Socialization
of Symbols
Representing the Idea
of Country

"White, Blue, and Emblazoned,"
"the Five-Pointed Star," the Ubiquity of Flags and
Signs Proclaiming "¡Viva Cuba Libre!"

When the armistice between the United States and Spain brought an end to military actions, the sidewalks and plazas of the island's cities became the scene of a different kind of war—a war of symbolic skirmishes over how civic rights and Cuban national identity should be taken up and publicly expressed within the transitory new political order. More particularly, the combatants fought over how to politically represent the citizenry and institutionalize patriotic memory. Rivalries thus shifted from the real, material terrain of armed conflict to the vaporous, rhetorical environment of argument and symbols.

This "war after the war," which centered on inventing a national community in the midst of the problematic circumstances of this period "between empires," was not waged solely by educated groups. Indeed, my interest here is to go beyond the horizon of activities pursued by the intellectual and political class and explore how common people, the majority of them illiterate, took part in this conflict over symbols. Lacking education, social advantage, or wealth, and thus finding closed to them the traditional avenues of making speeches in elite political forums or arguing ideas through written contributions in the press, thousands of unknown Cubans participated in the symbolic construction of the nation on a more visceral level, taking part in rallies, marches, and impromptu street gatherings where they made their feelings known, collectively, through chants, cries, and gestures.

As midday approached on 12 September 1898 in Havana, where the Spanish authorities still exercised power, ten working class Cubans who ranged in age from eighteen to twenty-four were arrested for issuing the "subversive cries" of "¡Viva Cuba Libre! [Long Live a Free Cuba!]" as they rode in a third-class coach on the urban train between the Concha station and Marianao. The transgressors were taken by the police to the fortress of La Cabaña, and remanded to the authority of a military judge.[1]

A month later, on 11 October, a young black prostitute, scarcely seventeen years of age, was dragged off to a police station and later confined to Havana's Casa de Recogidas (a home-cum-jail for destitute and fallen women) on the strength of another prostitute's denunciation. The young Habanera was accused of causing "a scandal in public" and of "insulting Spaniards" by unleashing a string of "nationalist abuse" at a Spanish soldier ambling in a drunken state past the doors of one of the many bordellos on Calle Samaritana.[2] On the night of that same day, the owner of a small café called La Reina was taken, along with the man who played piano in the café, to the Vivac prison (a civilian jail run by the police) in Havana, on the grounds of upsetting public order. In his declaration, the police warden alleged that he had reproved the owner on numerous occasions for allowing the "Bayamesa" to be played on the café's piano. Although the owner swore he had ordered "that the anthem not be played in the establishment" and the pianist declared that it was not the anthem that he had played but rather the tune of "a *danzón* with a very similar-sounding part to it" that a client had been whistling near the café that day, the two were nonetheless assessed a heavy fine.[3]

On 9 November 1898, a young man, eighteen years of age, was arrested and sentenced to a prison term in the El Morro castle, charged with "using his finger to draw five-pointed stars and letters spelling *Viva Cuba Libre* on a dusty shopwindow" outside the grounds of a cigarette factory on Paseo de Tacón.[4] During the last months of Spanish rule, incidents such as these occurred almost daily on the streets and in the plazas of the capital. Demoralized government officials tried to stop them but were powerless to do so. On the busiest street corners, underground newspapers, bearing names like *El Grito de Baire*, *Cuba Libre*, *La Estrella Solitaria*, and *El Machete*—names that in themselves stood and propagandized for independence—were hawked by a steadily growing number of vendors.[5] One such individual, Nicolás Valdés, a thirty-three year old Havana resident who lived on Calle Monserrate, was imprisoned on 9 December 1898 for "having subversive newspapers in his possession." According to the police report, at the time of his detention Valdés had thirty-three copies of *El Grito de Yara*, with a picture of Antonio Maceo on its front page, seventy-two copies of *Himno Bayamés*, thirty-three of *La Guásima*, five of *El Grito de Baire*, eleven of *La Estrella Cubana*, five of *La Independencia*, two of *El Machete*, five of *Cuba Independiente*, one copy of *La Linterna*, and one of *La Victoria*.[6]

Swamped by a rising tide of protest, the police could not possibly arrest all the people who appeared on the streets holding little Cuban flags in their hands, or sporting a shiny star on their chests or belt buckles. Even businesses, such as the prominent Wilson's Book Store located on the busy commercial strip of Obispo, displayed in their store front windows copies of *La Independencia* and *El Grito de Yara*, featuring blown-up pictures of Céspedes, Estrada Palma, and Maceo on their front pages.[7] Some merchants got a step ahead of the official transfer of power by painting the facades of their businesses white, blue, and red or by replacing their Hispanophile signs with nationalist ones.

The flare-ups between Spanish authorities, who tried to suppress the expression of nationalist sentiment even as they prepared to depart the island, and Cubans intent on making such feelings known, ranged from the innocuous to the serious. In December 1898, *La Guásima*—a nationalist newspaper published in Marianao—denounced the rough treatment received by a Cuban woman, María Betancourt, who had a silver star ripped off her chest as she walked along the street. The same issue of the paper also reported the ludicrous skirmishes that broke out between some Spanish soldiers stationed at a public square and a group of shoeshine boys who provoked their ire by wearing small Cuban flags and emblems on their clothes. A confrontation between an agitated crowd of Cubans walking down the streets waving a Cuban flag and a detachment of Spanish soldiers patronizing a grocery at the intersection of Infanta and San Miguel ended more dramatically, resulting in a brawl that left one person dead and several wounded from stabbings with bayonets.[8]

Thus, even in Havana—where contingents of Spanish troops had encamped in the streets and plazas awaiting repatriation in the last days of Spanish colonial rule—public demonstrations of *cubanía* could not be held in check. On the afternoon of 26 December 1898, a member of the Spanish police force dejectedly described the scene to his superiors: "Since this morning, various groups have been cruising through the neighborhoods of Peñalver, Chávez, San Nicolás, Vives, Ceiba, Jesús María, and Arsenal, their cries of "¡Viva Cuba Libre!" filling the air in every direction. Most of the houses are decorated with Cuban and American banners and flags, and the San Nicolás and Jesús María churches are ringing their bells."[9]

Indeed, over the final months—not just days—of Spanish rule, the existence of a Cuban nation was given effective life, publicly and spontaneously, through the uninhibited display of flags, stars painted on walls and shopwindows or worn on brooches and belt buckles, the colors blue and white emblazoned on clothes and the sides of buildings, cries of Cuba Libre! and patriotic songs heard on the streets or in cafés, and nationalist signs posted on the front of businesses. Thus the common people of the capital—workers, newspaper vendors, shoeshine boys, piano players in bars and cafés, even prostitutes participated by one means or another in molding and reiterating the symbolic language through which a discourse of Cuban nationhood was articulated and spread.

Furthermore, after the withdrawal of the Spanish and the arrival of the North Americans, and the threat represented by a continuing U.S. military presence, the need to demonstrate the reality of the nation and avert stumbling into a symbolic void, became all the more vital. The question *Who are we?*, critical at a time of confusion when the end of Spanish sovereignty had not brought independence but only a new imperial relationship, was posed through a welter of gestures and images steeped in allegorical meaning.

On returning to Havana from the United States during the first days of January 1899, an émigré Cuban journalist wrote of his expectation that he would find a sad, dispirited city, full of U.S. flags, with soldiers of the occupation stationed at all points. To his amazement, the man related, "our beloved Cuban flag flew everywhere." "Were you to ask us what sound predominates at this unique hour we would say that it is the sound of the Anthem of Bayamo." Without venturing out very far, in fact by not going any further than the balcony of the house in which he was composing his article, the man could hear the strains of the anthem, interpreted in a different way, "according to the musical temperament of the person playing it," on seven or eight pianos at the same time.[10]

As contemporary sources make clear, the outpouring of flags, signs and images, patriotic music, and national colors occurred everywhere, underlining that a significant popular consensus had formed around a discrete set of symbols which conveyed the idea of a "country," or Cuban nation. This consensus flowered and was nurtured during the years of war against the Spanish metropole. As such, it preceded by many years the official establishment of the Cuban Republic in 1902.

The Symbolic Legacy of the Wars

In Cuba, as in many other places, the experience of anticolonial rebellion and revolution was the principal source of the myths, representations, and symbols that helped fuel and concretize a discourse of national identity. Yet the construction of a metanarrative that places the hallowed origins, foundational exploits, and emblematic images of the nation in its struggles to achieve independence has been little examined in Cuban historiography. Nationalist-minded historians have simply taken what Ramiro Guerra calls "the national sentiment" associated with the independence campaigns as a spontaneous, self-contained phenomenon, without investigating the manner and mechanisms through which such notions of belonging to a national community are diffused and reiterated, become embedded in emblems or symbols, and get translated into patriotic practices and rituals.[11]

In a probing sociological study of Mexican national identity, Roger Bartra refers to the aura of invisibility that envelops the process through which national values are created: "The myth of the national character would seem to have no history; it is as if national values had been plummeting out of the sky over the fatherland to become unified in a substance in which the souls of all Mexicans are eternally and equally bathed." Bartra, however, circumscribes his analysis to the production of nationalist myths that stem from and serve a hegemonic political culture. In his view, the creation of a metanarrative about the nation is exclusively the outcome of a self-serving will to power on the part of nationalist groups committed to the process of unifying and institutionalizing the modern capitalist state.[12]

Ángel Rama, in his influential work *The Lettered City*, similarly ties the emergence of an autonomous narrative about the formation of nationality in Latin America to the work of educated urban elites. At the end of the nineteenth century, in parallel fashion to the making of its national literatures, Latin America witnessed the impulsive flowering of a school of historical writing which "constructed a cult of heroes, placing them above political factions and turning them into symbols of the national spirit."[13]

In the Cuban case, the contribution of the educated elite to the development and furtherance of a discourse about nation and country is undeniable. The traditional historiography locates the genesis of Cuban national consciousness in the first decades of the nineteenth century. If we take that claim to be valid, then the separatist rhetoric and ideology of the second half of the century must be understood as the inheritance of earlier-developed discursive strategies. These earlier strategies were necessarily the foundation on which the idea

THE SOCIALIZATION OF SYMBOLS

that Cuba differed from the mother country was built. At the beginning of the century, according to this scheme, Cuba possessed a nucleus of prominent creoles who constituted a class of "people well adapted to their environment, anxious to attain progress and political autonomy, and to play the preponderant role in their country to which their enlightenment, their background, and their individual and collective worthiness entitled them."[14] These ambitious and high-minded men directed themselves to formulating and debating social reform projects, a central element of which was to define the essence of cubanía: the elaboration of an archetypal national culture, with its heroes, landscapes, emblematic images, and characteristic "types and customs."

This educated circle, including members of first-rate intellect, laid the cornerstones of nationality by refashioning the creole self-image. Through various writings and representations, what had until then been the "ever faithful Island of Cuba," prodigal daughter of the Mother Country, began to be thought of as "the creoles' country," with the right, if not to sovereignty, then at least to autonomy within the colonial framework.[15] Throughout the nineteenth century, several generations of politicians, poets, journalists, novelists, historians, and critics contributed to what gradually but inexorably came to be perceived as Cuba's national culture. This culture was projected onto and inscribed in a past; it was made the object and outgrowth of certain "origins," the expression and high point of a "genealogy" and a "tradition," which were now viewed as the seedbed and justification for campaigns for political autonomy.

Outside and woven around the conflicts internal to this narrative, the conflict between visions at once reformist and radical, elitist and populist, traditionalist and modernizing, is a central unifying thread: that national identity takes shape against and in contrast to an oppositional referent—in Cuba's case, Spanish control and domination.[16] Consequently, a major influence in nineteenth-century Cuban political history was the idea, promulgated and nurtured by the educated elite, that Cubans belonged to an "imagined community of the nation," possessing its distinctive history, traditions, emblems, and virtues. This idea was at the core of the creoles' growing dispute with the metropolitan power, culminating in the outbreak of the wars of liberation, which in turn provoked a rupture with a culture and a past that had been shared for nearly four centuries.

On the terrain of the "Republic in Arms," whether during the course of the wars themselves or from the quieter bastions of cultivated opinion, and both in earlier years and later during the period of the "bountiful truce," as well as through the efforts of Cuban exiles in the United States, an epic narrative of the history of the homeland was being constructed, containing its foundational figures and defining moments and episodes, with their attendant heroes, symbols, and archetypal tales. Owing to the power of the written word, military events were turned into History, and their protagonists, dead or alive, became the subjects of a heroic campaign, reified in poems, narratives, and commemorative speeches.

The marked liberalization of political and cultural life on the island in the years that followed the signing of the Pact of Zanjón in 1878 (ending the Ten Years' War) led to an unprecedented boom in publishing. At the end of the 1880s, more than five hundred periodicals were being published in the capital alone.[17] Magazines such as the *Revista de Cuba*, *Revista Cubana*, and *Hojas Literarias*, as well as the Havana newspaper *El Fígaro*, frequently served as forums in which ideas about the formation of a Cuban nation were debated, along with related topics, such as the Ten Years' War and its consequences, or the character—often represented in starkly negative terms—of the Spanish colonial regime. Works such as Manuel de la Cruz's *Episodios de la Revolución*, Ramón Roa's *A pie y descalzo*, and Enrique Collazo's *Desde Yara hasta el Zanjón*, appearing as they did between the two wars of liberation, were among the first written accounts of the military conflict of 1868 to be distributed on a national scale. As such, they in large measure laid the groundwork for the conventional wisdom that the Cuban nation was born out of the War of Independence and its legacy.[18]

Newspapers and other writing that promoted the cause of independence, whether published on the less than stable presses of the hinterland or produced by persons in exile, played a critical role in disseminating and fomenting acceptance of these fundamental representations of the nation. The anecdotal recollections of those who participated in the wars, articles commemorating national days, patriotic poetry, accounts of battles, and biographies of heroes—all these and more were passed from hand to hand along routes than went from the rugged countryside of eastern Cuba through Kingston and Key West all the way to New York or Paris, and vice versa.[19]

This foundational narrative of the nation was enriched at the same time by visual imagery which also had its origin in the independence struggles. As pictorial representations of the nation, the escutcheon with the palm tree (the national tree) and the flag with its single star were reproduced and circulated not only in drawings, engravings, and photographs, and printed on letterhead, bonds, currency, and stamps issued by the Republic in Arms, but on objects of daily use as well, such as rosettes, brooches, animal yokes, and buckles.

However, the historiographical line which locates the symbolic construction of *cubanidad* (the constituent elements of cubanía) in the vanguard actions undertaken by the educated creole elite minimizes or relegates to a secondary plane the active participation of popular sectors and the important weight borne by subaltern political culture in fostering the "imaginative community of the nation." The role played by oral tradition in transmitting the memory of the independence struggle has received scant attention from historians. If, as is the case, the "invention of tradition" and nationalist symbolism resulted largely from a process steered "from above," it is no less the case that the popular classes made this symbolic and iconographic repertoire their own by endowing nationalist representations with multiple new-begotten meanings.

Moreover, as Ada Ferrer has emphasized, the fact that as of 1887 only 37 percent of the country's white population and barely 12 percent of those classified as being "of color" were able to read or write does not mean that the illiterate majority was automatically excluded from absorbing ideas originating in and disseminated through books, pamphlets, and newspapers. The most important news of the day reached the ears of the common people through the cries and shouts of newspaper and penny press vendors. Then later, with the help of relatives and friends, in casual settings such as family gatherings; by meeting people in grocery stores, barber shops, or the market; through soirées and parties in clubs or educational societies, or in worksites themselves, as in the collective reading of news practiced in the tobacco shops, the uneducated participated in the discussion of topical issues.[20] These outlets and mechanisms in turn gave rise to chains of oral transmission and, more important, to different "communities of interpretation" in which the original messages were often recast or reinterpreted in keeping with the dissimilar experiences of the new recipients of the information.[21]

By utilizing oral history techniques and painstakingly reconstructing, on the basis of testimonial sources or data obtained in local archives, the life histories of persons low in the social hierarchy, Rebecca Scott recently documented the case of a woman born a slave around 1860 on the plantation of Santa Teresa, near the city of Cienfuegos. As a child Barbara Pérez was taught to read by the mistress of the house. Freed from slavery years later, she became a central figure in Arimao, the small rural community where she lived for most of her life. Her ability to "take in the press" soon became known, and whenever a newspaper reached the hamlet, all of its inhabitants collected outside her house to listen to the news and, more than likely, discuss it.[22] In this case, in place of the classic Habermassian public space with its "salons," refined gatherings, and bourgeois cafés set in urban environments, we are dealing with a kind of "plebian" public sphere, in which—by "translating" accounts of the news to her illiterate fellow villagers—a humble black woman (who in other settings might be a barber, a municipal employee, the local pharmacist, or schoolteacher), creates a space for the exchange and spread of opinion, a space which also links political deliberations occurring on a national level, as synthesized in the newspaper reports, with the concerns and interests of a small, outlying community. It is precisely in such arenas of "plebian" opinion, rather than in the lofty public forums of "enlightened" opinion, that my interest in analyzing the symbolism of Cuban patriotic sentiment and dialogue lies, insofar as it took hold during the period of the U.S. occupation.[23]

Patriotic Literature and National Identity during the Years of the Intervention

With the cessation of Spanish rule, the generally unrestrained freedom enjoyed by the Cuban press, together with the relatively benign position taken by the U.S. military authorities toward public demonstrations of nationalism, opened a critical space for disseminating the images and representations that permeated the discourse about national identity. A plethora of newspapers, many very short-lived, some appearing even before the Spanish troops had fully withdrawn from the island, served as a vehicle for the diffusion and socialization of the symbolic legacy of the independence struggles and its embrace by societal groups.

These ephemeral newspapers, operating without official license and lacking a publisher's imprint, began to circulate widely in Havana and other cities during the last days of 1898. Along with carrying news that focused primarily on the withdrawal of the Spanish army and the presence of U.S. military forces in the eastern part of the country, they invariably (based on my selected consultation of them) included pictures and biographical sketches of prominent patriots, reproductions of the Cuban flag and escutcheon, as well as patriotic poetry, songs, and serialized histories. Unlike the major Havana dailies, these penny press newssheets and newspapers were affordable to at least some poor Cubans.

On the front page of its 24 September 1898 issue, one such paper, *La Estrella Solitaria*, included a biographical piece on the mambí general Mayía Rodríguez, as well as an engraving of him. Like its companion newspapers, *La Estrella Solitaria* advertised the sale of rosettes and little Cuban flags. "In some establishments," it added "ladies' belts that have the Cuban flag and five-pointed star on them have been put on sale."[24]

An issue of *La Independencia*, dated 12 October 1898, offered its readers—for the anniversary of the *Grito de Yara*—a picture of Carlos Manuel de Céspedes, the "father of the Country," along with an article dedicated to his memory. "His name," it asserted, "will remain engraved on the History of Cuba with indelible letters." The article concluded by referring to both Martí and Céspedes as apostles and redeemers of the people, who "have laid the foundation of the grand edifice of Cuban freedom." Cuba in the future will be "eternally happy" because of their efforts. An ode extolled the virtues of the machete, the mambise weapon par excellence, which occupied a privileged place in the iconography of the revolution. In a florid metaphor of continuity, Quintín Banderas's polished and sharpened machete, a "symbol of the redemption" of the Cuban people, was also described as heir to the "poisoned arrows of the Cibonay." Now, the article asserted, "everything signifying immorality and oppression will be swept onto the ground in Cuba by the two-handed thrusts of its honed blade," and "the effect of the well-tempered edge of its burnished blade will make the single-starred flag flutter, proudly and gallantly."[25]

This issue of *La Independencia* also reviewed the first celebration in Guanabacoa and Marianao, both located on the doorstep of the capital, of the anniversary of the Grito de Yara on 10 October. In addition, it reproduced in full the words of the "Bayamesa," in a version identical to the one that is sung today, as well as another revolutionary anthem, long since forgotten, called the "Holguinero."[26]

As was customary at the time, another newspaper, *La Guásima*, offered its readers a popular history published in serialized form, under the heading "Reminiscences of the Past." Following a tradition already established in the exile press of rendering the episodes of the wars of liberation in a literary mode, the newspaper serial provided a narrative of the death of Antonio Maceo, written by the Catalonian mambí José Miró Argenter, whose epic poems would later become among the principal chronicles of the revolutionary era.[27]

Although many of the narratives and short biographies published in the press during these years were factually incorrect or prone to fantasy, they nonetheless played an important role in helping to spread the patrimony bequeathed by the wars of liberation.[28]

Newspapers were not only the source for the remarkable diffusion of the corpus of nationalist symbols, constructed out of memories of the independence struggles, that were evident everywhere in this period. Magazines, printed ephemera, novellas, and song collections also functioned as outlets for the dispersion of images and representations of and about the nation.

During these years, inexpensive, small-format storybooks—broadly analogous in structure and techniques of production to *literatura de cordel* (popular poetry pamphlets)—achieved a considerable readership among Cubans. Classified as "historical novels," they typically dealt with patriotic themes and subjects. In a pair of such works, published in 1900 and 1901 respectively, the lives of José Martí and Antonio Maceo were fictionalized in a way that mixed the real and the invented in the style of the serialized adventure stories then in fashion. In the pages of *Martí: Novela histórica por un patriota* (1901), actual events in the life of the Apostle, such as his incarceration in the Havana prison and his departure to live in exile, are intermingled with imagined episodes in which, for example, a fellow supporter of the independence struggle saves Martí's life by turning into his double and running through the streets of Paris chased by a Spanish agent he ultimately kills in a duel on a bridge over the Seine. A similar conceit is found in *Antonio Maceo: Vida y hechos gloriosos de este heroico general cubano* (1900). Its anonymous author imagines that the future mambí general endures an experience which leaves a traumatic mark on him. Maceo, while still a child, is forced to look on helplessly as an old slave woman, who had been his "nanny," is tortured and killed. This incident compels him to dedicate the rest of his life to the struggle for the emancipation of Cuba's slaves. Following this path, moreover, he avenges the memory of his unfortunate nanny and wet nurse, so brutally executed by a cruel master. Incorrect facts and imagined events aside, by disseminating and popularizing —in the manner of the adventure novel—episodes in the lives of the country's foundational heroes, this type of storytelling helped spread the symbolic patrimony of the wars of liberation.[29]

The poems and songs contained in songbooks and collections of *décimas*, such as *El Tiple Cubano* (1901) or *La Nueva Lira Criolla* (1903), provide clear evidence of the marked politicization of daily life in Cuba during this period. In contrast to their counterparts in the 1897 edition, the majority of the songs and popular poetry in the 1903 collection of *La Nueva Lira Criolla* carry a definite political message. Décimas, songs, and even the more stylized *guarachas* explicitly refer to the heroic campaigns of the wars of liberation, the defeat of the Spanish and their withdrawal from the island, the controversial presence of the U.S. forces, and Cuba's need to secure its long-sought independence. Both collections contain numerous anthems, songs, and poems celebrating the Cuban flag as well as paeans to the brave mambise soldiers. Within the inner circle of heroes of the independence struggles, Martí, Maceo, and Gómez—in that order—are sung and written about the most, followed closely by Céspedes and Calixto García.[30]

Textbooks were another genre that played a decisive role in diffusing the symbolic patrimony of the independence struggles, in both their military and civil phases. As I noted earlier, the national-level reorganization begun in 1899 of the country's system of primary education expanded school enrollment considerably. Across the island in both rural and urban settings, thousands of children, irrespective of race or class, began to learn about national history according to a more or less standard lesson plan. The adoption in 1901 of Vidal Morales's influential textbook, *Iniciadores y primeros mártires de la Revolución cubana*, as the basic manual for teaching history in Cuba's public schools paved the way for the later institutionalization and standardization, in the republican era, of the teaching of Cuban national history.[31]

A letter found among the papers of Máximo Gómez summons up these initial years of the twentieth century, when things which today are common knowledge to all school-age children were still uncertain and questioned. The letter was written to Gómez in 1902 by several residents of Cienfuegos who wanted to commemorate the death of José Martí. They were uncertain whether his death had occurred on 19 May, as reported in the press, or on 21 May, the date taught to children in the city's public schools.[32]

To receive certification, Cuba's schoolteachers took a uniform examination, and the text or manual which they used to prepare for this test had been published by 1902. It was written by a group of distinguished figures in Cuban letters, including Manuel Sanguily, Nicolás Heredia, Carlos de la Torre, Valdés Rodríguez, Esteban Borrero, and Vidal Morales himself. One of the virtues of this work was that it put in place, for the first time, a common set of themes and topics to be covered by teachers of Cuban history in the first years of the Republic.[33]

Another factor in the equation was the U.S. military occupation and U.S. presence on the island, which boomeranged by intensifying nationalist sentiment in the public schools. The public schools had been reorganized on the U.S. model, but this was purely a matter of form and did not dictate content. There was a notable proliferation, during the years of the U.S. intervention, of demonstrations of nationalism in the schools, such as the commemoration of patriotic anniversaries, the ritualized saluting of the flag, and classroom singing of the "Bayamesa," well before it became the official national anthem.

Descriptions of the celebrations of the national days, when schoolchildren —clutching little Cuban flags—took part in marches, are an example of this affirmation of nationalist sentiment by the schools. Havana's Board of Education reported that on 24 February 1900—the fifth anniversary of the Grito de Baire—children in the public schools sang anthems in their classrooms, "above all of Bayamo and of the Invasion"; they listened as the origin of the

Cuban flag and escutcheon was explained to them; and they heard "short but substantive evocations of praise of the most brilliant figures and heroes of our revolution." In addition, children in the lower grades received little Cuban flags and pictures of the country's founding leaders and heroes.[34]

The following year the 24 February anniversary was celebrated in more lavish style. The city's schoolchildren marched along the Prado from the Campo de Marte down to La Punta, on the western edge of Havana's harbor, "each child with a Cuban flag in his or her hand." Several musical bands could be heard playing the strains of the "Bayamesa," as the children "found themselves in the midst of the vibrant military sounds which, when heard, always put us in the presence of the intangible, of greatness, of the everlasting, of what constitutes the ideal: the Fatherland."[35] In a letter written in 1900, Máximo Gómez describes how, in the company of his family while visiting the gravesites of his son and Antonio Maceo, he came upon a group of more than four hundred children who had gone there and were "lined up in a most orderly way to place flowers on the heroes' graves."[36]

Thus, against the annexationist cultural initiative promoted by the U.S. military government, Cuba's public schools served as a focal point for the dissemination and reenactment of nationalist-directed practices in general and of a body of patriotic symbols in particular. Ironically, the introduction into Cuba of practices followed in the U.S. educational system, which were aimed at fostering a sense of national community among students and—in certain places, such as New York City—were also conceived as an instrument for assimilating immigrants who would later be converted into "citizens" imbued with the "American spirit," became an important vehicle for instilling patriotic sentiment in future "Cuban citizens."

This process was furthered not only by the strong nationalist feelings held by members of local boards of education and by teachers themselves, but also by the fact that the U.S. superintendent of Cuban public schools was a man of progressive ideas and was inclined to espouse them in opposition to those advocated by the typical neocolonial administrator, such as the U.S. governor of Cuba, Leonard Wood.

Indeed, remarkable as it may seem, the first large-scale publication on the island of the "Bayamesa"—a printing of one hundred thousand copies—occurred in December 1900 on the initiative of Alexis Frye, paid for out of his personal funds. The letter which accompanied the distribution of the pamphlet emphasized that "Cuba must teach its children that any nation which tries to trample on human liberty is tyrannical and that every tyrant is a coward. It must teach them that it is mandatory that Cuban heroes shall be ever alert to defend the independence of the country, with their life and treasure, against every foreign power, whoever it might be, which in years to come tries to ascend the tyrant's throne." The pamphlet, bearing the words of the anthem, was handed out to schoolchildren throughout Cuba, with the intention that on "the first day of this new century . . . the National Anthem is heard everywhere on the Island, so that children from every home can lift their voice in chorus, and learn the highest lesson of patriotism, which will forever shield this beautiful and heroic land from all danger."[37]

Biographies of the "founding fathers"—Céspedes, Martí, Maceo, Calixto García, and Máximo Gómez—thus quickly found their way into Cuban textbooks, assuming the prominent place occupied by accounts of Washington, Jefferson, and Lincoln in the U.S. texts on which they were modeled. In addition, the ceremonial rituals practiced in U.S. schools, such as saluting the flag and singing patriotic songs, were also assimilated into Cuban schools. They were seen to be an indispensable part of creating in young Cubans a firm sense that they belonged to a single community. For the moment, given the absence of a national state possessing the authority to standardize the history curriculum and institutionalize civic rituals in the schools, it fell to the teachers themselves and to the nationalist-minded school boards, often aided by the actions of local municipal councils or the "extraofficial" initiatives of veterans' associations, to lay a foundation for the systematic teaching of *historia patria* (history of the national past), through which schoolchildren everywhere on the island became familiar for the first time with the basic symbols and representations that helped foster in them the idea of belonging to the nation.

In sum, a narrative about the origins of the nation, with its accompanying iconography—both vitally important to the confection of nationalist imagery and ideology in the first years of the century—emerged in stages from a wide range of sources: the periodical press, serialized newspaper histories, and novellas, song collections and printed ephemera widely distributed among the lower social strata; reproductions of patriotic emblems, engravings with the images of heroes and mambise chiefs, textbooks with the words to anthems and revolutionary songs, patriotic décimas, celebrations of the principal dates marking the revolution for independence, and chronicles of heroic episodes in the wars and in the lives of patriots.

Cuba's Museums during the Interregnum:
From Colonial Life to the Creation of a National State

The island's museums, several of which were founded in these years, served as another arena for the consecration and institutionalization of patriotic memory. Paralleling the process by which Cuba's history was reinterpreted on the basis of nationalist premises, as articulated in the press, commemorative speeches, textbooks, and other expressions of written culture, a concerted effort also got under way to locate, identify, and collect "relics" from the past, objects of material culture that carried within them a record of historical experience.

Places laden with patriotic significance, such as the Foso de los Laureles (the moat and the grassy area around the La Cabaña fortress) and the wall adjoining it against which the medical students had faced a firing squad, were identified in Havana with commemorative signs and plaques. The U.S. military government named Vidal Morales director of archives for Cuba, and Morales began the work of assembling, preserving, and publishing documents considered essential to reconstructing and rewriting the history of the former colony from a nationalist perspective.[38]

In this atmosphere and context, numerous objects—many perfectly pedestrian in themselves—were turned into historical "relics." The rifles and machetes used in the recently concluded war were perhaps the most pertinent example. Diaries and memoirs of participants in the war portray a relationship between the mambí soldier and his weapon that bordered on the intimate. Many a soldier had acquired his weapon at considerable risk to his own life by wrenching it from the hands of the enemy. Once the military conflict ended and the Liberation Army, under pressure from the U.S. authorities, was discharged, soldiers were ordered to give up their arms. The collection of rifles and machetes, which the soldiers viewed as virtual extensions of themselves, was a traumatic process. It required more than three months to settle negotiations between the Cuban side, which wanted the arms to be delivered to Cuban army officers and kept in arsenals protected by Cuban guards, and the U.S. authorities, who had stipulated that each Cuban soldier needed personally to give up his weapons, at which time he would receive a seventy-five peso remuneration, "generously" awarded by the McKinley administration. All of these weapons, under the U.S. plan, would be handed over to the nearest detachment of the U.S. Army. The agreement finally reached, however, privileged the Cuban position; the weapons could be given up to Cuban officers or, failing that, to mayors.[39]

Many soldiers flatly refused to part with their weapons, however, and others declined the seventy-five peso payment, believing that the U.S. "handout" sullied their honor as soldiers and Cubans. Some brigades handed over only part of their weaponry, secreting the rest in case it should be needed in the event of an armed conflict with the occupying army.[40]

When the discussions between the two sides threatened to boil over, the "nongovernmental" Cuban-American League tried to intervene and find a middle ground. Its president, William McDowell, who did not otherwise conceal his organization's annexationist agenda, proposed that all of the weapons collected should be carefully labeled, with a card also attached to each, recording the name and service record of the soldier to whom it had belonged during the war. The weapons would be sent to the "Pantheon of Cuban Liberty," where they would be preserved as sacred relics of the Cuban homeland. It would thus be guaranteed that "the children of the heroes of Cuba Libre, to the latest generation, can know with certainty and see the instrument with which their ancestor fought for the cause to which he gave the full measure of devotion."[41]

It is not clear whether McDowell's proposal was merely a stratagem, meant to convince the soldiers to hand over their weapons, and thus achieve the rapid disarming of an army that could threaten the exercise of U.S. power in Cuba, or whether it was in fact a well-intentioned idea aimed at preserving part of the memory and record of the war. What is certain, however, is that labeled and stored away, removed from the hands of the soldiers or officers who had wielded them in the war, these weapons became nothing more than museum artifacts with no potential to be used.

In the aftermath of the war, it was not simply flags and soldiers' weapons which were transformed into collector's items, but a wide variety of objects of personal use, such as handkerchiefs, clothing, watches, and billfolds belonging to distinguished patriots or martyrs of the independence cause. Patriotic clubs, private individuals, and state institutions like the national archive or the national university collected or became repositories for such "relics."[42]

The concern manifested by Cubans to preserve their historical patrimony was by no means misplaced. Authorities of the U.S. military government quickly approved, as official policy, the collection and removal of objects of historical interest found on the island. An 1899 order issued by the military governor expressly stipulated that U.S. Army officers serving in Cuba "take possession of as many objects of historical, ethnological or artistic interest as they can obtain through licit means" and send them to the military intendant of the Cuban Division to be loaded on ships, transported, and deposited "among the existing collections of the 'Smithsonian' Institution in Washington, D.C."[43]

In November 1898 Emilio Bacardí, then mayor of Santiago de Cuba, conceived the idea of establishing a museum, with a library attached to it, "realizing that founding [such an institution] was indispensable and urgent, before many historical relics of priceless value, coming out of our wars of independence, disappear or get smashed up."[44] Bacardí sought and obtained the support of Leonard Wood, the city's military governor. Wood not only authorized the founding of the museum but also granted it a monthly subvention of two hundred pesos. Over the next two and a half months, the planned museum received "donations of books, antiques and art objects and, of special note, historical relics of a patriotic nature." During his travels in Egypt, Bacardí had acquired an interesting mummy. He put the mummy on exhibit to raise funds to construct a proper building for the museum. He also authorized the exchange of six gold medallions, which had been used on special occasions in colonial times by members of the municipal council, for a group of art objects in order to enlarge the museum's holdings.[45]

With this groundwork accomplished, the first museum of the postcolonial era in Cuba was inaugurated on 12 February 1899. Bacardí's museum project had become a reality by getting support from two radically different sources. Born of a private patriotic initiative, with donations received and funds raised from the community, it was also aided by and in this initial phase counted on support from the government of military occupation.

Santiago's museum mounted one of the first public exhibits that attempted to portray the colonial period through all of its major phases. In a kind of symbolic reconciliation of the old antagonisms, objects representing competing powers and interests were placed in proximity to each other: pre-Colombian ceramics were exhibited next to a Castilian banner and a stone belonging originally to the tomb of Velázquez; weapons and insignias of the Spanish army shared space not only with machetes, rifles, and flags of the Liberation Army but with shells, fired by the U.S. Navy, which helped sink Admiral Cervera's fleet in Santiago's harbor.

The display of numerous objects (including sculptures, stone utensils, and ceramic vases) representative of the culture of Cuba's indigenous population served a dual purpose. Offering a vindication of the Amerindian legacy on its own terms, it provided an alternative tradition—one different from the Hispanic—for the origins of the country's "national" culture. With respect to rehabilitating the older indigenous civilization, archaeologist Enrique Gómez y Planos had written in 1901: "It is only right that our prehistory claim the place that belongs to it. . . . to know that the men of our past possessed such knowledge, that the fairness and justice of historical science demands [acknowledgment] of their worth, aiming to grant them their bravery and do away with the stigma of savages which they have borne up to the present, is a good thing."[46]

The museum also housed a separate department of unique, irreplaceable artifacts, in which it exhibited a collection of "patriotic relics." These included a pair of gaiters, a hammock, a saddle, and a bloody shirt which had belonged to Antonio Maceo, as well as various objects which had been the personal property of José Martí, Francisco Vicente Aguilera, generals Flor Crombet and José Maceo, and other notable Cuban patriots. The library annex complemented the museum's holdings by housing collections of maps, photographs, newspapers, and manuscripts, along with letters written by Antonio Maceo, José Martí, and other well-known figures.[47]

Another pioneering Cuban museum was founded in 1899 in Cárdenas, a port city located on the northern coast in Matanzas province. Thanks to the diligent work of the museum's planning commission, directed by Oscar M. Rojas, by the time the U.S. occupation was drawing to a close the institution had amassed a substantial collection, including an important group of objects associated with the campaigns for independence. In March 1902 the museum wanted to acquire the stairs which had been attached to the scaffold on which Narciso López was garroted in 1851. At the time, they lay abandoned on the grounds of the Havana jail. In a letter to Leonard Wood, the Museum Commission's secretary argued for the city's right to exhibit the object in its museum, since "Cárdenas was the first place in Cuba where, in front of selfless devotees of freedom, General López ran up the Cuban flag." A regionalist-centralist rivalry, or tension between the preservation of distinctly local historical memory versus the shaping of such memory on a national scale, was clearly evident in the U.S. authorities' response. After consulting with Cuban civic leaders, the headquarters of the military government denied Cárdenas's petition. The stairs, it ruled, "should be preserved in a national museum and not in one that lacks this character [because] the object in question carries undeniable value for the history of the Island as a whole, given that the events to which it pertains, in which that person [Narciso López] was to figure with such ill-considered motives, involve all of the Island, not simply one locality."[48]

In December 1899, the municipal council of Cienfuegos—spurred on by Pedro Modesto Hernández, a prominent intellectual and civic leader—decided to establish a museum "in which to preserve all that which has an ethnic or historical character." Since the city lacked a suitable structure for this purpose, it proposed, until one could be built, to use one of the halls in the municipal council building. Two days after the councilors' decision, a newspaper in the nearby town of Trinidad carried an appeal by those appointed to run the new museum, requesting that people send "weapons, flags, letters, etc. which have some historical interest to the offices of the Veterans of Independence, and Sr. Alemán [president of the veterans' center] will register them pending receipt of supporting documentation." It is not clear whether the museum in fact ever opened to the public, but a year after the initial steps taken to found it, a note was inserted in the minutes of the Cienfuegos municipal council indicating that the museum had acquired, among other objects, the Mayarí cannon, an imposing piece of artillery, from the 1895 war, which had been cast in metal in one of the workshops on Mayarí Hill, which lay within a mambise-controlled district.[49]

These incipient museums, founded during the interregnum between the colony and the creation of a national state, served not only as ground for the preservation of memory but also as focal points for political and cultural negotiation, where images of the past—whether immediate or remote—were adjusted and recast to suit new realities. For the museums' visitors, moreover, the defining themes of Cuba's historical narratives (both national and local) came to life in the exhibited objects and artifacts. They ceased to be the patrimony of only a few or the exclusive subject of scholarly research carried out by narrow groups of specialists or the highly educated and instead became part of the public sphere, accessible and visible in cabinets or cases, contextualized through the explanatory labels set next to the materials being displayed.

Sacred Relics and Patriotic Merchandise

Arjun Appadurai has hypothesized that material things possess a kind of social existence; as such, they carry different meanings that change from one context to another and are complemented by narratives that explain their identity and diverse social functions.[50] In this respect, Cuba's years "between empires" bear witness to a revealing metamorphosis of different signs. On the one hand, as we have seen, mambise regimental flags which once fluttered freely in the wind turn into relics framed and exhibited under glass, and weapons of war like rifles and machetes are "mummified" by being made into museum objects. The dress worn in the field by Liberation Army soldiers (which in reality often consisted of nothing more than rags) is referred to as though it were standard military issue and idealized into expressing the spirit and substance of cubanía. On the other hand, however, this type of sacralizing reification of the artifacts and "relics" of war, a process which accompanied the institutionalization of memory, was matched by an equally prominent—and opposite—tendency: the rampant commercialization of all objects classified as "historic."

On this latter score, the memoirs of a resident of Santiago describe how, while the city was under U.S. occupation in 1898, bands of North American tourists bought Cuban flags and rosettes and mambise machetes with the same abandon as they did crosses, insignias, sabers, badges, and cuffs belonging to the Spanish army. Their hunger for acquisition embraced the spent shells of artillery fired by the U.S. naval forces in the battle for Santiago no less than the spoils of the defeated Spanish fleet. Mundane objects such as pieces of crockery, lamps, and ashtrays taken off the Spanish warships which had run aground on the coast fetched very good prices.[51]

The salesmanship and "business" sideline of a Santiago inhabitant illustrate the opportunities for profit generated by the North American thirst for "patriotic" souvenirs. The small enterprise founded by this individual in 1898 involved buying new machetes in hardware stores, burying the blades and scabbards in a humid spot, waiting a short while until their metal had oxidized, then flecking them with some nicks and scratches, and, finally, selling them to North American tourists—for five or ten pesos each—on the claim that they were the *quimbos* (a short-handled machete) of mambí chieftans.[52]

Newspaper advertisements during this period are likewise a good measure of the escalating traffic in "patriotic" objects. Toward the end of 1898, the papers began to run notices of sales of red, white, and blue–striped belts with buckles that had the "single star" on them, pictures of Cuban patriots, flags of varying size, and rosettes and brooches decorated with Cuban emblems.

An announcement appearing in *Patria*, under the heading "Long Live a Free Cuba! Independence or Death," advertised for sale a "complete offering of Cuban novelties and jewelry," including pins, brooches, buttons with insignias, cuff links, high-waisted belts, painted plates, and more. "Everyone," the advertisement sermonized, "should wear the emblem of the Fatherland and be a patriot."[53] This same issue of the paper informed its readers that portraits of José Martí, done in crayon, were on sale in its business office.[54]

In February 1899 the *Diario de la Marina* also advertised flags for sale. No fewer than "12,500 Cuban and American flags of all sizes" were being offered by the Los Americanos shop on Havana's Calle Muralla.[55] In June 1899 *El Reconcentrado* invited its subscribers to purchase, for one silver peso, with a discount given to wholesale buyers, an allegorical Cuban picture photo-engraved on corduroy cloth, which—the newspaper avowed—was executed "to great effect" and "ought not to be missing from any Cuban house."[56] Still another advertisement, this one appearing in the Havana paper *El Nuevo País*, invited future fathers to acquire baptismal cards decorated with patriotic Cuban emblems.[57]

With respect to the buried remains of patriots fallen in the wars of liberation, *El Cubano*—the publication of the Havana branch of the Center for Veterans of Independence—advertised the sale of Cuba brand funeral wreaths, "dedicated to the heroes of the Cuban Republic," made of a hard porcelain and guaranteed to last for one hundred years.[58] In a somewhat lighter vein, so that the city's tailors could "without difficulty make the dress uniforms ordered from them by their customers," who needed them when participating in celebrations and other patriotic events, the Sáenz tailorshop, located on Havana's Calle Aguiar, sold "colored illustrations," priced at one and a half pesos each, representing the "true uniform of the Cuban Army, approved by the executive commission of the Cuban Assembly."[59] As the U.S. intervention was about to end, a business with a machine for making soda fountain drinks introduced—to accompany the traditional fruit drinks and fashionable North American *Coca Kola* [*sic*] on its menu—a novel nationalist drink, the *ponche bayamés helado* (Bayamo ice cream punch), with which to salute the fiestas celebrating the inauguration of the Cuban Republic.[60]

Other merchants used endorsements by prestigious independence leaders to boost their sales. Under the heading "To rejuvenate yourself!," *La Guásima* carried an advertisement for a product called Oil of Barrinat, a natural hair dye to whose effectiveness both Major Gaspar N. Betancourt and Lieutenant José L. Concepción of the Liberation Army testified. General Quintín Banderas pitched the products of Crusellas, a Cuban manufacturer of soaps and fragrances.[61] None less than Máximo Gómez featured in an advertisement for a pharmaceutical product: "Saving the illustrious caudillo! The strong asthma attacks from which Generalissimo Máximo Gómez suffers will stop as soon as he's given the inimitable and infallible revivifying potion, the one and true remedy for this malady."[62]

Thus, through their direct connection to a stream of commercial products, the "patriotic" meanings of nationalism and its discourse took on concrete form and were woven into the familiar routines of everyday life. Transformed into objects of consumption, flags, emblems, and portraits of Cuba's civic and military heroes were reproduced everywhere, converted into images of the larger society. Printed on product labels, embroidered on clothes, handkerchiefs, and belts, engraved on plates, ashtrays, buckles, buttons, and brooches, these "symbols of the Fatherland" coursed their way through all the avenues of commercial traffic, taking on new "worldly" meanings in the process.

In the charged political atmosphere of the period, small details, such as the colors and design of clothing or of dishware, the ribbon on a hat or the style of button worn on one's lapel, acquired a transcendent importance. For example, when he made his entrance into Havana on the anniversary date of 24 February, Máximo Gómez wore a lapel button with José Martí's portrait on it. On the following day, in another vivid demonstration of nationalism, the guests at a banquet in Gómez's honor were served on plates, ordered especially from London for the occasion, with portraits of both Gómez and Antonio Maceo glazed in black.[63] The typical dress of the mambí or of the Cuban woman, incorporating the colors of the flag, were not just worn by children and girls for celebrations and special school events on the national days. When the Treviño Circus barnstormed the island in 1901, one of its most successful shows involved a woman tamer dressed "in the typical Cuban outfit, white, red, and blue with a palm fiber hat" who subdued the starved circus lion, serving as a proxy for the 'Spanish' lion, in a popular parody of the solution to the conflict between the two nations."[64]

An "ill-chosen" or indiscreet element of one's clothing often caused tension or provoked a confrontation. A newspaper reported in 1900 that a man sailing across Havana Bay from Casablanca was accused of being an agitator and taken to the Vivac prison by a security officer. His crime, for which he was fined five pesos, consisted of wearing a hat ribbon with yellow and red colors resembling those on the Spanish flag.[65]

Another conflict, with far more serious implications, involved an aide-de-camp to the Afro-Cuban general Quintín Banderas. In January 1900 the aide attended a Liberation Army veterans' banquet wearing a "button of concord" on his lapel. The button, which he had acquired in a pharmacy on the Plaza de Dolores in Santiago de Cuba, depicted the Cuban and Spanish flags tied together. This gesture was considered offensive by the majority of guests at the banquet and produced a bitter dispute which laid bare the clashing views of racial differences and what it meant to belong to the nation prevailing among groups that had waged the independence struggles. The aide was immediately and severely reprimanded by a white general, Carlos González, while Quintín—according to the press account—came to the defense of his subordinate, arguing that in the new order brought about by the U.S. occupation, perhaps only the Spanish flag would prevent black Cubans from once again becoming slaves of the whites. The division of opinion set off a heated controversy which all but turned the banquet into a brawl. Ultimately, a highly respected black general, Jesús Rabí, stepped in to mediate, and his efforts tamped down the dispute. In Rabí's opinion, the issue transcended the pros and cons of propaganda about the peace settlement and a policy to promote harmony between Cubans and Spaniards. He took the unyielding position of a strong patriot. "It is degrading," Rabí said, "for a veteran to link himself to the flag of a country which slaked its hateful thirst on ours." In his view, idealistic as it may have been, "Cuba doesn't have blacks and whites, but only Cubans. . . . Jesús Rabí," the general finished with a flourish, "is just Cuban."[66]

Objects and relics classified as "patriotic" thus frequently served as sign and symbol of a contradictory relationship; they and the treatment accorded them illustrated the strange collusion during this period between nationalist attitudes and discriminatory practices.

For example, La Popular—an educational and recreational society in Camagüey—made a show of its devotion to cubanía by preserving as a relic, among its most valued possessions, a small piece of one of Antonio Maceo's uniforms. Nevertheless, when the society's directors were asked if they would allow their meeting hall to be rented for an evening event to celebrate Alexis Frye's forthcoming visit to the city, they turned down the request, on the grounds that there would be persons of color among the invited schoolteachers. The racism displayed by the club's leaders was criticized by a local paper, which highlighted the obvious paradox implicit in La Popular's stance, whereby it venerated "as a sacred relic" a piece of clothing which had belonged to this hero of the wars of liberation, though at the same time "if the heroic Maceo were alive, he would be denied entrance into its halls which are so clearly an extension *of the people.*"[67]

Another example of this interweaving of patriotism and racism that crept into the process of identifying patriotic "relics" was the exhumation of the remains and subsequent anthropological study of Antonio Maceo's cranium, carried out by a national commission at the end of 1899. Maceo's remains were exhumed, together with those of his adjutant, Francisco ("Panchito") Gómez Toro, on 17 September 1899, so they could be interred, after an elaborate funeral ceremony on 7 December, in a mausoleum located on the hilltop of El Cacahual. Taking patriotic symbolism to an extreme, many of those attending the exhumation collected small fragments of clothing which still adhered to Maceo's remains, as well as bullets from a repeating rifle and pieces of earth from where he had been buried.[68] These "relics," the authenticity of which was confirmed in the presence of a notary at the very moment of exhumation, became prized objects given to honor or show appreciation to friends and comrades in arms. Salvador Cisneros Betancourt, who as president of the Comisión Popular Restos de "Maceo-Gómez," directed the disinterment, had a kind of certificate printed up on cardstock on which, under the heading "Keepsake," small fragments of the bloody blue jersey, worn by Maceo on the day he died, were affixed. Various friends of Maceo received these patriotic relics in testimony to the "deep sympathy" which the Marquis of Santa Lucía professed for them.[69] In a letter sent to a friend at the end of September 1899, General Pedro Díaz, who was also present at the exhumation and earlier played an important role in helping rescue the bodies of Maceo and Panchito following the Battle of San Pedro, confirmed that he had shipped under separate cover "a handful of the earth that was collected after the remains of the venerable Maceo were cleaned," as a reward for the services rendered by his friend during the revolution.[70]

A report prepared by the Comisión Popular Restos de "Maceo-Gómez," reproduced in the press at the beginning of October 1899, accounts for how parts of the "relics" gathered up at the burial site were treated and dispersed. Three of Panchito Gómez's teeth would be set in pieces of gold and a button off his uniform as well as cuttings of his hair placed in a locket made of the same precious metal "for their perfect preservation." All of the items would then be presented, "with a special dedication," to Maceo's widow. In addition, two bullets found in Maceo's grave were also to be set in gold and presented as a gift to "Panchito Gómez's mother."[71]

Privileged individuals were not the only recipients of Maceo's clothing. An undershirt belonging to the general had also been found in his grave. The commission decided, in this case, "to preserve it intact behind a glass frame for eventual donation to the Museum of Havana." On the day of the exhumation, a Doctor Casuso had collected a part of one of Maceo's shirts. This shirt, a newspaper reported, was given to the commission by its "owner [to be divided up] into equal parts among all of the members of the Commission," with the corresponding notarized certificate attesting to their authenticity."[72]

As these examples demonstrate, there was no real logic behind the dispersion of the mortal remains of the two heroes. In keeping with agreements reached by the commission, part of the relics were ceremoniously given to family members, another part to a museum (yet to be established), and still a third distributed, as "mementos," among commission members present at the exhumation.

At the same time that shreds of Maceo's clothing and clods of earth from his burial site were turned into sacred relics and passed from hand to hand, testifying to the reverence for the everlasting memory (as phrased in the language of that time) of the independence hero, his cranium became an object of anthropological interest, the subject of an organized "scientific" study. According to a published pamphlet, "at the moment at which the casket that contained Maceo's skeleton had to be welded shut forever," the members of the exhumation committee came to the realization that "those remains deserved something more than a dry anatomical description or a mere certificate of identity." That "something more" was nothing other than a "deep anthropological study" carried out by prominent people in the Cuban scientific community, such as Carlos de la Torre and Luis Montané, employing the arsenal of craneometric techniques utilized in the racially tinged anthropology then in vogue.[73]

The study combined, in a splendidly paradoxical way, the "patriotic" motivation to glorify the memory of the independence hero with the application of techniques developed by the French anthropologists Paul Broca and Paul Topinard, both ardent defenders of "scientific racism," a dogma founded on the belief that cultural inequalities among human beings are a direct consequence of their racial differences.[74] "Fortunately," the Cuban research team claimed, the anthropometric evidence derived from Maceo's remains showed that the hero's white inheritance predominated over his black ancestry. If indeed the proportions of his bones corresponded to the characteristics of the black race, his great cranial capacity "which can be confused with that of the better endowed European," would explain his great innate intelligence as well as his notable intellectual faculties and leadership qualities.[75]

After comparing the dimensions of Maceo's cranium and bones with those of "African blacks" and of "modern-day Parisians," the commission reached the conclusion that "given the race to which he belonged and the sphere in which he nurtured and pursued his activities, Antonio Maceo can, in all rightness, be considered as a truly superior man."[76]

Clearly, it was only because Maceo was of mixed blood that an anthropological study had to be made of his cranium in order to validate his status as a "truly superior man." In his case, intellectual merits, exceptional military feats, and strength of moral character demonstrated over a more than thirty-year period devoted to the struggle for Cuba's independence were not enough. While white national heroes like José Martí or Calixto García were canonized on their death as central figures in the pantheon of "heroes of the Nation" purely on the basis of their individual achievements, without any need to meet additional requirements or offer further evidence, Maceo's incorporation into the national pantheon was accompanied by an anthropological examination of his mortal remains and, even more remarkably, by a kind of back-handed testament of his *limpieza de sangre* (purity of blood). At the same time that the commission of experts was carrying out the examination of his remains in Havana, in Santiago de Cubà Maceo's original birth certificate was being belatedly amended. As recorded in the *libro de pardos* (the registry reserved for persons of mixed white and black or Indian and black ancestry) of the parish of Santo Tomás, the information on that certificate had clearly specified that Maceo was the "natural" son of Mariana Grajales. On the orders of Archbishop Francisco de Paula Barnada, however, the *provisor* (chief ecclesiastical judge) and vicar-general of the parish altered Maceo's baptismal and marriage certificates on 23 September 1899, declaring him—three years after his death—to be the "legitimate" son of the Maceo marriage.[77]

Two divergent attitudes, or ways of thinking, governed the handling and the socialization of "patriotic" objects in this period. The first, oriented toward the conversion of common, domestic things into objects holding patriotic memory, turned them into museum artifacts and sacred "relics" worthy of reverence and worship. The second, directed toward integrating the "sacred symbols of the Fatherland" into the worldly markets of commercial exchange and the streams of everyday life, turned them into vulgar objects of consumption.

Both constructs, however, had the same end result: embodied in objects, whether in the form of relics or of products for the marketplace, the symbolic patrimony of the nation was "displayed where it could be seen," publicly exhibited, a phenomenon which contributed in large measure to its extraordinary diffusion and popularization.

The experiences and memories of the struggles for independence, with their epic narratives, their music, poetry, and patriotic iconography, were transformed during the years of the period "between empires" into the fundamental symbolic capital that underlay and supported the construction of national identity in the face of the threatening presence of the "other," embodied in the government of U.S. occupation.

If one considers that precisely during these years, in the course of patriotic ceremonies, the majority of the island's inhabitants witnessed for the first time the raising of the national flag in public or sang, again for the first time, the "Bayamesa" out loud, one will grasp the significance of studying these forms of public, collective affirmation of a sense of belonging to the nation years before the national state officially came into being. The widening acceptance of the flag and the "Bayamesa" as the representative emblems of the nation, the consolidation—not without conflict and tension—of a national pantheon of heroes and martyrs revered, in newspapers, textbooks, pamphlets, and collections of songs and décimas, as the founding figures of the nation's history, are critically important milestones in the genesis and diffusion of collective sentiments of national identity.

The belief that one belonged to the nation was also expressed during these years in chants, slogans, and bodily gestures; conveyed spontaneously on clothes, banners, placards, and triumphal arches and realized in nationalist rituals and ceremonies. At the same time, the recent memory of the wars began to be reified in a selective way on signs and monuments; it was "adapted" and brought to life in museum exhibits, crystallized in an endless series of objects having "patriotic" meanings, and revered in the form of relics or—conversely—purchased in shops and market stalls.

SIX
Public Culture
and
Nationalism

The "Production" of the Nation: Ceremonies and Monuments

The patriotic demonstrations that constantly occurred during this period opened a privileged space for the public expression of Cubans' feeling that they constituted and were members of a national community. The diffusion through the press of a symbolic nationalist patrimony was accompanied by its public representation in marches, meetings, acts of homage, celebrations, and funerals. These ceremonies enabled the symbolic codes I noted in chapter 5 to be fleshed out and consummated on public occasions in which music, flags, triumphal arches, dress featuring the national colors, and banners featuring portraits and allegorical depictions were dynamically intermixed. The debates over patriotic memory, national tradition, and what was most authentic in each also took place through the more limited channel of written texts. Yet this source, too, reached a wider audience, with its arguments advanced via the programs of public spectacles which often drew large numbers of people.

Although historical accounts of the period of U.S. occupation have traditionally represented Cubans as the victims of systematic humiliation and marginalization, forced to witness the U.S. flag flying everywhere on the island, in reality these years saw a prodigious number of nationalist ceremonies and demonstrations, events that were critical in creating a shared body of national symbols. Nonetheless, the symbolic "production" of the nation was not realized without discord and violence. Even as the nation's existence was made explicit in a wealth of rituals, practices, and emblems, a complex maneuvering took place in which patriotic memory and the national tradition, the Spanish colonial legacy and the "modernizing" element tied to the U.S. presence, were each verbalized, written about, and acted out in widely varying ways.

In *Imagined Communities*, Benedict Anderson emphasizes the role of print culture, the periodical press especially, in the development of the bonds of solidarity which constitute the imagined community of the nation.[1] Nevertheless, my emphasis here on patriotic ceremonies, with their elements of speechmaking, celebration, and performance, and on marches or public gatherings, with their myriad flags, salutes of gunfire, triumphal arches, portraits, and music, all intended to be seen and heard rather than read, is justified in virtue of the fact that nearly 70 percent of the Cuban population was illiterate at this time. This kind of public "production" of the nation thus furnished both the social space and the type of occasion in which thousands of Cubans lacking formal instruction could participate in collective affirmations of the existence of a national community and in the creation of the symbolic languages through which this community took shape. In this period, therefore, the unlettered majority was not reduced to being mere spectators at events orchestrated from above by an intellectual elite. On the contrary, the years of the intervention were marked by the proliferation of small-scale ceremonies, conducted in pueblos and other locales, rich in both popular creativity and the spontaneous expression of a sense of national identity.

Furthermore, these ceremonies, with their visual and auditory props and movement, combine an aesthetic expressiveness and an emotional power absent from the simple written formulation of ideas and values. The participation of large numbers of people in patriotic celebrations throughout the island also indicates that a public consensus had formed around a particular set of national values and emblems. This level and degree of attachment by the populace would be far more difficult to ascertain, much less verify, in the case of a written text and its contents.[2]

Through their displays of *cubanía* in the midst of patriotic celebrations, people from all walks of life not only marked the break with the Spanish colonial past but also—in publicly reaffirming the existence of the nation—called into question the legitimacy of the U.S. imperial presence. When men and women, holding flags and singing anthems, took part in a patriotic march, they effectively put themselves in the category of "citizens" of a future independent republic, rather than one of "natives" or "inhabitants" of a conquered territory, as the U.S. authorities persisted in calling them. Moreover, the official status of "patriot" conferred by having joined in the independence struggles and proudly exhibited during these celebrations gave hundreds of people of humble origin the social prestige and consideration needed to demand unequivocally the recognition of their civic rights, whether before the U.S. authorities or in dealing with power groupings and coalitions among the "higher" classes.

Thus, like other modes and methods for expressing the nationalist consensus and Cubans' conviction that they belonged, individually and collectively, to a nation, patriotic ceremonies also became a vital ground on which to press for civic rights and democratic freedoms and a space in which contrasting viewpoints on matters of race, citizenship, class, and gender could be counterposed and negotiated.

U.S. authorities administering the occupation, very likely influenced by the size and intensity of nationalist demonstrations, adopted a reticent attitude toward them, falling in the middle between repression and tolerance. The Cuban entities that organized patriotic ceremonies—municipal authorities, veterans' councils, the local committees of political parties, patriotic clubs, and others—frequently did not even bother to consult U.S. governing officials, especially in the interior of the country, where the practice of reaching decisions unilaterally was a source of pride.

A Captain General's Requiem Mass and Rites for Antonio Maceo

On 7 December 1898, in Santiago de Cuba, where the U.S. military occupation began nearly six months before it did in the western part of the country, a mass was said and solemn funeral rites performed in the basilica of the metropolitan cathedral for the soul of General Antonio Maceo.

According to a witness's account, the church's bells starting ringing the day before the event, to signal its importance. On the morning of 7 December, in a most unusual gesture, they were rung twice fifty times, repeating a ceremonial practice followed in the colony to announce the period of official mourning which began whenever its highest authority, the captain general, had died. A catafalque, surrounded by candles and "covered with wreaths," lay in the center of the cathedral, and behind the empty coffin (the location of Maceo's remains, which had been buried during the war, was a carefully guarded secret), a number of important leaders of the War of Independence, including the esteemed black generals Silverio Sánchez Figueras and Quintín Banderas, could be seen in the choir stall, "occupying the places of honor which, under the colonial regime, were reserved for persons ennobled by the Spanish monarch."[3] A formation of armed troops from the Mambí Army stood outside the packed church, where an enormous crowd also waited, and saluted the end of the religious ceremony with a round of gunfire. The next event, a civic gathering, began at noon in Santiago's Reina Theater, where those assembled listened to a series of fervent patriotic speeches. The last event on the program was a ceremonial procession, in which hundreds participated, to the Maceo residence on Calle Providencia (later renamed Calle Antonio Maceo), where a commemorative stone plaque was placed.[4]

In my judgment, this solemn remembrance and celebration of Antonio Maceo, which has never received much attention, possesses tremendous symbolic importance. That Maceo—a Cuban mulatto and *mambí*—would be granted the rites of a captain general, not only as the U.S. occupation was getting fully under way but within the walls of the Catholic Church, the most colonial-minded, pro-Spanish, and hidebound institution on the island, is scarcely conceivable. At bottom, it demonstrates the depth and reach of nationalist feelings, which had solidified during the recently concluded war, and is emblematic, furthermore, of a shift in political power and prestige: the former "criminal ringleaders" of the Liberation Army had supplanted the families endowed with titles by the Spanish monarchy. The effect of seeing the black general Quintín Banderas seated in the place once reserved for nobles of the Crown is not difficult to imagine and was obviously heightened by the crude stereotypes of colonial racist propaganda, according to which the general and his kind were the living image of savagery and incivility.[5]

As I observed earlier, nationalist ceremonies like the one conducted in Santiago often became vehicles for the questioning and subversion, at least on a symbolic level, of distinctions of class, race, or social standing inherited from colonial society. The tribute rendered to Maceo on the anniversary of his death, however, manifests a peculiar symbiosis between the old ceremonial codes of colonial times (the Catholic ritual of a requiem mass and the performance of the funeral rites for a captain general) and the symbolic language of nationalism, still in the process of consolidation.

Furthermore, when one considers that the ceremony took place in a city under U.S. military occupation, barely four months after Spain and the United States had signed an armistice, the question naturally arises of how the U.S. authorities, who up to this point had kept Cuban soldiers at arms' length, denying them the right to participate in the ceremonies formalizing Spanish capitulation and stopping them from even entering the city, could have allowed an event with such overtones to take place. The answer is disarmingly simple: taking advantage of the temporary absence of Leonard Wood, the city's military governor who was on a trip to the U.S. mainland, the organizers of the ceremony, supported by the municipal council, simply chose to ignore the military government. According to a U.S. wire report, reproduced in the *Diario de la Marina*, the U.S. authorities only learned of the event "when they saw Cuban soldiers and civilians marching through the city's streets, preceded by a hundred cavalrymen and infantrymen armed with Remington rifles" and the church's bells had begun to peal. En route to the basilica, followed by a crowd of people, the *mambíse* troops passed defiantly in front of the very doors to the headquarters of the government of occupation.[6]

According to Emilio Bacardí y Moreau (who in all likelihood personally witnessed the event), the people who spoke in the Reina Theater "made virtually no reference to the Americans; while saying much about the independence which Cubans had won." The U.S. wire story also reported that the several thousand Cubans who attended the event in the theater were "almost all of color," as were the Mambí Army troops who participated in the church ceremony; the latter were described as being composed primarily of "Negroes . . . armed with machetes and revolvers."[7]

The disquiet and paranoia felt by the U.S. authorities at any demonstration of nationalism which might cause them to lose their grip on public order is patently clear in the tone and slant of the wire report, with its emphasis on "mobs of armed Negroes." Only days after such defiance of U.S. rule, the prohibition against members of the Liberation Army entering the city and circulating through it with arms in hand was reiterated.

The mass and patriotic march held in Santiago de Cuba to honor the memory of Antonio Maceo is a clear indication that even within the restricted bounds of life under an occupation imposed by military force, a public sphere could be carved out for the open expression, in ceremonies often involving hundreds or thousands of people, of feelings of national identity.

Nationalist Appropriations of the Ceremonies Marking the Transfer of Sovereignty

If we scrutinize the history of the celebrations held at the end of 1898 to commemorate the change in sovereignty closely and carefully, we will find that they were indeed appropriated to express nationalism. The centerpiece in the transfer of power, carried out in Havana on 1 January 1899, remained in the memory of later generations as an unmistakable symbol of the humiliation of Cubans before the assertion of U.S. imperial power. The image of the U.S. flag flying over Havana's El Morro castle, an image preserved in photographs and prints as well as in verse, still stands as the most graphic representation of the frustration and powerlessness inherent in Cuba's new neocolonial predicament.[8] Yet a deeper examination of sources from this period reveals an interesting and little-studied phenomenon—the subversion, in nationalist terms, of the original meaning behind the imperial ceremony.

Carefully managed by the U.S. authorities, the ceremonial transference of powers, capped by a solemn military parade, the firing of a cannon at precisely twelve noon, and the exchange of flags on the El Morro castle, was designed to confirm symbolically, through an impressive visual spectacle, the United States's recently acquired military power over the island.[9] The agreements ratified by both powers in a private meeting in Paris were stamped with a public character through this staged outdoor ceremony. The Spanish side had acted out its role in the script days before by carrying the supposed remains of Christopher Columbus onto one of the warships in its fleet. Thus Spain left Cuba, the last enclave of what had once been its immense New World empire, taking with it, as a kind of coda to its long presence there, what were then believed to be the mortal remains of the Americas' "illustrious discoverer."

Ignominiously brushed aside during the official ceremony, the Cubans nonetheless made it their own by giving it a different meaning. Far from limiting itself to validating the legitimacy of U.S. power, the Junta Patriótica of Havana, in a broadside it published on 31 December 1898, encouraged the city's residents to celebrate the formal end of Spanish sovereignty, long the symbol of oppression and tyranny, with as much fervor as Cubans had brought to freeing themselves from the colonial yoke. This piece interpreted the raising of the U.S. flag as the "beginning of a new epoch of freedoms . . . under whose aegis the single star must soon radiate over the citizens of the great Cuban Nation."[10]

The official prohibition issued by the military government against such celebrations[11] intimidated the Junta Patriótica, which in a new broadside a day later, urged people to be moderate and to celebrate "by themselves," and "with calm rejoicing."[12] And yet people in the capital thronged the streets on the first day of January 1899, the city's houses were decorated with flags and portraits, and their doors were thrown open for parties and patriotic dancing that lasted until sunrise the next day. Martínez Ortiz has described the scene for us: "The people's happiness was immense, it overflowed everywhere, was expressed in as many ways as such a feeling can be externalized. Cubans were delirious; there was not a home, modest as it might be, that was not decorated in some way, and the fireworks, the cries, the applause, the songs and music greeted, from the very break of day and with deafening joy, what for all was the dawn of gratifying hopes, the definitive fulfillment of many years of longing."[13]

In this way, a sober and stately commemoration, from which Cubans were meant to be excluded and during which "order and the due respect that the solemnity of the circumstances demand" was expected, turned into an orgy of fiercely patriotic fiestas and demonstrations that the U.S. authorities, despite all their efforts, could not contain.[14] Paradoxically, the raising of the U.S. flag, an act wounding to national dignity and which, because of its powerful symbolism, had already sparked numerous conflicts between North Americans and Cubans during the war, was now interpreted as "the springtime of a new era of freedom," "the dawn of gratifying hopes," and the "prelude to the independence" desired by Cubans for so many years.[15]

As we have seen, the public, including a smaller contingent that participated directly in the Havana ceremony as well as people in general who learned of it via coverage in the press, was invited to witness and thereby indirectly sanction the solemn installation of the new imperial power by succumbing to the seductions of a theatrical set piece, with its military parade, anthems, flags, and cannon fire. The Cubans, in this script, were relegated to the role of spectators, since in the eyes of the U.S. military they were nothing more than the "inhabitants" of a conquered territory, a people without the legal right to determine the political destiny of their own land. Outside the prearranged lines of the script, however, the exchange of flags unleashed a host of strong feelings and emotions.

The reception given a speech, spectacle, symbolic gesture, or other such event is always a dialectic, entailing creative appropriations in which the matter being treated, or material presented, is transformed, reformulated, and surpassed by the person encountering it. Consequently, texts or spectacles never possess in themselves a stable, univocal meaning; rather, they are invariably "read," interpreted, in shifting, pluralistic, and contradictory ways. The transfer-of-sovereignty ceremony was intended by the U.S. military authorities to display the force and power of the island's new masters, but this meaning was recast in different ways: in "patriotic" but prudent and conciliatory terms in the broadside issued by the Junta Patriótica and in unrestrained nationalistic terms by the people of Havana who, despite the prohibition announced by the U.S. authorities and the urging of "calm rejoicing," spilled into the streets to celebrate wildly, as if true independence were at hand.

The formality and solemnity of the commemoration, and the oppressive character which these qualities brought to its initial symbolic meaning, were dissolved and overturned in the joyousness and self-confident irreverence of the street crowds, in songs and dances with *décimas* or *guarachas* such as this one, which was used to open and close a work of vernacular theater popular in this period:

Party away Habaneros:
Domination is no more,
and the Spanish colors
must come down at midday.
In their place will go up
the American flag;
but soon will it yield
to the Cuban.
Habaneros, party away![16]

The showy atmospherics of the transfer-of-sovereignty ceremony carried out in the capital, and the heavy coverage given to it in the press, have, however, obscured the importance of the hundreds of more modest celebrations held in numerous cities and small towns across the country to mark the end of Spanish colonial rule. The evacuation of the Spanish army from Cuban territory took place in stages during the fall and winter of 1898 and was accompanied, as it occurred, by small-scale ceremonies held in military barracks, mayors' offices, municipal council buildings, public offices, and other places throughout the island to commemorate the transfer of power.

Unlike the situation in Havana, Santiago de Cuba, and other important cities, where Cuban soldiers did not participate directly in ceremonies acknowledging the transfer of power, in many towns and communities it was the mambise forces who took up the positions of the Spanish army as it withdrew. In these locations, it was not the U.S. but the Cuban flag which replaced the Spanish on the flagpoles of public buildings. Communities in the provinces were decorated with flowers and flags to receive the Cuban troops, and they celebrated with processions, banquets, gatherings, and patriotic dances.

These fiestas and functions marking the end of Spanish sovereignty, organized by patriotic clubs—many of them composed of women and established in the days following the signing of the armistice—were probably the first public demonstrations of patriotism in urban areas in the western part of the country, where the sphere of action of the government of the Republic in Arms had never reached. When people in this region witnessed the Cuban flag raised for the first time they were often overcome with emotion. In some localities, both flags—those of Cuba and the United States—were run up simultaneously by the mambise troops, in a voluntary gesture of deference to the North Americans.[17]

On 30 December 1898, the Liberation Army entered the northern coastal municipality of Corralillo. In his memoirs, a mambí officer sketched a vivid picture of the soldiers' reception:

> Masses of men and women, children and old people, blacks and whites, left the hamlet and headed toward a country house located a few hundred yards away, the place had already been prepared for our reception. ... We still had some distance to cover when the thunderous cries to a free Cuba, to peace, to the United States, and to our flag and my regiment rang out loud and clear. Over here, Cuban and American flags were unfurled; over there, bouquets of flowers tossed by a huge group of young ladies. Dressed from top to bottom in blue and white and wearing the triangle and star of our insignia on their chest, they came right up to the ranks of my soldiers, who, filled with pride and happiness like me, choked up to see such enthusiasm and patriotism. In the middle of those stupendous cries of "Viva!" and that jumble of people waving their handkerchiefs and hats, the beat of the classic *zapateo* was heard, drowning out the noisy shouts of all those people crazed with joy and satisfaction. In those moments one experienced what there had never been an occasion to feel: the sublimity and the magnificence of liberty; in other words, the baptism of the national homeland which had just been born.[18]

On 29 December 1898 a patriotic procession was organized in Rancho Veloz, a short distance southeast of Corralillo, to greet the Cuban forces:

> At two in the afternoon, a bustle of activity like none seen before erupted on the streets of this pueblo, especially in the front of the municipal council, where the festivities and rejoicing to honor the Cuban Army were set to take place. At 2:30, the signal to start was given, and four Cuban soldiers, riding spirited horses, broke away, clearing the streets, and following them came the band playing the "Bayamesa," the "Evangelina Cossío" club with a magnificent flag, exquisitely embroidered, and a banner, the work of the young Rojo ladies, with this dedication: "To the Liberation Army"; then [came] a horse-drawn carriage with the girls María C. San Pedro and Emelina Díaz, representing, respectively, the United States and Cuba, wearing fancy allegorical dress and covered by the flags of both nations, two Cuban soldiers and four beautiful women on horseback, Blanca and Mercedes Lastres, Ramona Díaz, and Clara Aruca serving them as an honor guard; [after that

appeared] the "Martí" club with the Cuban flag and a splendid banner . . . with this dedication: "To the heroes of Independence" the "Maceo" club with its flag and banners bearing dedications to the Liberation Army; and closing the march were the Mayor, Council members, and other authorities, followed by more than two thousand people, among whom every social class was represented.[19]

Closer to Havana, indeed on the very doorstep of the capital, in the community of Guanabacoa, a reception was organized and carried out for the Cuban forces commanded by Brigadier Rafael de Cárdenas, despite the massive deployment of U.S. troops just miles away. Every street in the town, as a newspaper report put it, "was garlanded like the young maiden who awaits the man to whom she is engaged." Several bands played the "Himno Invasor," along with *danzones* and zapateos, and people gathered for a procession that left from the main plaza. "The march was started by three young men, on spirited horses, one carrying the American flag, another the Cuban flag and in the middle [a third holding] a white flag with red letters that read 'Honor to the Army.' A musical band, a group mounted on horseback, and two companies from the Liberation Army followed behind." After them came a young girl representing Cuba, dressed "in an outfit of silk, blue and white–striped skirt, red bodice with a silver star, and a Phrygian cap." Further behind, a young lady carried "a beautiful Cuban flag from which hung two cords secured by two children dressed in the uniform of our warriors." They were followed by the representatives of various associations, a delegation of people from both the Junta Patriótica and the local fire department, and, finally, by Brigadier Rafael de Cárdenas, accompanied by his general staff and his battalion's combat flag, together with the rest of the soldiers under his command and the townspeople. The procession was closed, in the words of the newspaper article, by "the most beautiful of the beautiful ladies of the locality," who rode in several cars and carriages adorned and canopied with Cuban flags. The commemoration ended with a banquet celebrated in the town's main plaza, where tables had been arranged in the shape of the "single star."[20]

I have included these extensive descriptions of local ceremonies organized to celebrate the transition to a new system of domination as a way of spotlighting the particular circumstances under which a date chosen to mark the accession to power of a foreign military intervention could be confused with, or transformed into, "the baptism of the national homeland which has just been born," or the break of a "new dawn spreading a torrent of freedoms." As we have seen, the translation of the event into nationalist terms, as evidenced in the profusion and worshipful use of flags, banners, anthems, dress, and patriotic songs, took place not only in towns and communities where the Liberation Army had replaced the Spanish forces, but in those places, like the capital, where the heavy concentration of U.S. soldiers made that nation's imperial presence impossible to overlook or ignore.

In these early celebrations, contrary to what is frequently claimed, the people who hailed the U.S. as well as the Cuban flag were neither a minority of "unabashed admirers of America" from the annexationist bloc nor renegades abandoning the cause of independence. The representation of both flags tied together was an oft-recurring image in these years, found not just in photographs and prints but also in décimas and songs of popular inspiration.[21] The visual similarity between the two flags (the colors white, blue, and red in combination with stars and stripes) was exploited during this brief "honeymoon" period. Indeed throughout 1898, both during the war and after Spain's capitulation, many Cubans—no matter their social class—looked on the North Americans positively, as the bearers of a tradition of order and progress whose intervention would make possible an end to the bloodshed and, after that, the installation of a modern, democratic republic. The mythical image of the United States as the Western Hemisphere's summit of freedom and liberty and model country of democratic virtues was so widely accepted in this period that many people saw no contradiction whatever in the simultaneous hoisting of the two flags and, moreover, naively placed their confidence in the good intentions of Uncle Sam, who held Cuba's independence "in safekeeping."

Within several months, however, the arrogance and blatant racism of the U.S. soldiers and civilian bureaucrats of the military occupation, as well as the nakedly imperialistic motives underlining the policy of the McKinley administration, would disabuse Cubans of these simplistic hopes. For the time being, though, as the next century edged closer, they rejoiced in celebrating not merely the end of a devastating war and four hundred years of Spanish colonial domination but the imminent arrival of what they believed would be a period of notable social progress, followed shortly by their definitive political independence.

In this sense and for these reasons the end of Spanish sovereignty could be interpreted by many Cubans in seismic terms, as the advent of a "radiant era of the freedoms of citizenship," initiated under the aegis of the continent's "champion of democracy," the United States.[22] In this new order, the rights and prerogatives corresponding to the inhabitants of a "democratic republic" would be enjoyed by all those who until now had been the victims of colonial oppression. Both the images of freedom and democracy associated with the

U.S. model and the promises of an egalitarian republic that had helped inspire the independence movement led people to think that the end of Spanish rule over Cuba would bring a new life for everyone: poor and rich, blacks and whites, men and women. In the midst of this generalized optimism, however, some among the crowds of celebrants noticed much sooner than others that, for all the slogans about freedom, the gatherings in favor of democracy, and the show of flags calling for independence, the colonial past did not fade with the last sunset of 1898.

On the night of 1 January 1899, the police in Havana swept through the streets of the city's poor neighborhoods and broke up the partying where the "beat of drums" betrayed the revelers' "distinctly uncivilized" celebrations. According to the account given many years later by Amador Prio Rivas, a long-time Havana police officer, many *ñáñigos* (Afro-Cuban men belonging to the Abakuá secret religious society), who had been feared and suppressed under the colonial regime "took advantage of the period of the revolution for freedom, and realizing that, with the disappearance of Spanish sovereignty over Cuba and Spanish governmental control of the Island, they could dedicate themselves with renewed passion to the religion and practices which they professed, agreed to organize anew, for which purpose they met on the first day of January 1899."[23]

The members of this society who joined the festivities that night paid dearly for their mistaken belief: imprisoned, tried, and convicted, they were sentenced to a year in jail for the crime of "illegal association."[24]

In the interior of the country, even as groups of "peaceful" Spanish troops were cheered on by the call for "peace and concord," in some pueblos black Liberation Army soldiers found themselves stopped from sharing in the community celebration by a wall of segregation: separate dances were held for whites and blacks, delivering what must have been a clear message that the dreamed-of democratic republic "that included all and was for the good of all" was still far away.[25]

The Construction of a Pantheon of Heroes and Martyrs

During the months that followed the formal change in regime, Havana's residents gave free rein to their anxieties about the direction of the country by joining multitudinous demonstrations. The first such event, on 28 January, was a civic procession commemorating the birth of José Martí, universally recognized by Cubans as the "apostle and martyr of the glorious revolution."[26] Despite the day's breaking cold and wet, "it could be said that all of Havana took part in it."[27] Societies, clubs, committees, unions, schoolchildren, representatives from the University of Havana, the lawyers' association, the Secretaries' Council (whose members had been appointed by U.S. Governor-General John R. Brooke a few days before), and municipal council members participated in the event, as did Martí's widow, son, and elderly mother. According to a newspaper report, "banners and Cuban flags appeared everywhere [while several musical groups] played the national tunes." To further honor Martí, a marble plaque (the first one consecrated in the capital to the memory of a martyr of the independence struggle), paid for by tobacco workers in Key West, was placed on the wall of the house in which the Apostle was born.

A little more than ten days later, thousands of Habaneros gathered once again, this time for the funeral of Calixto García. The general's remains, brought to Cuba from the United States, where he had received full military honors at Arlington National Cemetery, were placed on view in the hall of the municipal council, through which "a silent and solemn crowd" filed past to pay its respects.[28] The number of people at the burial was astounding, "Havana had never seen anything like it," Martínez Ortiz would later write.[29] An unfortunate incident, however, soured the mood surrounding the otherwise smoothly executed funeral rites. An abrupt change in the order of the cortège heading to the cemetery provoked one of the first confrontations between officials of the U.S. military government in Havana and Cuban civil authorities. Although the order of the funeral procession had been arranged and agreed to in advance, when the carriage occupied by the governor-general passed by, a group of U.S. cavalry soldiers (Brooke's general staff and some men from the guard escorting him) stepped in and occupied the place belonging to the key Cuban revolutionary group, the Asamblea del Cerro.

As a result, the Asamblea's representatives not only decided to withdraw from the procession but decreed that the rest of the Cuban military forces which had gathered for the funeral ceremony should abandon it as well. A considerable number of Cuban generals and high civil officials proceeded to do just that. When the party arrived at the cemetery, it fell to the U.S. side, led by William Ludlow, to render the customary gun salute in final homage to the Cuban general.

Máximo Gómez, who at this time was undoubtedly the most prestigious living figure among those who had led the struggle for independence, made his entrance into the capital on 24 February, the anniversary of the *Grito de Baire*, amid a great wave of nationalist demonstrations. To greet Gómez, "a compact mass of thousands upon thousands of men, women, and children filled the streets, balconies, terraces, and rooftops."[30] The number of people who gathered to witness Gómez's entrance into Havana was estimated by *La Discusión*, one of the city's daily newspapers, at 150,000:

> An outpouring of the public onto the streets and plazas such as had
> never been seen, inexhaustible; a delirious enthusiasm on the part of
> all who saw the procession; triumphal arches put up in various places
> through which the Liberation Army and its leader had to pass; flags and
> banners on houses and on streets; flowers flung like a veritable rain,
> from female hands, at the undefeated caudillo and his heroic soldiers
> and officers; doves beribboned with the colors of the national flag and
> launched into the air from numerous residences; and, on a final note, as
> the sublime realization of everything that historic moment signified, the
> flag, torn and bloodied, that accompanied the Generalissimo from East
> to West during the triumphant campaign of the Invasion, drawing forth
> at his passage an incessant stream of applause, tears, and acclaim.[31]

The new practice of honoring heroes of the wars of liberation, whether living or dead, kept its momentum. In September 1899, Havana's citizens assembled once again, on this occasion to attend the exhumation of the remains of General Antonio Maceo and his aide-de-camp, Captain Francisco Gómez Toro. The remains of both patriots were disinterred from the site where they lay, on the farm near Havana of an ordinary campesino who had zealously guarded the secret until the end of the war. The degree to which Habaneros became emotionally caught up in the funeral rites performed for Maceo and Gómez Toro can be judged by the extreme reaction of the inhabitants of Regla (located across the bay from Havana) in the face of what they considered a profanation of the memory of the two patriots. On 18 September, as stated in the charges brought before Guanabacoa's Court of First Instance, the local police had to intervene in order to rescue eleven Spaniards threatened with lynching by an enraged mob which accused them of having organized a luncheon "to celebrate, as a fiesta, the exhumation of general Maceo and his adjutant." These protestors were not mollified by the Spaniards' submission to the court, in which they claimed that they had met, in their condition as bakers, to come to an agreement on the price of bread, and the accused had to be removed from the building where they were meeting under a police escort, making their way past "a huge gathering of people" yelling out that a lesson was called for to avenge the alleged profanation.[32]

After the exhumation, wakes were held over the remains of Maceo and Gómez Toro in numerous parts of Havana, organized in "funeral chapels" set up for this purpose and attended by hundreds of the city's residents. As I have noted, their bodies were laid permanently to rest on 7 December 1899 in a mausoleum on the hilltop of El Cacahual, in a ceremony witnessed by thousands of the capital's residents.[33]

The great crowds of people who marched in the procession that marked José Martí's birthday, or joined the street celebrations on the occasion of Gómez's entrance into Havana on 24 February 1899, or shared their sorrow at the burial of Calixto García or the funeral service for Maceo, represented the public expression of the commitment to the cause of the revolution for independence, a cause embodied in the tributes rendered to those whom they had collectively recognized, for some time, as their principal leaders.

During the time of the U.S. intervention, that is, years before the historical reconstruction of the wars of liberation ordained them as great national figures or the Cuban Republic canonized them as heroes in bronze and marble, men such as Martí, Gómez, Maceo, and Calixto García were publicly revered as the most important leaders of the 1895 revolution. Their exploits and triumphs were lauded in speeches and articles, recreated and written about in textbooks, described in ephemeral imprints and popular literature, sung about in anthems and décimas, and memorialized in street signs, stone plaques, and monuments. The repeated coverage of these honors and commemorations in the local as well as national press helped consolidate and generalize people's memory of them throughout Cuba.

Yet the creation of a national pantheon of heroes and martyrs, as a way of rendering tribute to these relatively few founding figures, may have come at some cost. Although it certainly formed a basic element in the construction of a political ethos and consensus shared throughout the country, it could also have contributed to the shrinking or even complete loss of local and regional historical memory.

The first symptoms in the "homogenization" of the country's recent past can be traced back to these years, an offshoot to the process of devising an all-embracing version of the history of the national past in which both class conflict and tension based on race and gender could be ignored and regional particularities and differences minimized. The first signs of this attempt at "sealing" the cracks in the "body" of the nation, intensified by the urgent need to forge a consensus in the face of the U.S. military presence, appeared not only in publications of one type or another but surfaced as well in the public "production" of patriotic rituals and ceremonies or in the inscriptions on plaques and monuments.

Despite the strong political wind behind it, however, this reductionist tendency did not sweep away all the countervailing currents pulling against it.

As determined as minority political groups may have been to impose a single sweeping metanarrative of Cuban life and history that would squeeze out and eliminate the dissonant versions of subaltern classes, their path was blocked by the U.S. military government's total control over the apparatus of state power. What is more, any attempt to compress Cuban social and historical reality into an artificially uniform ideological mold and explain it on similar terms would encounter several obstacles: the proximity in time of the recently concluded revolution for independence, which left its victories and high human cost fresh in the minds of those who had fought it, the strength of the popular sectors, radicalized by their experience of the revolution, and the decentralized character of political participation, which was exercised through myriad organizations and impelled by varying circumstances and conditions.

Nowhere were the changes wrought by the wars of liberation more evident than in the country's smallest communities, where the prestige and honor accrued by the common man who had participated in the wars and gained the appellation of patriot gave him access, for the first time, to the political arena, which in turn changed the class and—not infrequently—the racial composition of municipal councils. Newly created organizations such as the veterans' centers and patriotic clubs that had not been founded on the basis of wealth or class or level of cultural attainment began to insert themselves into local political life and to influence its content and direction by collaborating closely with the municipal councils.

In the aftermath of the revolution, the countryside witnessed a second phenomenon which helped check the drive to extend the power of central authority and impose a version of national history that helped justify it. The bodies of hundreds of foot soldiers killed in the uprisings and wars against Spain lay in shallow, hastily constructed graves or—in some cases—still lay unburied on the fields of battle. These patriots were now honored and remembered in proper funeral ceremonies. Throughout the island, the bodies of the fallen were located, exhumed, and identified. As part of the ceremony of moving them to a permanent burial ground, people organized masses and civic processions and put up temporary funeral chapels, in addition to placing commemorative plaques and constructing small pantheons and monuments. These efforts, spread across the entire country, formed a local counterweight to the much more grandiose ceremonies celebrated in the capital to honor the central figures of the national revolutionary pantheon.

In the majority of cases, the humble gravesites and burial mounds which began to appear during these years in pueblos and rural communities resulted from popular initiatives taken on the local level. In stark contrast to the mausoleums erected in the same period for the "martyrs of the fatherland" and the pretentious monumentalist style which, under the impetus of state sponsorship, would soon come to characterize the Republic, these local efforts were financed by money collected door to door, raised in raffles and charity affairs, and donated by patriotic clubs or municipal councils. The veterans' centers coordinated the search for soldiers' remains and, together with the revolutionary clubs, organized the collection of funds, while municipal authorities supported part of the costs and ceded land for the construction of burial sites or the placement of memorials.

The popular foundation on which these patriotic initiatives rested is seen, for example, in a local newspaper account of the preparations being undertaken for the funeral ceremony and burial of the remains of persons killed in the war of 1895–98. The report appeared in a newspaper published in Batabanó, a fishing community located south of Havana. In January 1901 the paper published an appeal by the local veterans' center that the community join an undertaking, set for 10 February, to locate and move the remains of local martyrs of the nation. The remains of forty-seven patriots fallen on the field of battle were to be placed in a "funeral chapel" in the building of the municipal council. The paper informed its readers that Máximo Gómez and other revolutionary figures would come from Havana to participate personally in the ceremony. The announcement invited "official leaders, army soldiers, worker's unions, societies, political groups, and all residing in the vicinity" to attend the burial. In addition, it asked that people living in Batabanó place the proper signs of mourning on the front of their houses and that shops and commercial establishments, if possible, not open for business on that day out of respect for the solemn occasion.[34]

On 3 February a note in the paper mentioned that the veterans' center had commissioned Antonio Arredondo, a lieutenant colonel in the Liberation Army, to acquire in Havana, with funds raised by a popular auction, a stone plaque and the ossuaries and sarcophagi needed for the internment. Members of Batabanó's fire department and employees of its municipal council contributed money to have the front of the mausoleum wreathed in porcelain. The same issue of the paper requested that the girls and young ladies of the locality make paper wreaths and artificial flowers and get them to the municipal council to decorate the coffins, and that they also have them on hand to throw as the remains of the liberators were being taken for burial. The girls were also urged to volunteer as members of an honor guard that would be maintained around the coffins in the council's "funeral chapel."

Several days later, according to another report in the paper, a modest mausoleum was installed in Batabanó's central plaza to "perpetuate the memory of the patriots" and "to inspire new generations." The mausoleum was decorated with a porcelain wreath from the well-known Havana company Palais Royal, purchased with funds raised by popular subscription. As a patriotic gesture, the company donated the balance between the retail price of the wreath and the sum of money collected for its purchase.

On 10 February, the date chosen for the burial ceremony, the community's homes all wore signs of mourning. The Liceo Martí and the local headquarters of the National Party flew Cuban flags at half-mast, with strips of black crepe. Even the Casino Español (Spanish Club) joined in the mourning by flying both a Cuban and Spanish flag at half-mast and draping black banners from its windows and doors. People kept vigil over the coffins in the "funeral chapel" which had been set up in the council's main meeting hall. During the vigil, the honor guard standing watch over the remains of the soldiers alternated between the girls who had volunteered and members of the Rural Guard and local fire department. The coffins were surrounded by a great many wreaths furnished by unions and workers' groups, the municipal council, the veterans' center, the National Party, the firemen, and teachers and children from Bata-banó's schools.

At midday, the funeral cortège set off. In its ranks—as the paper had an-nounced—was Máximo Gómez, who had arrived by train from the capital to attend the burial. The procession was begun by a detachment of cavalry from the Rural Guard, followed by the members of the fire department. Groups of young girls, scattering flowers, waited along the route for General Gómez, who covered the distance to the burial site on horseback, trailed by his party. Further behind, flanked on either side by young ladies with flowers and schoolchildren carrying wreaths with ribbons tied to them, came relatives of the dead and soldiers who had fought alongside them, shouldering the coffins and ossuaries. Members of the veterans' center, authorities of the municipal council, representatives of the National Party, the Worker's Federation, and recreational clubs, as well as union members representing longshoremen, sea-men, woodcutters, bakers, carpenters, and sponge cutters marched behind fol-lowed by the orchestra, cavalry, and a long line of carriages. When the cortège reached the plaza, the soldiers' remains were placed in the tomb together with a mass of wreaths and flowers. Father Luis Mustelier, a Cuban priest who had also come from Havana and was renowned for his deep nationalist sympathies and his oratorical skills, delivered the funeral oration before a multitude of people, their grief written on their faces. The entire population of Batabanó filed past the patriots' "final resting place," after which the tombstone that "separated them from all other mortals" was set in place.[35]

In addition to demonstrating the consensus around national values that existed on a local level, expressed for example in the success of the community-based campaign to raise funds and later in the size of the crowd that attended the burial, the rituals of the funeral ceremony and its planning are a case study of the organizing power that a "nongovernmental" group like the Center for Veterans of Independence had come to wield in these years. The composition and order of those marching in the funeral procession (which also served as a nationalist celebration) reflected not only the general social structure of the community but a dominant workers' presence as well. The participation of women, an important feature to note for this period, was not confined purely to activities considered as "befitting the fairer sex," such as making paper wreaths and artificial flowers. The presence of a female honor guard at the wake, on an equal footing with veterans, firemen, and soldiers from the Rural Guard, can be interpreted as a sign of greater recognition for the social role of women in the locality.

The close collaboration between the veterans' center and the municipal council is especially noteworthy and underscores a point I made earlier; namely, that in contrast to the capital, where political and other institutions were controlled by U.S. officials, municipal councils in the interior of the country were in the hands of Cubans, many of whom came from the ranks of the Liberation Army.

Institutionalizing Local Memory in Plaques and Monuments

Although municipal life during these years possessed an exceptional richness and heterogeneity, it has not been the focus of much study. Replacing colonial emblems, such as portraits, flags, escutcheons, and seals, in municipal councils with nationalist symbols; giving streets new patriotic names; organizing fiestas, tributes, and other types of commemorations to celebrate key dates on the nationalist calendar; and placing plaques or modest monuments on streets and in public parks and squares were initiatives that frequently originated and were endorsed and approved on the municipal level.

The commitment of the majority of municipal councils to a nationalist political agenda was strengthened after the first elections for municipal offices. Held in June 1900, despite the limitations imposed by the electoral law, they witnessed a clear victory for the country's nationalist sectors. In many of

Cuba's municipalities, the newly elected mayors were former officers of the Liberation Army, ranging in rank from lieutenant and captain up to general.[36]

The minutes of municipal council meetings are an excellent source for examining how a sense of patriotism, articulated and embraced on a country-wide scale, interfaced with nationalist politics locally and regionally. The postal service and a greatly improved telegraph system, as well as the recently installed telephone network, enabled municipalities not only to be in ready contact with each other, their provincial capitals, and the national capital, but to work together and, if it served their purposes, mount a common front. The hundreds of telegrams sent by councils throughout the country to the headquarters of the military government or the secretary of interior and state, or both, as part of the campaign to win approval for making the 24 February and 10 October anniversaries official national holidays, or to protest the attempt to replace the military administration of Cuba with a U.S. civil administration and government are good examples of this type of concerted action.[37]

Of course, municipal council sessions were also the scene of intense debates over matters tied closely to the political life of the community itself and not just the nation. The nationalist leaning of local politics was manifested in various ways; for example, by selecting Liberation Army veterans for positions funded out of municipal budgets, organizing tributes, fiestas, burials, and other nationalist ceremonies, and granting funds, out of a sense of patriotic obligation, to support pensions for the widows and families of martyred soldiers or the erection of monuments and plaques in memory of the wars of liberation and their heroes.

The actions taken by the authorities of Cienfuegos illustrate this pattern. According to the minutes of its council, between January 1899 and 1901, the municipality contributed funds to national campaigns organized to underwrite the construction of three edifices: a monument to Antonio Maceo in Santiago de Cuba, a mausoleum for Calixto García in Havana, and the pantheon for Maceo and Francisco Gómez Toro in El Cacahual, as well the acquisition of the home in which José Martí was born, so that it could be given to his mother. It also approved a monthly contribution of two pesos in gold to help guarantee a pension for María Cabrales, Maceo's widow; helped support, monetarily, the orphaned daughters of Generals Felix Borrero and Francisco Adolfo (Flor) Crombet and the elderly mother of General Guillermo Moncada; and agreed to designate funds to help "reward with some object the fidelity of the patriot Pedro Pérez, who faithfully guarded [the bodies of] those heroes who fell at Punta Brava."[38]

In addition to participating in these projects of national scope, the authorities of Cienfuegos used the power of patronage to give jobs in municipal offices, the jail, and the police force to many Liberation Army veterans. They also donated some fortifications constructed on the outskirts of the city during the war years to soldiers' families in need of housing and subsidized the purchases of prostheses for those disabled in the War of Independence.[39]

In July 1900, once the popular election of municipal officials had taken place, Cienfuegos's municipal council sent a message to the U.S. military government, informing it that, inasmuch as the municipality is "by its nature, origin, and tendencies a genuinely Cuban body, its desire was to fly only the Cuban flag from the municipal building." The council concluded its message on an assertive note by saying that should its request not be agreed to, it would opt to not fly any flag from the building.[40]

After the war, the city began to renovate several of its urban spaces. The municipal council participated in these distinctly patriotic projects. The old Paseo de "Vives" was renamed the Avenida de la Independencia and, thanks to municipal funds, lined with palm trees, universally recognized as an emblem of Cuba's national identity. The municipality also provided monetary and other support for projects originated by local associations. For example, on the initiative of several of the city's unions, a popular subscription was taken up to collect funds for the construction of a park on a triangular piece of land lying between "Castillo, "O'Donell," and Cuba streets. As originally conceived, there would be a statue placed in the center of the park, with an allegorical motif to symbolize victory, and busts of Céspedes, Martí, and Maceo attached to its pedestal. In support of the proposal, the municipal council agreed to assume control over the targeted land and see to completion the construction of the park. In the near term, however, the cost of the statue was beyond the means of the community, so a palm tree and a jagua fruit tree were planted on the land instead. Since these appeared on the insignias of the nation and the city of Cienfuegos, respectively, they were seen to represent the harmony between the local and the national.[41]

The tensions that predictably cropped up between the desire, in the abstract, to preserve patriotic memory in the form of monuments and differences of opinion about which "patriots" deserved to be immortalized in that way and which did not, surfaced in the elusive attitude displayed by the municipality toward another popular-based park proposal for the city.

This proposal was tied to an event which distilled and symbolized many of the tensions and contradictions in Cuban society. On 29 December 1899,

Dionisio Gil, a black general in the War of Independence, was killed by pistol shots fired by two municipal police officers mounted on horseback, following a violent argument which the mambí general had in a restaurant with a hygiene inspector and another police officer. The assassination, the circumstances of which were not made clear, sparked an organized public protest on the day after Gil's death. Inspired by the arrival in the city of another notable black general, Jesús Rabí, a large number of people, presumably "of color," came together in front of the veterans' center and demanded that the murderers be brought to heel. Despite the assurances of Rabí and other mambise leaders that justice would be done, the crowd was not appeased. The demonstrators continued to protest vocally, until the local police waded in, beating them with sticks and leaving three men wounded.[42]

A year after these events, a commission began to collect funds for the purpose of constructing a park and monument as a memorial to the general. In contrast to the interest it took in other proposals, the municipal council did not evince much enthusiasm for the project. In February 1901, after the members of the commission had failed on two previous occasions to bring municipal authorities aboard, the council came to an ambiguous agreement which authorized a sum of money to be donated in "the amount that the council's president considers appropriate." The funds were to be drawn from an account maintained by the council for "unanticipated or incidental expenses," and only when its balance was deemed sufficiently large.[43] The council's agreement does not seem to have had any material effect, since nowhere in the group's minutes is it recorded that any money was ever actually donated for the construction of a monument to General Gil.

Ultimately, the money collected from all sources for the project was barely sufficient to cover the cost of constructing a small park, which was officially opened to the public (without a statue of the general) on 29 December 1901— the second anniversary of the patriot's death.[44]

The history of the successes and failures of the project to erect a statue of General Dionisio Gil can undoubtedly be read in different ways. On the one hand, the reluctance of the Cienfuegos municipal councilors to support the project, despite their clear nationalist orientation, may be seen as yet another instance of racial or class prejudice or as a sign of the subjectivity that permeated the institutionalization of historical memory not only in Cienfuegos but throughout the country. On the other hand, the fact that the park became a reality, albeit without a statue, through the individual contributions of manual and other workers in the city demonstrates that the popular sectors possessed an authentic capacity to exert pressure, pursue a common objective, and—despite the significant obstacles they faced—interpose their own remembrance of what happened in the past and who made it happen and thus their own sense of historical justice.

The circumstances of the mambí general's death—its occurrence not in the course of a battle against the enemies of the country but at the hands of a municipal police force composed primarily of former Liberation Army members—foreshadowed a conflict destined to repeat itself many times in the coming years. One-time comrades in arms who had fought together for independence would confront each other as members of opposing groups: workers against owners, liberals against moderates or conservatives, and soldiers of the National Army against insurgents belonging to the Partido Independiente de Color (Independent Party of People of Color).

As the nationalist alliances forged during the period of the revolution for independence began to unravel, the need to create the illusion of consensus increased proportionately, made more acute by the threat contained in the U.S. presence. After the founding of the Cuban Republic in 1902, the construction of a "national epic," free of imperfections, contradictions, and dissenting views, became a pillar of the process through which the country's new political elites legitimized their hold on power. This official history was institutionalized, awarded canonical status in the first decades of the Republic through multiple forms of representation; it was carved into public monuments, statues, and commemorative plaques, engraved on postage stamps, coins, and currency, and hung as portraits in classrooms, state offices, and museum galleries.

Within this hegemonic metanarrative, the manifold experiences of the anticolonial struggle were steadily reduced to a few stereotyped accounts, as its thousands of protagonists disappeared from the scene, leaving only a handful of "heroes," with spotless records, whose "antiseptic" biographies—always narrated in exactly the same terms—were repeated ad nauseum in homages, commemorations, and textbooks.

The complex, richly textured memory of the wars of liberation thus began to be reified in ostentatious monuments and official celebrations where the "invention of tradition," as embodied in the state, turned what were once emblems of rebellion into rituals of consensus and agreement. Nevertheless, despite the marginalization of Cuba's popular sectors in the "official" version of events in the wars of liberation, the battle scars of those years were burned into memory, and their traces can still be found, in both the written record and in material form, as archival documents and printed matter, as inscriptions on facades and walls, and as unpretentious monuments and commemorative plaques erected in the country's smaller communities and cities.

Of the insistent need to relive the past through commemorations, Hannah Arendt observed: "Experiences and even the stories which grow out of what men do and endure, of happenings and events, sink back into the futility inherent in the living word and the living deed unless they are talked about over and over again. What saves the affairs of mortal men from their inherent futility is nothing but this incessant talk about them, which in its turn remains futile unless certain concepts, certain guideposts for future remembrance, and even for future reference arise out of it."[45]

The institutionalization of the memory of both the wars of liberation and the nation's founding fathers, through a kind of symbolic repeating of the heroic circumstances of the one and the origins of the other in the course of patriotic ceremonies and commemorations, was a major factor in creating and molding Cubans' nationalist imagination during the period "between empires." After 1902 the political elites heading the state attempted to exercise control over these processes of forming, diffusing, and reproducing the memory of the wars of liberation by "officializing" a particular set of national characteristics, institutionalizing patriotic rituals and a calendar of national celebrations, and producing, or trying to produce, a single, uniform version of the multiple, heterogeneous discourses concerning the nation. The state took charge of organizing national commemorations and homages, defrayed the costs of constructing monuments, regulated the renaming of streets and communities, and financed the founding of museums and memorials.

Nonetheless, during the interval between the end of Spanish colonial rule and the creation of the national state, the contributions of popular groups were critical to the development in Cuba of a sense of national identity and the process of institutionalizing patriotic memory. Thousands of individuals, the majority of whom were illiterate, participated actively in the debate and struggles over the symbolic construction of the nation and their rights and representation as citizens. Singing anthems in unison, marching with flags, dressing in the national colors, paying tribute to soldiers fallen in the battles for independence, and celebrating the national days, Cubans rejected the foreign military presence and, in equal measure, publicly represented themselves as "citizens" of a future independent republic.

NOTES

Abbreviations

AHMT	Archivo Histórico Municipal de Trinidad
AHPC	Archivo Histórico Provincial de Cienfuegos
AHPS	Archivo Histórico Provincial de Santiago de Cuba
ANC	Archivo Nacional de Cuba, Havana
BCUH	Biblioteca Central de la Universidad de La Habana
HUA	Harvard University Archives, Cambridge, Mass.
LC	Library of Congress, Washington, D.C.
RG140	Record Group 140, Military Government of Cuba, U.S. National Archives and Records Administration, College Park, Md.

Introduction

1. Pérez, *Cuba between Empires.*
2. Certeau, *Practice of Everyday Life.*
3. In the sense in which I use the term, *popular culture* is by nature a complex and changing construct, defined by its fundamental difference from its conceptual and social "other": elite or high culture. It should therefore be understood that elites and masses, "high" and "low" culture, are examined as entities whose borders are mutually and equally porous, and as a system of demarcating cultural forms in service of different criteria: class, ethnicity, race, gender, the aesthetic, the market-driven, etc., all of which are historically conditioned and subject to constant change and reactualization.
4. Anderson, *Imagined Communities.*
5. Pérez, *On Becoming Cuban.*
6. Herzfeld, *Cultural Intimacy*, 30.

Chapter 1

1. Martínez Ortiz, *Cuba*, 1:19.
2. Ibid., 14.
3. *El Independiente*, New York, no. 5, 29 October 1898, 2.
4. Isaac Carrillo y O'Farrill, "El 24 de febrero," *Cuba y América*, Havana, 2, no. 545 (March 1899): 6.
5. See *Informe sobre el censo de Cuba, 1899*, 102, 107.
6. Geertz, "Después de la revolución."
7. Emilio Núñez, "El pasado y el presente," *El Fígaro: Número album consagrado a la Revolución Cubana, 1895–1898*, nos. 5, 6, 7, 8, February 1899, 79. Following the armistice,

the last Spanish flag to grace an official structure in Cuba was lowered from the building that housed the military headquarters in Cienfuegos. As Arturo Alsina Neto, a Spanish official present at the ceremony, relates, this act signaled "the definitive end of our occupation of the last tiny piece of American territory." From the deck of the steamship *Cataluña*, which was carrying the last battalions of Spanish soldiers back to the Iberian Peninsula, the U.S. flag was visible above the military quarters on the port, along with a "multitude of flags, showing the single star," flying from the buildings that dotted the town. Meanwhile, the Spanish flag "had been ignominiously tucked away in the suitcase of one of the returning soldiers." The ill fortune suffered by the "repatriated flag," preserved as a treasured relic by Alsina, changed in 1906 when he donated it to the Museo de Artillería in Madrid, where it was displayed next to the flag Hernán Cortés had carried with him to Mexico in 1518—a conjunction that symbolized "the two epochal events which marked the onset and the conclusion of Spanish domination in America." See Alsina Neto, *Última bandera*, 25–26, 52.

8. García Álvarez and Naranjo, "Cubanos y españoles," 112–13.

9. Leonard Wood to Emilio Barcardí, 4 July 1902, APSC, Fondo Emilio Bacardí, legajo 4, expediente 12. I am indebted to John-Marshall Klein, who informed me of Wood's letter and kindly provided me with his transcription of it.

10. There are several documents, dating from November 1899, belonging to the Court of First Instance of Havana's Belén neighborhood which exhibit this treatment—the Spanish stamped paper for 1898–99 has been used but has had the Spanish coat of arms excised. See ANC, Fondo Asuntos Políticos, legajo 173, signatura 3.

11. "Extractos y noticias de las actas del Ayuntamiento," in Martínez-Fortún y Foyo and Rodríguez Arce, *Monografías*, 105. Concerning the state of juridical and administrative disorientation which characterized municipal life during the first months of the U.S. occupation, the newspaper *El Independiente* wrote the following: "There are scarcely two municipalities on the island which are organized in the same way and have the same authority. Some have based themselves on universal suffrage, others on limited suffrage, and in still others the councilors have been named by the district military authority. Some enjoy almost unlimited power and authority and others have virtually none. The right of habeus corpus has been recognized in Santiago de Cuba; Gibara has trial by jury; and here in Havana we are at the mercy of the old system, so signally in contradiction with the supposed current state of things, and without certain of the guarantees which previously existed. The Manzanillo municipal council has instituted new levies and increased some of the older ones; the collector for the Trinidad municipal treasury has invented new procedures with which to pursue taxpayers who are delinquent in paying what they owe; and in Havana the chief of police believes that he is called upon to intervene in disputes between bosses and workers, and has tried to scuttle a strike by the workers by replacing them with other people." *El Independiente*, New York, no. 5, 4 March 1899, 1–2.

12. Ponte y Domínguez, *Matanzas*, 259.

13. Villanueva, *Colón*, 3:57.

14. José Antonio González Lanuza, "Rótulos trascendentales," *El Fígaro*, Havana, 3 May 1903, 210–11.

15. Lubián, *Club*, 32; and Martínez-Fortún y Foyo, *Anales y efemérides*, 18, 21, 24.

16. The symbolic significance of moving the university from its location in a section of Old Havana to the old military explosives building on the outskirts of the city is addressed in the institution's annual bulletin corresponding to the 1900–1901 term: "The building, which over the course of so many years was used to prepare and construct instruments of death and destruction, will have attained, by a strange opposition of destinies, a splendid and admirable vindication; appropriately sheltering the highest educational institution of the Cuban state, [an institution] devoted at its core to producing the most worthy elements of our progress, of our culture, and of our civilization." Note the contrast between the "instruments of death and destruction" attributed to the former regime and the elements of "culture," "progress," and "civilization" as distinctive of the new era. See Universidad de La Habana, *Memoria anuario*, 17. For more on the conversion of military barracks into primary schools, see Montori, "Educación," 540; and Venegas Fornias, "Arquitectura," 60–64.

17. For a study of the educational project carried out under the sponsorship of the U.S. military government, see Pérez, "Diseño imperial."

18. Manuel Márquez Sterling, "El problema de la educación," *Cuba Pedagógica*, Havana, no. 2 (November 1903): 66.

19. See ANC, Fondo Secretaría de Gobernación, "Expediente sobre reparación en el Archivo General de la Isla," legajo 95, expediente 681, 1901; and legajo 96, expediente 728, 1901.

20. Venegas, "Arquitectura," 59. See also Sánchez de Fuentes, *Cuba monumentaria*, 381.

21. For a graphic picture of the sweep of urban redevelopment projects in Havana, see a set of maps—dated 1900 and 1901 and printed by the Office of the Chief Engineer, City of Havana, Military Government of Cuba—which illustrate the progress made in remodeling and constructing parks, developing garbage collection routes, designing the sewer system, and paving the city's streets. ANC, Mapoteca, maps 483, 484, 485, 486.

22. Ramón Meza, "Parques públicos," *Cuba y América*, no. 109 (February 1902): 313. The plans by the U.S. military government to redevelop urban spaces and improve conditions of hygiene as well as Meza's own thinking and preferences on these matters were both clearly influenced by the ideas underlying two urban trends then in vogue: the "City Beautiful Movement" and the "Park Movement." Through their renovation of the urban landscape, endowing cities with tree-lined open spaces that acted as the "lungs" of the metropolis, these two movements also served a "regenerative" function, implanting "civic" elements into open urban spaces, elements that would stimulate a more democratic form of interaction and participation among the city's inhabitants. Thus, the "civilizing" campaign for improved hygiene in Havana undertaken during the years of the U.S. intervention should be read against the background of U.S. domestic efforts to "civilize" and "regenerate" its own densely populated urban "jungles," plagued as they were by pockets of poverty, violence, and unhygienic conditions. See Olmsted and Sutton, *Civilizing American Cities*; Boyer, *Dreaming*; and Domosh, *Invented Cities*.

23. Meza, "Parques públicos," 315.

24. Héctor de Saavedra, "La terraza," *Cuba y América*, no. 100 (May 1901): 3–6. Note the contrast between colonial "darkness," with its emphasis on the "gloominess" of the site prior to its redevelopment by the North Americans and the civilizing "illumination"

that accompanied its modernization, in this case realized in the form of electric lighting. On the impact of electricity on daily life and its importance as an icon of modernization, see McQuire, "Immaterial Architectures," 126–40.

25. Saavedra, "Terraza," 6.

26. Decree of Municipal Mayor Perfecto Lacoste, 30 September 1899, *Colección legislativa*, 2:70 (appendix).

27. Venegas, "Arquitectura," 69–70.

28. Sánchez de Fuentes, *Cuba monumentaria*, 381.

29. Ramón Meza, "El cerro," *Cuba y América* 9 (June 1902): 95.

30. Ibid., 96.

31. Ibid., 94.

32. The *solar*, or *ciudadela*, is a type of collective housing, with rooms opening onto a corridor or central patio and communal kitchens, lavatories, and bathing facilities. In 1902 there were more than two thousand *solares* in Havana, housing nearly a third of the city's population. In the words of Carlos Venegas Fornias, the *solar* in Havana was "the foundation of a neighborhood popular culture, with a mature identity that infused life into an urban culture peopled by such stereotyped figures as the *gallego* [the term was applied to Spanish immigrants as a whole], the *mulata*, or the *negrito*, all of whom were stock characters in comedic or popular theatre." Venegas Fornias, Menocal, and Shaw, "Havana between Two Centuries," 17. See also Tamayo, "Vivienda," 23–31; and Chailloux Cardona, *Síntesis histórica*.

33. Ramón Meza, "El vedado," *Cuba y América*, no. 6 (June 1903): 380–81.

34. The Spanish flag came down in Santiago de Cuba on 17 July 1898. A mere four days later regulations were issued informing residents of all of the city's neighborhoods of their obligation to clean both the interior and exterior of their respective domiciles, and to collect garbage and waste, which could serve as the source of infection. Those in violation of the regulations were subject to heavy fines. Teams of six hundred men spent days sweeping the city's streets. The payment earned for this work (one peso and three servings of food per day), not to be gainsaid by people living in a community suffering from hunger and illness, caused many (including university professors, public employees, barbers, and schoolteachers) to take broom in hand. Bacardí y Moreau, *Crónicas*, 10:133. Regarding the regulations on public hygiene, the rounding up of the indigent population, and the ordinances pertaining to stray animals, see *Colección legislativa*, 1:41 and 2:5 (appendix) and 2:61 (appendix). The Havana newspapers went to the extreme of publishing a daily account of the exact number of stray dogs put down. According to the daily paper *La Guásima*, between 17 August and 4 December, 174 dogs met their death in the municipal animal morgue. *La Guásima*, 4 December 1899.

35. Venegas, "Arquitectura," 66–67; *Diario de la Marina*, Havana, no. 47, 24 February 1899, 4; "The Sanitation of Buildings," *El Independiente* (bilingual edition), Havana, 2nd ser., no. 3, 18 February 1899, 1.

36. Fray Candil, "Muecas de España," *El Fígaro*, no. 47, 22 December 1901, 552.

37. McClintock, *Imperial Leather*, 207–31. The cartoon was published in the 30 March 1901 issue of *Literary Digest*; I am indebted to Louis Pérez Jr. for supplying me with a reproduction of it.

38. For an excellent though controversial analysis of how the ideas of modernity and progress associated with U.S. society and culture became enmeshed in the discussion in nineteenth-century Cuba of the question of nationality, see Pérez, *On Becoming Cuban*.

39. The role played by visual material in helping diffuse the material culture so closely intertwined with the U.S. presence has yet to be studied. Nevertheless, a simple reading of the contemporaneous periodical press, with its many advertisements accompanied by photographs and illustrations, indicates the magnitude of such activity during these years. The decrees issued by Havana's municipal council in 1900 also demonstrate the spread of advertising and marketing initiatives and the corresponding need to regulate them. A decree dated 26 January 1900 made it illegal to attach advertisements to the walls and columns of both private residences and public and government buildings. Violators were subject to a fine. Henceforth, advertisements could only be placed by merchants or owners of industrial concerns on the site of their own establishments, on the wooden fences of empty lots, and on buildings still under construction. Two months later, in March 1900, a companion decree was issued regulating how advertisements and signs could be placed, in order to protect walls from being defaced, the city as a whole from being cheapened, and passersby from being inconvenienced. The municipal authorities, furthermore, took steps to correct mistakes in grammar on labels and signs and to block the use of advertisements which "violated decorum" or "offended decency and public morality." Reference in the text of the decree to "advertising agents or executives" (the forerunners of companies such as the Havana Advertising Company and the Tropical Advertising Company, which would later monopolize the business) reveals just how professionalized the business of advertising had become. The requests submitted to the Department of State and Interior for permits to organize raffles and drawings as a way of promoting a higher volume of sales in shops and other businesses is a further indication of the aggressive commercial approaches taken during this period. See "Disposición de la Alcaldía prohibiendo fijar anuncios en las paredes y columnas de casas particulares," 26 January 1900, and "Acuerdo del Ayuntamiento del 12 de marzo de 1900," in both Duque and Bellever, *Jurisprudencia*, 230; and ANC, Fondo Secretaría de Gobernación, legajo 96, expediente 766, and legajo 97, expediente 789.

40. Roig de Leuchsenring, "Aventuras y peripecias," 257.

41. "La vida de las estatuas," *El Fígaro*, Havana, no. 4 (28 January 1900): 40. "¿Qué estatua debe ser colocada en el Parque Central?," *El Fígaro*, no. 16, 30 April 1899, 18. Obviously, far from reflecting popular opinion, the survey expressed the ideological orientation of the "better classes" of Cuban society in general and of the capital in particular. The magazine's readership was drawn from this social group.

42. *El Fígaro*, Havana, no. 20, 28 May 1899, 36. See also "La vida de las estatuas," *El Fígaro*, no. 4, 28 January 1900, 40; Enrique José Varona, "A la nueva estatua del Parque," *El Fígaro*, no. 21, 1 June 1902, 242; and Iglesias, "José Martí: Mito," 201–26.

43. *El Fígaro*, Havana, series commemorating the Cuban Revolution, 1895–98, nos. 5, 6, 7, and 8, February 1899.

44. For an interpretation of the importance of the myth of Martí to the process of consolidating the republic during its first decades, see López and Iglesias, "José Martí," 38–43; and Lillian Guerra, *Myth of José Martí*.

45. See Asociación Monumentos "Martí-Céspedes," *Reseña*.

46. González Lanuza, "El aspecto social," *El Fígaro*, Havana, nos. 20–21, 20 May 1903, 48.

Chapter 2

1. See *Calendario del Obispado de La Habana* for the years 1861, 1867, and 1893; and *Almanaque del maestro* for 1883.

2. Regarding the calendar as "locus of memory," see Backzo, "Calendrier." On the value of almanacs as a source for the study of patriotic celebrations and the relationship between them and the rise of nationalism (in the United States), see Waldstreicher, "Rites of Rebellion."

3. Anonymous handwritten notes in *Almanaque Baillo-Bailliere*.

4. Ibid.

5. Ibid.

6. Andrés Clemente Vázquez, "El año cubano," *El Fígaro*, [special album devoted to the Cuban Revolution, 1895–98], Havana, nos. 5, 6, 7, and 8, February 1899, 30.

7. Decades later, in contrast, the Cuban Revolution would assign allegorical names to years in order to emphasize the break between the period of the Republic, "subject to the interference" of U.S. interventionism, and the advent of the new revolutionary era that began with its "Year 1": 1959.

8. Compare the *Almanaque del maestro* for 1883 with the *Calendario del Obispado de La Habana* for 1899, as well as with the *Almanaque del maestro* for 1901.

9. *Calendario del Obispado de La Habana* for 1899.

10. *Calendario del Obispado de La Habana* for 1900.

11. *Calendario del Obispado de La Habana* for 1901.

12. Order 176, issued by military headquarters, 21 September 1899, signed by Adna R. Chafee, printed in the *Gaceta de La Habana*, 22 September 1899.

13. *Gaceta de La Habana*, 12 November 1899. In an article appearing during 1900 and tellingly titled "Things That Fade Away," the author referred sarcastically to the replacement of celebrations dating from colonial times with the "more democratic" commemorations linked to the U.S. presence: "Festival days that include the practice of kissing the hand have disappeared, because in democratic societies such as ours, one does not take delight in kissing anyone's hand, though this doesn't preclude kissing the feet of someone who might grant you a favor. We, on the other hand, have the Day of Giving Thanks to God for blessings received during the year, even though such blessings haven't been received: but in any case it's a day of jubilation and of democratic practice." Wen Gálvez, "Cosas que se van," *El Fígaro*, Havana, no. 14, April 1900, 177.

14. Álvarez Curbelo, "Fiestas," 216–17.

15. On 21 February 1899, General Máximo Gómez, passing through Matanzas on his way to Havana, where he would make his entrance three days later, was feted with a great banquet in his honor. On the following day, Gómez, accompanied by James Wilson, the military governor of Matanzas, presided over a reception and a dance organized in celebration of George Washington's birthday. See James H. Wilson to William Potler, 22 February 1899, Wilson Papers, box 43, LC. (I am indebted to Ada Ferrer for generously sharing this information with me.) Concerning the celebration of the 12 August

holiday in Matanzas during 1901, see a telegram from the civil governor of Matanzas to the secretary of state and interior, sent on 9 August 1901, in ANC, Fondo Secretaría de Gobernación, Expediente sobre la declaración de días festivos en la Isla de Cuba, legajo 94, expediente 518.

16. *Diario de la Marina*, Havana, no. 47, 24 February 1899, 1.

17. *El Telégrafo*, Trinidad, year 23, no. 40, 22 February 1899, in AHMT.

18. Ibid.

19. "El baile de la Tertulia," *El Telégrafo*, Trinidad, year 23, no. 140, 7 July 1899, 2–3, in AHMT.

20. "Las fiestas de la paz," *El Telégrafo*, Trinidad, year 23, no. 171, 15 August 1899, 2, in AHMT.

21. Ibid.

22. *Calendario 1900, obsequio*; *Calendario Obispado de La Habana* for 1899 [similarly for 1900, 1901, and 1902].

23. Quoted in Williams Brooks to the secretary of state and interior, Santiago de Cuba, 30 September 1899, ANC, Fondo Secretaría de Estado y Gobernación, legajo 94, expediente 512.

24. Telegram dated 22 July 1899 from Demetrio Castillo, civil governor of Santiago de Cuba to D. Méndez Capote, secretary of state and interior, ANC, Fondo de Secretaría de Estado y Gobernación, "Expediente sobre la declaración de días festivos en la Isla de Cuba," legajo 94, no. 518. In Santiago, as in other areas of the province of Oriente, the days of Saint John, Saint Peter, Saint James, and Saint Anne coincided with carnival celebrations. Even a century earlier, in 1800, Santiago's carnivals were mistrusted by authorities, who considered them disruptive of the public order. An official edict indicated that during carnival time not only did people celebrate horse races in a "wild" way, but in addition "some entertained themselves by getting drunk, with the result that lots of them sustained falls and committed abuses, and with the confused intermixing of social classes, they took license to insult anyone and everyone with indecent songs and risqué quips, starting brawls." Bacardí y Moreno, *Crónicas*, 2:77. See also, on pages 98 and 181 of this same volume, reference to the prohibitions placed on the "fiestas de mamarrachos" (Santiago's summer carnival celebrations). The conditions which led to disruptive behavior in the carnival celebrations made them propitious dates for uprisings against the established powers. For example, 24 February 1895 was designated as the date of an uprising because it coincided with carnival celebrations in western Cuba. Half a century later, in 1953, in Oriente province, one of the dates of carnival, 26 July, Saint Anne's Day, was chosen as the day for the assault on the Moncada Barracks, turning it into the most important civic celebration on the official revolutionary calendar, the Day of National Rebellion.

25. Actas Capitulares, Ayuntamiento de Cienfuegos, AHPC, vol. 42, fols. 18 and 93–94. The U.S. soldiers and civil officials involved in the incident were subject to a military trial, the record of which is contained in RG153, Office of the Judge Advocate General. I am indebted to Rebecca Scott for providing me with a photostatic copy of the documents.

26. *El Vigilante*, Guanajay, no. 70, 7 October 1900.

27. Ibid. According to the 1899 census, Mariel, located in the province of Pinar del Río,

had a population of 3,631, and the municipal area of Guanajay, in the same province, had 8,796 inhabitants. *Informe sobre el censo de Cuba, 1899,* 206.

28. María Escobar to Máximo Gómez, Remedios, 29 December 1899, ANC, Fondo Máximo Gómez, legajo 30, no. 4167; Martínez-Fortún y Foyo, *Anales y efemérides,* 12–13, 25.

29. Ortiz, *Virgen,* 251. The legend of the "mambisa" disappearances of the Virgin of El Cobre during the Ten Years' War was probably a nationalist rereading of the original myth. From the seventeenth century on, these legends alluded to the "peripatetic" character of the Virgin, who on occasion would miraculously disappear from the sanctuary that sheltered her. See ibid., 64–69.

30. Portuondo Zúñiga, *Virgen,* 226–32. I am indebted to Olga Portuondo Zúñiga for these anecdotes regarding the Liberation Army.

31. "La Virgen de septiembre," *El Güireño,* Güira de Melena, no. 58, 9 September 1900. Among the popular classes, the propagation of the cult of Our Lady of Charity was also connected—at least in the western part of the country—to the veneration of the Yoruba deity Ochún. In light of the new freedom of religion, and as a clear expression of the syncretism discussed above, an Afro-Cuban society or council, which in 1901 petitioned the military government to allow it to celebrate its rituals and drum beating on Sundays and other festival days, gave itself the name "Mutual Aid Society of African Lucumís of Our Lady of El Cobre and Saint Lazarus." Portuondo, *Virgen,* 257–58; RG140, entry 3, no. 640.

32. Ibid., 231; "En el Cobre," *El Porvenir,* Santiago de Cuba, 1 October 1898.

33. Portuondo, *Virgen,* 245.

34. In a conversation we had about the close connection between the image of Our Lady of Charity and Cuban revolutionary iconography, Jorge Lozano, a specialist in the historiography of Martí, described having seen an almanac, presumably dating from the early years of the twentieth century, whose cover was illustrated with a picture of the Virgin of Charity. The curious thing in this case is that the boat appearing at the foot of the Virgin was being sailed not by the three Johns, as is customary, but by the three leading heroes of Cuba's revolutionary campaigns: José Martí, Máximo Gómez, and Antonio Maceo. More than half a century later, the photographs and televised images of the youthful rebels who descended triumphantly in 1959 from the Sierra Maestra confirmed this association which, as we have seen, goes back to the period of the wars of independence. Many of the rebels, among them Fidel Castro, wore medallions and reliquaries of the Virgin of El Cobre around their neck.

35. "Las fiestas en Marianao," *Patria,* Havana, no. 51, 27 February 1900.

36. Portuondo, *Virgen,* 241, 245; Ortiz, *Virgen,* 267–71.

37. *La Luz del Hogar,* Güines, no. 20, 22 September 1899, 7.

38. *El Vigilante,* Guanajay, no. 27, 6 May 1900.

39. *El Occidente,* Guanajay, no. 8, 26 January 1901.

40. *El Nuevo País,* 7 February 1900.

41. *El Telégrafo,* Trinidad, 23, no. 127, 21 June 1899, 3, in AHMT.

42. Benedict Anderson emphasizes the importance of alterations in the perception of time for the creation of an imagined nationhood in his *Imagined Communities.* The representation of the nation as an organism that moves through homogeneous empty

time, measured by clock and calendar, in which—analogous to the narrative thread of a novel—the principal events in the life of the community are rationalized and accommodated, is, according to Anderson, one of the images of modernity that has most influenced the formation of a sense of belonging to a national collectivity. The role of ceremonies and other highly ritualized events in expressing collective cohesion and identity and in structuring social relations is examined in Hobsbawm and Ranger, *Invention of Tradition*.

43. Martínez Arango, *Cronología crítica*, 87.

44. See the imprint titled "Ciudadanos," signed by the neighborhood committee of Guadalupe, for the reception given General Máximo Gómez, dated 23 February 1899, Havana, in ANC, Fondo Academia de la Historia, box 106, sig. 243. For a description of Gómez's entrance into Havana on 24 February 1899, see *Diario de la Marina*, Havana, nos. 47 and 48, 24 and 25 February 1899 respectively; and Souza, *Generalísimo*, 291–92. On the songs as well as other manifestations of the popular mood, see Piedra Martel, *Memorias*, 143–45.

45. Rousseau and Díaz de Villegas, *Memoria descriptiva*, 267. An undated letter sent to Máximo Gómez by Vicente Goytisolo, a black descendant of slaves who identifies himself as "lucumí king," appears to allude to this episode. Goytisolo, whose prose and handwriting mark him as barely literate, mentions having fulfilled a promise that he made to Santa Bárbara Bendita (the deity, or orisha, Changó in the pantheon of Afro-Cuban Santería) to remove her from his head and display her as he walked through the streets of the city on the day on which his *mambise* brothers should enter it. It is thus very likely that one of the "allegorical banners" to which these local Cienfuegos historians refer in their memoir was precisely this image of Santa Bárbara that was venerated in the city's *lucumí* meeting hall. Vicente Goytisolo to Máximo Gómez, ANC, Fondo Máximo Gómez, legajo 36, no. 5012.

46. "Las fiestas del aniversario," *El Telégrafo*, Trinidad, year 23, no. 42, 26 February 1899.

47. Pedro P. Pérez to Leonard Wood, Guantánamo, 14 February 1899. AHPS, Fondo Gobierno Provincial, legajo 875, expediente 29.

48. RG140, Military Government of Cuba, letters received 1899–1902, file 420; and ANC, Fondo Secretaría de Gobernación, "expediente relativo a que se declaren días de fiesta el 10 de octubre y el 24 de febrero," legajo 94, expediente 521.

49. In a communiqué of 10 January 1900, J. N. N. Richards, assistant to the military governor, informed Diego Tamayo, the secretary of state and interior, of Leonard Wood's ruling: "No action will be taken on the subject of holidays until after the municipal elections, when the people will have an opportunity to express their wishes." ANC, Fondo Secretaría de Gobernación, legajo 94, expediente 521.

50. "El día de hoy," "En el matadero," *La Lucha*, Havana, no. 48, 24 February 1900; "El gran meeting," *Patria*, Havana, no. 49, 25 February 1900.

51. "El 24 de febrero en las escuelas," *Patria*, Havana, no. 51, 27 February 1900.

52. Ibid.

53. On the opposition to the naming of the new bishop, see Martínez Ortiz, *Cuba*, 1:108; and "Manifiesto al pueblo de Cuba del Comité Popular de Propaganda y Acción," 1 January 1900, ANC, Fondo Adquisiciones, legajo 86, 4390.

54. Printed flyer titled "Conmemoración del 24 de febrero: Al pueblo cubano," dated 21 February 1900, Havana, ANC, Fondo Academia de la Historia, box 498, sig. 539.

55. Telegrams signed by Fernando Figueredo, assistant secretary of state and interior, to the civil governors of Santa Clara, Havana, Pinar del Río, and Matanzas, dated 9 October 1900, ANC, Fondo Secretaría de Gobernación, legajo 94, expediente 521.

56. Universidad de La Habana, *Memoria anuario*, 32.

57. Letters from the mayors of Abreus, Bahía Honda, Sagua, Santa Isabel de las Lajas, Sabanilla, Los Palacios, Santiago de Cuba, Holguín, etc. to Leonard Wood, January–February 1901, RG140, Military Government of Cuba, Letters Received, 1899–1902, file 420.

58. Diego Tamayo to Leonard Wood, 31 May 1901, RG140, Military Government of Cuba, Letters Received, 1899–1901, file 420; and ANC, Fondo Secretaría de Gobernación, legajo 94, expediente 521.

59. J. B. Hickey, official of the general staff, to Diego Tamayo, secretary of state and interior, 9 February 1901, ANC, Fondo Secretaría de Gobernación, legajo 94, expediente 521.

60. *La Solución*, Surgidero de Batabanó, no. 8, 10 October 1900. Scott McQuire has described the range of emotions evinced by people witnessing a display of electric lighting for the first time. In Cuba, the recollection of this moment of enrapturement (which McQuire calls "the technological sublime") when the "wonders" of such modern artifacts as electric lamps, telephones, or moving pictures were revealed to people, is associated with the period of the intervention, when many Cubans had their first exposure to electric light bulbs or to the movie clips invented by the "magician" Edison in his Menlo Park laboratories. McQuire, "Immaterial Architectures," 128.

61. *La Solución*, Surgidero de Batabanó, 28 February 1901.

62. *La Aurora*, Consolación del Sur, 24 February 1901.

63. For a suggestive study of the changes affecting deeply rooted Cuban cultural practices, such as cockfighting, see Riaño San Marful, *Gallos y toros*.

64. ANC, Fondo Secretaría de Gobernación, legajo 96, expediente 702.

65. For an indication of the largely negative opinions held by the Cuban elite, see the responses published by *El Fígaro* to a survey it conducted in 1902 on whether it would be appropriate to reestablish cockfighting: "Qué opina usted de la lidias de gallos?," *El Fígaro*, Havana, no. 44, 16 November 1902, 543–45. Several of the respondents, members of the animal protection society—whose activities gained importance during the U.S. occupation—denounced the gratuitous violence committed against animals. Others connected cockfights to the evils of gambling, which had been one of the arguments in favor of prohibiting them. In denying a petition to celebrate a cockfight as part of the festivities commemorating Our Lady of Candlemas, patron saint of the Río de Ay chapel in the community of Condado, the mayor of Trinidad cited the "immorality of the entertainment." Reporting on the matter, the local newspaper added, "As the country begins to rebuild itself, when workers and day laborers protest the deprivations from which they suffer, neither time nor money should be given over to this vice. Let us save the excellent roosters for what is practical and positive. They turn out very tasty and succulent with rice, butter, and saffron added to them, and what Cuba lacks is food, to restore the energy that is lost living in poverty." *El Télégrafo*, Trinidad, year 24, no. 23, 28 January 1900, 3, in AHMT.

66. RG140, Military Government of Cuba, Letters Received, 1899–1902, file 153.

67. Diego Tamayo to L. Wood, 6 February 1901, ibid.

68. Anonymous circular addressed to Cuba's campesinos, 8 January 1901 in RG140, Military Government of Cuba, Letters Received, 1899–1902, file 153; Emilio Acosta to Leonard Wood, 30 January 1901, in ibid.

69. *El Vigilante*, Guanajay, no. 71, 11 October 1900.

70. *El Vigilante*, Guanajay, nos. 72 and 73, 14 and 18 October 1900.

71. Quintero Rivera, "Modales," 65, 68. On the subject of music and social control, see Quintero Rivera, *Salsa, sabor y control*.

72. González Hechevarría, "Literatura, baile y béisbol," 35; Moore, *Nationalizing Blackness*, 23–26.

73. *Cuba y América*, Havana, no. 54, March 1899, 26.

74. In an article published in *Scribner's Magazine*, James F. J. Archibald of the United States managed, wittingly or not, to convey the moralistic and racist prejudices shared by many of his countrymen with regard to the *danzón*, while also attesting to the extraordinary popularity which it enjoyed during this period: "While speaking of dancing, I must not forget the famous 'danzon,' the national dance of the Cubans. It is a species of very slow round dance with something of the mechanism of our two-step, but a couple will dance it for any length of time in the space of a square yard, and the steps are not six inches in length. The music for it has no regularly marked time, but is a sort of barbaric rhythm, accentuated by the wild notes of the cornet and drum, which inevitably recall the sounds we heard on the Midway at the World's Fair. Almost nothing else is danced among the lower classes, and they seem passionately fond of this amusement. There are public balls every night many of which are given in the theatres after the performance is over, and which last until early morning . . . as rendered by these people the 'danzon' is exceedingly vulgar, and if tried in a dance hall in New York the police would probably not be needed to put the couple out. It was never popular among the upper classes until the war brought everything distinctly Cuban into prominence, and so in the last two years Havana society has learned the 'danzon' just as New York society has lately learned (at least the chorus of) the 'Star-Spangled Banner.'" James F. J. Archibald, "Havana since the Occupation," from *Scribner's Magazine*, items extracted from magazines of the Spanish-American period et seq. relating Cuba, Colección Facticia, Fondo de Libros Raros y Valiosos, BCUH.

75. Figueras, *Cuba*, 368. On the mockery directed at attempts to control dancing, in relation to the fines imposed by the courts on those dancing the danzón, see Plana, *Recuerdos*.

76. Sarachaga, *¡Arriba con el himno!*, 230. I am indebted to my colleague Pablo Riaño San Marful for suggesting this source to me. The following is another example of popular poetry devoted to the same theme: "The Two Steps" / "Where are you off to, Cubanita, / all drenched in sweat, / in the arms of that Yankee / running down the hall / dragged in a dizzying whirl / like a flower by the wind? Are you dancing? Falsehood! / (and pardon the expression) / to dance is not to be a martyr, / to dance is something better: / it's to move lightly / to the sounds of a *danzón* . . . / The two steps! What sort of dance is that? / that's done at such breathless pace / half collision, half thrown elbows / toes stepped on, cries of pain, / with chest thrust out / and nerves all on edge / frenzied, delirious /

whirling like a cyclone? / Is it a gringo dance? / And isn't there a better one? / Well, the girl who dances it, / if she has such inclination / and muscles of steel / and delights in its madcap movement, / and finds pleasure in leaping about / and thrills in all those blows. / But you so gossamer-like, / like a flower's open petals, / innocent as a daydream / so fragile in body / like the lily that perfumes / the brook around it / Don't you fear getting squeezed / or dying from being stepped upon? / Sweeter was your dance / and better your waltz, / more tender your *zapateo*, / more pleasant your *danzón*. / *Chica*, your feet have settled / our biggest problem / favoring McKinley / in his expansionist plans. / That indulgence of yours / flatters the one pulling the strings; / that isn't a protectorate, / that, *chica*, is annexation." *El Vigilante*, Guanajay, no. 100, 20 January 1901.

77. *La Independencia*, Havana, no. 3, 8 October 1898. Raimundo Valenzuela was the mulatto musical director of one of the most popular orchestras of the day.

78. Benítez Rojo, "Música y nación," 46; González Hechevarría, "Literatura, baile y béisbol," 35.

79. Decision of the Havana municipal council, dated 4 April 1900, in *Colección Legislativa*, 1:xxi (appendix). Regarding the censuring of "drum beating," see also the rejection by the U.S. authorities of the request made to them by the Mutual Aid Society of African Lucumís of Our Lady of El Cobre and Saint Lazarus, in RG140, entry 3, no. 640.

80. Actas Capitulares, vol. 47, fol. 12, 27 September 1900, AHPC.

81. Decision of the Cienfuegos municipal council regarding the petition submitted by the *moreno* (dark-skinned) Eulogio Abreu "requesting that, as a special favor and for one last time, drum beating be permitted tomorrow night in the area where the cabildo is located, in honor of its 'patron saint.'" Actas Capitulares, vol. 47, fol. 81, 3 December 1900, AHPC.

82. "Cúmplese la ley," *La Lucha*, Havana, no. 249, 13 October 1900.

83. León, "Fiesta," 61.

84. Moore, *Nationalizing Blackness*, 67–68, 92.

85. Even two decades on, a resolution adopted by the secretary of interior in 1922 instituted an island-wide prohibition against celebrations and ceremonial dancing reflecting Afro-Cuban belief, "in particular that known as 'Bembé' and any other ceremonies which, running counter to the culture and civilization of a community, are noted as symbols of barbarism and disruptive of social order." Quoted by Benítez Rojo, "Música y nación," 47.

86. For an excellent study of this evolution, see Moore, *Nationalizing Blackness*.

87. Piece signed by "una cubanita," 2 February 1900, *Patria*, Havana, no. 32, 7 February 1900.

88. "El Himno Bayamés," *El Telégrafo*, Trinidad, year 24, no. 43, 22 February 1900, 2.

89. *La Nación*, Havana, year 1, no. 67, 31 May 1900.

90. *El Occidente*, Guanajay, nos. 2 and 10, 6 January 1901 and 2 February 1901.

91. "Expediente que contiene copias mecanografiadas sobre disposiciones legales sobre el uso de la bandera, el escudo, y el himno nacional," in ANC, Fondo Donativos y Remisiones, legajo 567, no. 22. Despite the existence of this and other decrees from the late 1950s, Emilio Roig de Leuchsenring deplored the indiscriminate use still made of the national anthem and flag: "Free use of the flag was made by politicians and political types for every conceivable purpose and it turned up at celebrations of every sort as a

decoration for tables, meeting sites, buildings, etc. The same adornment served to grace a family dance that ended with thrown bottles or a cockfight no less than a genuine political function. . . . At every affair that sought to have a certain importance or tried to dress itself up as patriotic, the National Anthem became required music. The anthem was worked into all kinds of dance pieces and music advertising commercial and industrial products." Emilio Roig de Leuchsenring, "Por el respeto y justo uso de la bandera, el escudo y el himno nacionales," in ANC, Fondo Donativos y Remisiones, legajo 567, no. 22.

92. Hobsbawm and Ranger, *Invention of Tradition*, 263–307.

Chapter 3

1. Obviously, the presence of anglicized words and expressions in Cuban speech significantly predates the U.S. intervention of 1898. A decade and a half earlier, in 1882, Juan Ignacio de Armas, in his *Orígenes del lenguaje criollo*, had recognized English as "the foreign language which has contributed the most to enrich the body of our own homegrown language." Armas's recognition is a good signpost of the growing influence of North American culture on Cuban society in the second half of the nineteenth century. As might be expected, an analysis of English and English-sounding words, included in Armas's book, which had found their way into Cuban speech suggests a preponderance of technical words, such as *ingeniero* (engineer), *patente* (patent), and *kerosin* (kerosene); or words pertaining to the world of business and commerce, such as *bill* (payment due), *marchante* (merchant), etc. Somewhat surprisingly, the largest number of words mentioned by Armas has a gastronomic ring, indicating that food and drink of Anglo-Saxon origin had become a feature of the Cuban table. Words such as *lonche* (lunch), *sanduich* (sandwich), *bistec* (beefsteak), *rosbif* (roast beef), *queke* (cake), *panqué* (pancake), *ponche* (punch), *coctel* (cocktail), and *wisqui* (whiskey) suggest that—at least among the upper class—people frequently ate and drank *a la americana*. By including this "technical-culinary" slang in a text ostensibly dedicated to the analysis of characteristic forms of local, informal Cuban speech, Armas gave it a certain legitimacy. He was apparently an admirer of Anglo-Saxon ways and culture. Armas, *Orígenes*, 86–89.

2. Commenting on the prevalence of English-language notices in stores and barber shops, González Lanuza noted that, "at the present moment, and also going back some time, signs that use English to identify products, or employ that language to provide the name of a shop and describe what it sells, have a special impact and significance. In this arena, the prize—at least for frequency of use—goes to the barber shops: there is scarcely a single one which does not display a sign saying 'Barber Shop.'" José Antonio González Lanuza, "Rótulos trascendentales," *El Fígaro*, Havana, no. 18, 3 May 1903, 210.

3. Sarachaga, *¡Arriba con el himno!*, 284.

4. Wen Gálvez, "Un poco de fongueo," *El Fígaro*, Havana, no. 46, 9 December 1900, 560. On baseball-related words occurring in popular Cuban speech of the time, see the article "Vocabulario del *base-ball*," by Manuel Márquez Sterling, in the same issue of *El Fígaro*, 556.

5. M. Gómez to José L. Rodríguez, 12 April 1899; cited by Cordoví Núñez, "*La Independencia*," n.p.

6. *El inglés al alcance de todos* was recommended in the book section of *El Fígaro* as "an indispensable book, since, like no other, it will meet the urgent need faced by all Cubans, following the American occupation, to learn English in a rapid, assured manner." *El Fígaro*, Havana, no. 41, 29 January 1899, 4.

7. *New York Times*, 31 December 1898; cited in Pérez, *On Becoming Cuban*, 151.

8. Hernández Millares, *Obras*, 254.

9. *El Reconcentrado*, Havana, 14 June 1899.

10. Ibid., 125.

11. Ibid., 125–26.

12. Rafael M. Merchán, "El desmoronamiento del castellano," *Cuba y América*, no. 109 (February 1902): 363.

13. *El Occidente*, Guanajay, no. 7, 24 January 1901.

14. J. F. Pellón, "Hablemos castellano," *La Escuela de Verano*, Cienfuegos, year 1, 19 June 1901, 1–2.

15. "Lo del Café Washington," *El Independiente*, Havana, no. 4, 25 February 1899, 3; and "Disposición del Tribunal Supremo de la Isla de Cuba, 7 de marzo de 1900," in *Colección legislativa*, 1:475–79.

16. For an analysis of the U.S. military government's educational project, see Portell Vilá, *Estados Unidos*, appendix 2; Pérez, "Imperial Design," 33–52; and Almodóvar, "Escuela primaria," 467–77.

17. Letter from H. K. Harroun, secretary of the Cuban Educational Association, to General J. Wheeler, 19 October 1898, in Cuban Educational Association Papers, LC.

18. Letter of H. K. Harroun to F. Machado, 9 September 1899, in Cuban Educational Association Papers, LC; and Harroun, "Cuban Educational Association," 334.

19. Harroun, "Cuban Educational Association," 335.

20. In addition to the Cuban Educational Association and the Cuban-American League, a number of other "nongovernmental" or philanthropic organizations tried to influence—sometimes successfully—the institutional restructuring program carried out by the U.S. military government in Cuba. The Patriotic League, established to provide instruction about civic rights and responsibilities to children and adults and to instill "American ideas into the minds and hearts of Americans, natives and adopted," sponsored the introduction of the teaching of "civics" in the school curriculum through a project called *Ciudad Escolar* (City School), with the intent of fostering in Cuban children the "democratic" practices of government. For its part, the American Humane Association for the Prevention of Cruelty to Animals and Children undertook campaigns against "uncivilized" forms of entertainment such as cockfighting and bullfighting. A large number of individual citizens, along with several woman's associations and teacher's groups, as well as students and alumni of Harvard and other universities donated US$71,145.33 to a project that allowed almost half of Cuba's teachers to travel to Harvard during the summer of 1900 to learn about "American teaching methods." A study of the influence exerted by these organizations and their attendant philanthropic motives and activities in the broader process of "Americanizing" Cuba has yet to be done. On the "City School" project and the Patriotic League, see Cuba, Military Governor, *Civil Report*, 2:28–30. On the activities of the American Humane Association for the Prevention of Cruelty to Animals and Children, see letter from Laura Gill to Leonard Wood,

16 October 1901, in RG140, Military Government of Cuba, Letters Received, 1899–1902, file 153. On the donation of funds for the 1900 Harvard visit, see "Lista de los suscriptores para el fondo de los maestros cubanos," HUE83.100.9F (A, B), HUA. For this last source, as well as citations listed below to additional material in the same archive, I am indebted to my friend and colleague Lillian Guerra, who used her own research time at Harvard University to obtain copies of original documents for me.

21. William McDowell to Joseph Wheeler, 31 January 1899, Cuban Educational Association Papers, LC.

22. Ibid.

23. Correspondence of H. K. Harroun, "List of Cuban and Puerto Rican Students," Cuban Educational Association Papers, LC.

24. See "Memorandum for Mr. Harroun, concerning an educational system for Cuba," 28 November 1898," Cuban Educational Association Papers, LC.

25. Pérez, "Imperial Design," 43.

26. Ibid.

27. *New York Tribune*, 25 August 1899, 4; cited in Pérez, "Imperial Design," 43.

28. Frye, *Manual*, 80.

29. Letter of Leonard Reibold to H. K. Harroun, 31 January 1899, Cuban Educational Association Papers, LC; and letter of Leonard Reibold to González Lanuza, secretary of justice and public instruction, 22 August 1899, in ANC, Fondo Instrucción Pública, legajo 700, no. 49711.

30. Letter from Sam W. Small to Raimundo Cabrera, 12 April 1900, private archive of the Cabrera family.

31. Silver Burdett financed the publication of an educational journal called *La Escuela Cubana*. A rival publisher of teaching materials had this to say about one of the texts Silver Burdett was promoting in its journal: "This text is not suitable for our teaching. As hard as Mr. Small's periodical tries, Cuban children, when they look out on their country's beautiful countryside, don't see grapes, apples, pears, and apricots, but the 'refreshing coconut,' the 'sweet pineapple,' and 'great wild vines,' as Eusebio Guiteras, a Cuban teacher of recognized merit, notes." *La Escuela Moderna*, Havana, 1, no. 20 (30 November 1899): 23.

32. *Primera memoria*, 336.

33. Pérez, "Imperial Design," 41.

34. Pérez, *On Becoming Cuban*, 10.

35. *Datos demostrativos*.

36. Letter from the secretary of public instruction, Enrique J. Varona, to Leonard Wood, 9 April 1901, RG140, Military Government of Cuba, Letters Received, 1899–1902, file 440.

37. "La nueva era," *La Escuela Cubana* 1, no. 2 (1899): 50.

38. *Manual o guía para los exámenes*.

39. Harvard University, *La escuela de verano*.

40. Ibid., 2.

41. "Cubans in Cambridge: Accounts" (Report of the president of Harvard University, Charles W. Eliot, 23 November 1900, 38), CSS, HUE.83.100.le, HUA.

42. Ibid., 42.

43. Sanguily, "José de la Luz y Caballero," 31.

44. "The Cuban Summer School," 38.

45. Williams, "Boston's Cuban Guests," 137–38.

46. "Cuban Teachers Voyage up the Hudson," *New York Herald*, August 1900.

47. Julia Martínez, "The Cuban Teachers at Cambridge," *Independent*, 2 August 1900.

48. Ibid.

49. Ibid.

50. José Flías Torres, "Carta al director" ["Letter to the Editor"], 29 July 1900, *Revista de Instrucción Pública*, Havana, 24 August 1900, 15–16.

51. Ibid.

52. Ibid.

53. Proposal for a National Anthem; music: "La Bayamesa," by Perucho Figueredo; lyrics by public schoolteacher Fidel Miró, *Revista Pedagógica Cubana*, Havana, October 1900, 112.

54. Williams, "Boston's Cuban Guests," 138.

55. Ralph Waldo Gifford, "My Impressions of the Cuban Teachers," *Harvard Illustrated Magazine* (October 1900): 16–17.

56. From the autograph book left by the Cuban students at Harvard; HUE83.100le, HUA.

57. Ibid.

58. Cuevas Zequeira, *En la contienda*, 76.

59. Federico Salcedo, "Por donde viene la muerte," *El Fígaro*, Havana, no. 24, 25 June 1899, 213.

60. Manuel Sanguily, one of the most prominent nationalist voices in nineteenth-century Cuban letters, wrote that in the United States, "democracy has its magnificent fortress, and a sweeping freedom, its redeeming sword unsheathed, lifts her strong arm to the skies, brandishing the spotlight that illumines all consciences. Like a never-ending, utterly pure kiss of love, a tenuous ray of that life-giving brightness brushes the pallid forehead of Cuba." Anointed by that "light" and transformed by the northern "kiss of love," Cuba distances herself from Spain, and this antagonism forms the basis of what Sanguily calls "our social and political antinomy." "What is certain," [he affirms] "is that two peoples exist here, who represent, just like two hemispheres of the planet, two worlds of consciousness and two civilizations in history. . . . Why pretend otherwise? We Cubans are Americans as the Spaniards are Europeans." Sanguily, *Discursos*, 85–86.

61. Esteban Borrero, "Los cursos pedagógicos de verano," *El Fígaro*, Havana, no. 34, 9 September 1900, 408–9.

62. In a manifesto dating from September 1901, opposing the imposition of the Platt Amendment and advocating the designation of the nationalist leader Bartolomé Masó as a candidate in the next presidential election, an appeal was made for union between the former adversaries: Cuban and Spaniards should unite their forces in a double crusade "to save Cuba from foreign [*sic*] domination and the Latin race in America." "Manifiesto del Comité Central de Propaganda y Acción por Bartolomé Masó," 20 September 1901, ANC, Fondo Adquisiciones, legajo 86, sig. 4390.

Chapter 4

1. On the relationship between maps, censuses, and the mechanisms of colonial rule, see McClintock, *Imperial Leather*, 28–30; and Rafael, "White Love," 187.

2. On the changing of names in different Cuban pueblos, see Barceló y Pérez, Barceló y Reyes, and Peralta, *Recuerdo literario*; Alcover y Beltrán, *Historia de la villa*, 535; Martínez-Fortún y Foyo, *Anales y efemérides*, 13–14, 16–17, 21; Martínez-Fortún y Foyo, *Cosas*, 209; Pérez Rivero, *Historia local*, 91–92; *La Luz del Hogar*, Güines, no. 2, (25 December 1898): 5; *La Luz del Hogar*, no. 3 (April 1899): 2; Alonso, *Cartilla histórico-descriptiva*, 16; Ponte y Domínguez, *Matanzas*, 259, 272; Villanueva, *Colón*, 3:70–72.

3. Ephemeral imprint titled "Viva Cuba Libre," Alquízar, December 1898. The pueblo's old and new street names are both given on the handbill. I am indebted to my colleague Francisco Pérez Guzmán for bringing this item to my attention and reproducing a copy of it for me.

4. *La Luz del Hogar*, Güines, no. 3 (April 1899): 2. See also *La Luz del Hogar*, no. 2 (25 December 1898): 5.

5. In 1900 a female resident of Yaguajay commented to Salvador Cisneros Betancourt: "Here we live in a full-fledged republic. The pueblo's mayor is a colonel from the liberation army who, as far as things about the homeland go, thinks like you or me. The municipal council's staff is all from the army, too." Carta de mujer [signature illegible] a Salvador Cisneros Betancourt, fechada en Yaguajay, diciembre de 1900, ANC, Fondo Academia de la Historia, box 482, sig. 336. The woman's claims are confirmed by Jorge Ibarra: "It should be emphasized," he writes, "that ultimately the municipal councils found themselves in the hands of Liberation Army officials, who had been designated as mayors of the island's main towns by the interventionist government." Ibarra, "Máximo Gómez," 68. For an analysis of the complex relationships between these structures of local power and the U.S. authorities during the first year of the intervention, see Pérez, "Intervention and Collaboration," 20–22.

6. The decree of 6 September 1899, establishing a uniform process for requesting name changes, is found in *Colección legislativa*, 2:325–27.

7. Alonso, *Cartilla histórico-descriptiva*, 16.

8. *El Fígaro*, Havana, no. 24, 25 June 1899, 213.

9. Martínez-Fortún y Foyo, *Anales y efemérides*, 13–14, 16–17, 21; Martínez-Fortún y Foyo, *Cosas*, 209.

10. Alcover y Beltrán, *Historia de la villa*, 535. On Barton's humanitarian work in Cuba during 1898, see Pérez Guzmán, *Herida*, 125–27, 148–49, 154–56.

11. Ferrer, "Rustic Men," 4.

12. The testimony of Segundo Corvisón, who went from being a Havana dandy "on the sidewalk outside the Louvre" before the war to a lieutenant colonel in the Liberation Army, is a good example of the ambivalent attitude held by men toward the participation of women as soldiers in the insurrectionist campaign: "In Key West I heard about . . . the great exploits of the insurrectionist heroines who accompanied general Antonio Maceo in the invasion and shared in the much-talked about triumphs of that illustrious caudillo. And in truth, those imposing and audacious military actions, executed by women veterans, left me confused, even somewhat resentful." The divided image of one

of these *mambisa* women (as both tough soldiers and tempting sexual objects) which Corvisón goes on to provide confirms his conflicted feelings: The "capitana," whose name he omits, goes to sleep in a hammock "without taking off her clothes or putting down her weapons." Within a few minutes she starts snoring loudly like a man, and giving off some odor that Corvisón describes as "unpleasant" but which another adventurous young army mate immediately identifies—despite the masculine appearance of the woman in her military gear—as quintessentially feminine and exciting "earthy scents of foliage." Corvisón, *En la guerra*, 41.

13. Decree of 30 May 1899, published in the 7 June 1899 issue of the *Gaceta de La Habana*, and reprinted in *Colección legislativa*, 1:250. Weyler was the Spanish general who directed the brutal relocation of the colony's rural population into concentration camps during the War of Independence.

14. See "Relación de las calles de este término, cuyos nombres han sido cambiados desde 1899 a la fecha," in Duque and Bellever, *Jurisprudencia*, 382–85. In 1919 a journalist complained about the limited patriotic spirit of Havana's residents, who continued to call the streets renamed to honor Antonio Maceo and Máximo Gómez by their old names, San Lázaro and Monte, respectively. To remedy this situation and stimulate the cause of toponymic patriotism, he proposed that state agencies not accept official requests and correspondence that used the outdated addresses and that the post office keep letters similarly addressed. As part of this same campaign, a municipal decree was approved in 1922, under which businessmen who used the old street names, instead of the new ones, on the notices and advertisements they placed on streetcars, trucks, and other conveyances, were subject to fines. Despite these measures, as well as a new wave of name changes which occurred in Havana following the 1959 Revolution, the inhabitants of the capital have maintained their stubborn ways right up to the present, calling—as in colonial times—the "Paseo de Martí" "the Prado," or referring to "Avenida Carlos III" rather than "Avenida Salvador Allende." See Iraizoz, *Sensaciones*, 54–55; and Decreto del Ayuntamiento de La Habana, 27 December 1922, in Duque and Bellever, *Jurisprudencia*, 241.

15. González Lanuza, "Rótulos trascendentales," *El Fígaro*, Havana, no. 18, 3 May 1903, 210.

16. *La Estrella Cubana*, Havana, no. 3, 30 November 1898.

17. Ibid.

18. *La Independencia*, Havana, no. 4, 12 October 1898; *La Guásima*, Marianao, 14 December 1898. A similar incident had occurred in Santiago de Cuba in May 1898, when a mob attacked a tailor's shop, called Los Estados Unidos, located on Calle San Juan Nepomuceno, at the corner of Enramada. Some members of the mob tied a broom to a long pole; they soaked the broom in a bucket full of excrement and covered the business's signs with it. The tailor shop remained "decorated" like this until the city was taken by U.S. soldiers. Within a few days, some men could be seen standing on ladders, washing the shop's signs with sponges. Hernández, "Santiago de Cuba en 1898," 321 and 360.

19. *La Guásima*, Marianao, 14 December 1898.

20. González Lanuza, "Rótulos trascendentales," *El Fígaro*, Havana, no. 18, 3 May 1903, 210–11. A few weeks later, *El Fígaro* carried an article by Esteban Borrero, chronicling and ridiculing a similar case, involving the changes made to the name of a neighborhood

grocery store in Havana. Founded by a creole in the colonial period, the store was originally known by the thoroughly Cuban name El Aguacate. The store was subsequently purchased by a Spaniard, who changed its name to El Aguacate Español. Once the War of Independence began, he rechristened it "El Aguacate Español en Campaña." After Spanish rule came to an end, the new owner, wanting to have it both ways—that is, to stay current with the times but not lose his older customers—changed the name of the establishment once again, this time to El Aguacate de Martí Reformado. See Esteban Borreo, "Carta abierta al doctor José A. González Lanuza," *El Fígaro*, no. 22, 31 May 1903, 277.

21. Fernández Robaina, *Negro*, 36–45; and Helg, *Our Rightful Share*, 91–98.

22. *Cuba y América*, Havana, no. 65, 20 August 1899, 27.

23. *El Ciudadano*, San Antonio de los Baños, year 1, no. 3, 19 May 1900, 6–8, in ANC, Fondo Museo Nacional, box 32, sig. 78.

24. Calle San Tadeo in Santiago de Cuba was renamed Calle Leonard Wood, and a park in the city of Pinar del Río was given the name Parque Theodore Roosevelt. See Hernández, "Santiago de Cuba," 370; and Pérez Rivero, *Historia local*, 91–92.

25. Between 1890 and 1893, the bibliographer Domingo Figarola Caneda, who had assisted Francisco Calcagno in compiling information for the latter's celebrated *Diccionario biográfico cubano*, collected essential information about Cubans who had participated in the Ten Years' War against Spain, with the intention of publishing a biographical dictionary of the Cuban Revolution. To this end, he sent out a great many letters and circulars, in which he urged the veterans of the struggle to recount their experiences and provide personal details. The replies that he received demonstrate two things: the difficulty of writing a single cohesive narrative given the participants' divergent experiences, and the attempts to ignore the contributions made by numerous soldiers of humble background, many of them blacks or Chinese, by minimizing their achievements in the Mambí Army. In a letter to Figarola, the mulatto writer and journalist Martín Morúa Delgado countered the claims of "distinguished persons in the Revolution" who sought to deny that Chinese officers had participated in key events of the war, while also vouching for the fact that "capitán Liborio" was a real person (Morúa Delgado had personally met him while the two were in exile) and attesting to the respect generals Gómez, Maceo, Cebreco, and others commanded. In directing himself not only to the exploits of the Chinese soldiers but to the "heroic and noble acts of old, back-country blacks, who will never figure in any history," Morúa Delgado states: "As for 'the denial that there was any Chinese person who distinguished himself in the Cuban ranks,' that doesn't surprise me, because I constantly hear denied, by people considered to be serious and by highly distinguished peoples [*sic*] from different circles, things that are palpably the case and things that are better known than anything else; for which reason I believe that our history will have to come to be written by a Russian or a Turk." See Carta de Martín Morúa Delgado a Domingo Figarola Caneda del 29 de marzo de 1892, ANC, Fondo Academia de la Historia, correspondence addressed to Domingo Figarola Caneda and some of his replies concerning bibliographic, biographical, literary, and political matters. Colección Figarola Caneda 1890–99, box 168, sig. 474.

26. Burke, *Varieties*, 55–56.

Chapter 5

1. ANC, Fondo Asuntos Políticos, legajo 99, sig. 15. I am indebted to María del Carmen Barcia for her suggestion that I consult this file of papers.

2. The *parda* (mulatta) Ángela Cuevas, a seventeen-year old prostitute from Santiago de Cuba, was detained and sentenced in October 1898 for calling the Spanish "patones salaos" (foul-mouthed fools, or worse) and for telling them "to grab a suitcase" in preparation for getting out of Cuba. The case record is in ANC, Fondo Asuntos Políticos, legajo 99, sig. 22, and legajo 200, sig. 3.

3. ANC, Fondo Asuntos Políticos, legajo 99, sig. 21.

4. Ibid., sig. 32.

5. ANC, Fondo Asuntos Políticos, legajo 99, sigs. 24, 27, 28, 31, 34; legajo 165, sig. 3.

6. Ibid., sig. 34.

7. Ibid., sig. 24.

8. *La Guásima*, Marianao, 14 December 1898, in ANC, Fondo Museo Nacional, box 33, no. 2.

9. ANC, Fondo Asuntos Políticos, legajo 99, sig. 39.

10. "Crónica," *El Independiente*, Havana, 2nd ser., no. 5, February 1899.

11. Ramiro Guerra, "Difusión y afirmación," 22.

12. Bartra, *Jaula*, 27.

13. Rama, *Ciudad letrada*, 91.

14. Ramiro Guerra, *Azúcar*, 63.

15. For a paradigmatic analysis of the creation of "national consciousness" by educated elites in the Latin American context, see Martínez Peláez, *Patria del criollo*. I am indebted to María del Carmen Barcia for bringing this book to my attention.

16. National consciousness is always consciousness of difference. The notion of an "us" as entailing idiosyncratic distinctiveness takes shape through a distancing from an "other" with whom we perceive ourselves to be in conflict or whom we see as fundamentally different from us. The belief that there are values we share among "ourselves" which differ from those subscribed to by "others" is articulated in symbols, icons, or marks of identity present not only in texts (e.g., legal tracts, articles, or poems of a more or less political character) but also in visual imagery (e.g., lithographs, prints, and photographs), and through a pattern of repetition and diffusion they begin to channel and serve as instruments of memory and promote the reiteration of common values and practices.

17. Ferrer, *Insurgent Cuba*, 113.

18. Ibid. These three works are today considered classics of Cuban historiography.

19. For a documented history of the Cuban exile press, see Poyo, *"With All,"* 174–75. On the development of a transnational public arena which enabled opinion makers on the island to link up with the exile communities, see Ferrer, *Insurgent Cuba*, 116–17.

20. Ferrer, *Insurgent Cuba*, 116.

21. On the creation of new "communities of interpretation" as an element in the appropriation of meaning carried out by different communities of readers, see Chartier, "Texts, Printing, Readings," 154–75.

22. Scott, *Degrees of Freedom*, 12, 28.

23. The concept of a "public sphere" was given its classic definition and treatment in Habermas, *Historia y crítica*.

24. *La Estrella Solitaria*, Havana, year 1, no. 2, 24 September 1898.

25. *La Independencia*, Havana, no. 4, 12 October 1898.

26. Ibid.

27. *La Guásima*, Marianao, 14 December 1898, in ANC, Fondo Museo Nacional, box 33, no. 21.

28. Regarding the "falsehoods" which, in the opinion of Máximo Gómez, plagued a piece by Enrique Loynaz dealing with the death of José Martí, see Máximo Gómez to Vidal Morales, 13 July 1900, ANC, Fondo Máximo Gómez, legajo 21, no. 3039.

29. *Antonio Maceo: Vida y hechos*; and *Martí: Novela histórica*.

30. *El Tiple Cubano*; *Nueva lira*.

31. Morales y Morales, *Iniciadores*. Two other Cuban history textbooks published during these years were López, *Historia de Cuba*; and Biosca Comellas, *Nociones de historia*.

32. Eduardo Benet to Máximo Gómez, Cienfuegos, 8 April 1902, ANC, Fondo Máximo Gómez, legajo 21, no. 3091.

33. *Manual o guía para los exámenes*.

34. "El 24 de febrero en las escuelas," *Patria*, Havana, no. 51, 27 February 1900.

35. "Fiestas patrióticas: La parada escolar," *El Occidente*, Guanajay, no. 15, 27 February 1901.

36. Máximo Gómez to Lola Rodríguez Tió, 11 October 1900, ANC Fondo Máximo Gómez, legajo 21, no. 3049.

37. Leaflet titled "Himno de Bayamo," dated 17 December 1900, in Havana, and bearing the signature of Alexis Everett Frye, Superintendent of Cuban Schools, ANC, Academia de la Historia, box 496, sig. 509.

38. Sánchez de Fuentes, *Cuba monumentaria*.

39. On this topic, see the recent study by Ibarra, *Máximo Gómez*, 69–92.

40. Ibid.

41. William McDowell to Máximo Gómez, 24 May 1899, ANC Fondo Máximo Gómez, legajo 22, no. 3188.

42. The range of "aficionados" collecting "patriotic" objects went from a humble provincial woman to a nationally known figure such as Juan Gualberto Gómez. In 1901 a resident of Cienfuegos, Edelmira Guerra, wrote to Salvador Cisneros Betancourt to ask him for the pen he had used to sign the constitution, so that she might "add to a collection that I am forming of objects of historical value, or failing that, some object that you had with you during the war which I would preserve as a memento." In Juan Gualberto Gómez's correspondence there is a letter in which several generals from the Independence War certify that they have handed over to him a piece of "the glorious flag General Maceo set to flutter . . . during the memorable campaign of the Invasion." Edelmira Guerra to Salvador Cisneros Betancourt, Cienfuegos, 4 March 1901, Academia de la Historia, box 336, leg. 482; Pedro Díaz to Juan Gualberto Gómez, ANC, Adquisiciones, box 72, sig. 4266.

43. "Objetos históricos," *El Telégrafo*, Trinidad, year 23, no. 250, 22 November 1899, 2.

44. Bacardí y Moreau, *Crónicas*, 10:215.

45. Ibid., 213–16.

46. Enrique Gómez y Planos, "Prehistoria de la Isla de Cuba"; quoted in Bronfman, "Unsettled and Nomadic," 25.

47. Provincia de Oriente, *Memoria sobre el estado de la provincia*, 114–15.

48. "Expediente formado a virtud de escritos del Secretario de la Comisión promovedora del Museo y Biblioteca de Cárdenas solicitando se le entregue para dicho museo la escalera del patíbulo en que subió el general Narciso López cuando fue ejecutado en esta capital," ANC, Fondo Secretaría de Estado y Gobernación, legajo 97, no. 775.

49. Actas Capitulares de la ciudad de Cienfuegos, vol. 44, fol. 156, and vol. 47, fol. 24, AHPC; "El Museo de Cienfuegos," *El Telégrafo*, Trinidad, year 23, no. 28, 31 December 1899, 2.

50. Appadurai, *Social Life of Things*; cited in Bronfman, "Unsettled and Nomadic," 26. I owe the idea of considering the different treatment accorded "patriotic" objects during this period, their metamorphosis from one type of object into another, to my reading of Bronfman's suggestive text.

51. Hernández, "Santiago de Cuba en 1898," 363–64.

52. Ibid., 364.

53. *Patria*, New York, 31 December 1898.

54. Ibid.

55. *Diario de la Marina*, Havana, no. 47, 24 February 1899.

56. *El Reconcentrado*, Havana, 14 June 1899.

57. *El Nuevo País*, Havana, 7 February 1900.

58. *El Cubano*, Havana, 27 October 1899.

59. *Diario de la Marina*, Havana, no. 47, 24 February 1899.

60. *Cuba y América*, Havana, May 1902.

61. *La Guásima*, Marianao, no. 47, 4 December 1899.

62. *El Cubano*, Havana, no. 21, 14 October 1899.

63. Roig de Leuchsenring, *Lucha*, 57, 64.

64. *La Solución*, Surgidero de Batabanó, year 2, no. 4, 13 January 1901.

65. *El Vigilante*, Guanajay, no. 77, 1 November 1900.

66. *Patria*, Havana, no. 28, 24 January 1900 and no. 37, 3 February 1900.

67. *El Bobo*, Camagüey, no. 22, 29 November 1900.

68. Certificate signed by Salvador Cisneros Betancourt and Valentín Villar, president and secretary of the Popular Commission [for the] "Maceo-Gómez Remains," on which the authenticity of a fragment of Maceo's jersey, small bullet shells and the comb from a repeating rifle that came from San Pedro, and a clod of earth which had stuck to his head, are vouched for, 30 June 1901, ANC, Fondo Museo Nacional, box 17, sig. 14.

69. See Salvador Cisneros Betancourt's printed card, titled "Recuerdo," presented to Señorita Amparo Martínez y Montalvo, on which can be seen a fragment of the blue jersey that Maceo was wearing on the day he died at Punta Brava on 6 December 1896. "The day of the exhumation of such precious remains," the document confirms, "remains of the jersey were found with them; and a small section of it, to which the fragment that is here attached belonged, was then and there dedicated and handed to me, as set down in the minutes recorded by Sr. Gaspar Varona. And I, to vouch for the authenticity of this keepsake sign this document in my own hand in El Cacahual, in the funeral chapel, where I stand honor guard before the mortal remains of those heroes, 19 September 1899." Signed: Salvador Cisneros Betancourt, ANC, Fondo Donativos y Remisiones, box 308, no. 11.

70. General Pedro Díaz to Guillermo González Arocha, parish priest of Artemisa, Cacahual, 29 September 1899, ANC, Donativos y Remisiones, box 418, sig. 21.

71. *El Telégrafo*, Trinidad, year 23, no. 212, 5 October 1899, in AHMT.

72. Ibid.

73. Montalvo, de la Torre, and Montané, *Cráneo*; Bronfman, "Reading Maceo's Skull," 17–18; Helg, *Our Rightful Share*, 104–5.

74. Bronfman, "Reading Maceo's Skull," 17.

75. Montalvo, de la Torre, and Montané, *Cráneo*, 2.

76. Ibid., 4. The pamphlet was promoted by the Comisión Popular Restos de "Maceo-Gómez" and sold to the country's municipal councils as part of a nationwide patriotic campaign to raise funds for the construction of the mausoleum and the support of Maceo's widow.

77. Portuondo Zúñiga, "Marcos Maceo," 32.

Chapter 6

1. Anderson, *Imagined Communities*.

2. On the value of descriptions of parades and other public ceremonies as historical source material, see Ryan, "American Parade," 131–54.

3. Bacardí y Moreau, *Crónicas*, 10:201.

4. Ibid.

5. An interesting analysis of these stereotypes of the supposed "savagery and "boorishness" of the "rustics" who made up the black race, stereotypes held even in the ranks of the independence movement, can be found in the record of the court-martial to which Quintín Banderas was subjected in August 1897. See Ferrer, *Insurgent Cuba*, 173–87.

6. Bacardí y Moreau, *Crónicas*, 10:201.

7. Quoted in ibid., 202.

8. An example of this image as expressed in verse are the well-known lines of the modernist Cuban poet, Bonifacio Byrne: "On returning from the distant shore / somber and mournful of soul / I searched, all eyes, for my country's flag / another to see in its place."

9. Announcement "A los habitantes de la Isla de Cuba," Havana, 24 December 1898, signed by the U.S. government commission for the evacuation of the island of Cuba, in ANC, Fondo Academia de la Historia, box 106, sig. 211.

10. Announcement "Al pueblo de La Habana," signed by the Junta Patriótica, Havana, 31 December 1898, in ANC, Fondo Academia de la Historia, box 106, sig. 241.

11. On the denial of permission to celebrate the end of Spanish sovereignty, see the orders issued by Major General William Ludlow, U.S. military governor of Havana, 29 December 1899, cited in Roig de Leuchsenring, *Lucha*, 11.

12. Imprint titled "Al pueblo de La Habana," signed by the Junta Patriótica, Havana, 1 January 1899, postponing celebrations of the change in sovereignty, in ANC, Fondo Academia de la Historia, box 106, sig. 218.

13. Martínez Ortiz, *Cuba*, 1:14.

14. Announcement "A los habitantes de la Isla de Cuba," Havana, 24 December 1898, in ANC, Fondo Academia de la Historia, box 106, sig. 211.

15. According to Martínez Arango's account in his *Cronología crítica de la guerra his-*

pano-cubano-americana, an incident occurred between the Cuban and U.S. troops on 16 July 1899, the day of the Spanish capitulation and signing of the armistice in Santiago de Cuba. A Cuban army lieutenant, from the twelfth regiment under Cebreco's command, occupied the Socapa fort and battery, which were located next to each other at the mouth of Santiago's port. The Spanish flag was taken down and the Cuban flag run up in its place. A short while later, an official came off one of the U.S. ships and belligerently ordered the Cubans to take down their flag and fly the U.S. one instead. The Cubans, however, showed an equally firm resolve, so the U.S. official found himself obliged to withdraw and to hoist his country's flag in a nearby place. This incident produced a curious conjunction—the flags of the three countries engaged in military conflict flying simultaneously in the same area, since on the other side of the canal, in the bay, the Spanish flag could be seen waving, too (it would be taken down and replaced on the following day by the U.S. flag). Martínez Arango, *Cronología*, 73–74. For another description of a similar incident, see "Mi álbum de la guerra" (a mimeographed copy), by José Cruz y Pérez, Camagüey, 14 November 1931, p. 65, in ANC, Fondo Academia de la Historia, box 105, sig. 187.

16. Sarachaga, *¡Arriba con el himno!*, 284.

17. Sanjenís, *Memorias*, 318.

18. Ibid., 268–69.

19. Ibid., 328.

20. *Patria*, New York, 31 December 1898, in ANC, Fondo Asuntos Políticos, expediente 293, no. 36.

21. Some *décimas* found in a modestly printed leaflet, dated 1 August 1898 and similar to other imprints celebrating a Free Cuba, along with Máximo Gómez, Calixto García, and other independence heroes, contain the following lines: "Long live the Americans / who came to our aid: / let us embrace them / and love them like brothers. / Long live the Cuban flag / united with the flag of that nation / for which each Cuban / has a temple in his heart." See "A Cuba y mis hermanos," 1 August 1898, in ANC, Fondo Academia de la Historia, box 106, sig. 242. A published collection of verses, *décimas*, *guarachas*, and patriotic songs contains the following *décimas* dedicated to Cuban-American brotherhood: "Soon shall you see / united with the American / the Cuban flag / lifted high on El Morro / transfixing your gaze. / Nor shall you doubt, I believe, / the true shield, / that it pleased a foreign nation, / to give Cubans / to throw off the yoke / of a bellicose Spain. / United shall you see / two peoples of different race, / for adversity our lot / they tendered us a munificent hand / so to redeem Cubans / from an abject and perverse race." See the *décima* "Cuba para los cubanos," in *Nueva lira*, 161–63. I am indebted to Pablo Riaño San Marful for prompting me to consult this anthology.

22. Miguel de Carrión, "Ayer, hoy y mañana," *La Libertad*, Havana, 1 January 1899, 3.

23. ANC, Fondo Audiencia de La Habana, legajo 223, expediente 2. I am indebted to Lillian Guerra, who came across this case while conducting her doctoral research and kindly made her transcription of the original document available to me.

24. Ibid.

25. Sanjenís, *Memorias*, 331, 334.

26. *El Independiente*, Havana, 2nd ser., no. 1, 5 February 1899, 5.

27. Ibid.

28. Martínez Ortiz, *Cuba*, 1:38.

29. Ibid.

30. Ibid., 40.

31. Cited in Roig de Leuchsenring, *Lucha*, 61.

32. Causa no. 282, in the Juzgado de Instrucción de Guanabacoa, for the year 1899, in ANC, Fondo Donativos y Remisiones, legajo 563, no. 44.

33. Martínez Ortiz, *Cuba*, 1:78–91. The crowd that attended the ceremony was so numerous that several days later the owners of La Dificultad, a *finca* adjoining El Cacahual, demanded that its organizers compensate them for damage done to their fields. Letter of M. Villar to Salvador Cisneros Betancourt, Havana, 13 December 1899, ANC, Fondo Academia de la Historia, box 481, no. 334.

34. *La Solución*, Surgidero de Batabanó, no. 7, 24 January 1901.

35. Ibid.

36. *El Vigilante*, Guanajay, no. 45, 12 July 1900.

37. With reference to these issues in particular, see three documents in the ANC, Fondo Secretaría de Estado y Gobernación: "Expediente relativo a que se declaren días de fiesta el 10 de octubre y el 24 de febrero," legajo 94, no. 521; "Expediente relativo a acuerdos tomados por los ayuntamientos en solicitud de que se reconozca la independencia de esa Isla," legajo 95, no. 599; and "Expediente formado con motivo de las protestas a la implantación de un Gobierno Civil in esta Isla en sustitución del Militar que hoy existe," legajo 94, no. 595.

38. Actas Capitulares del Ayuntamiento de Cienfuegos, vol. 42, fol. 00204; vol. 43, fol. 30; vol. 44, fol. 63; vol. 45, fol. 22; vol. 46, fol. 87, AHPC.

39. Ibid., vol. 43, fols. 7, 9, 10, 17, 21, 25, 26; vol. 44, fol. 116; vol. 45, fol. 16.

40. Ibid., vol. 46, fol. 6.

41. Ibid., vol. 43, fol. 90; vol. 45, fols. 15–16; and Rousseau and Díaz de Villegas, *Memoria*, 270–71.

42. Rousseau and Díaz de Villegas, *Memoria*, 270–71.

43. Actas Capitulares del Ayuntamiento de Cienfuegos, vol. 48, fol. 45, AHPC.

44. See "Expediente relativo a la petición de permiso que solicita el señor Nicolás Valverde para establecer un bazaar en Cienfuegos cuyos productos se destinarán a la compra de una estatua que trata de erigirse a la memoria del general de ejército cubano Dionisio Gil," in ANC, Fondo Secretaría de Estado y Gobernación, legajo 96, expediente 754.

45. Arendt, *On Revolution*, 222.

BIBLIOGRAPHY

Archives

Cambridge, Mass.
  Harvard University Archives
    Autographs and Testimonials of Students
    Lista de los suscriptores para el fondo de los maestros cubanos
    Report of the President of Harvard University, 1900
Cienfuegos, Cuba
  Archivo Histórico Provincial de Cienfuegos
    Libros de actas capitulares del ayuntamiento (1898–1902)
College Park, Md.
  U.S. National Archives and Records Administration
    Record Group 140, Records of the Military Government of Cuba
    Record Group 350, Records of the Bureau of Insular Affairs
    Record Group 153, Records of the Office of the Judge Advocate General
Havana, Cuba
  Archivo Nacional de Cuba
    Fondo Academia de la Historia
    Fondo Adquisiones
    Fondo Asuntos políticos
    Fondo Audiencia de La Habana
    Fondo Donativos y remisiones
    Fondo Especial
    Fondo Instrucción pública
    Fondo Museo Nacional
    Fondo Secretaría y Ministerio de Gobernación
    Fondo Secretaría de Estado y Gobernación
    Fondo Máximo Gómez
Santiago de Cuba, Cuba
  Archivo histórico provincial de Santiago de Cuba
    Fondo Gobierno provincial
    Fondo Emilio Bacardí
Trinidad, Cuba
  Archivo histórico municipal de Trinidad
    Libros de actas capitulares del ayuntamiento (1898–1902)
Washington, D.C.
  Library of Congress
    Cuban Educational Association Papers

Official Documents

CUBA

Colección legislativa de la Isla de Cuba: Recopilación de todas las disposiciones publicadas en la "Gaceta de La Habana." 2 vols. Havana: Establecimiento Tipográfico Teniente Rey 23, 1900.

Cuba, Convención Constituyente, Diario de Sesiones. Havana: n.p., 1901.

Datos demostrativos del estado de la instrucción pública primaria en la Isla de Cuba al terminar el mes de noviembre de 1901. [Oficina del Comisionado de Escuelas Públicas] Havana: Rambla y Bouza, 1902.

Datos demostrativos del estado de instrucción pública primaria en la Isla de Cuba al terminar el mes de febrero de 1902. [Oficina del Comisionado de Escuelas Públicas] Havana: n.p., 1902.

Junta de Educación de La Habana. *Memoria anual de los trabajos realizados en las escuelas públicas del distrito escolar de La Habana.* Havana: n.p., 1901.

Ley electoral municipal adicionada con el censo de población y la ley de perjurio. Havana: Imprenta de la Gaceta Oficial, 1900.

Primera memoria anual del comisionado de escuelas públicas, 1900–1901. Vol. 2. Havana: Rambla y Bouza, 1902.

Provincia de Oriente. *Memoria sobre el estado de la provincia y los trabajos realizados por el gobierno y los consejos provinciales durante el año fiscal de 1904–1905.* Havana: Moderna Poesía, 1906.

UNITED STATES

Cuba, Military Governor. *Civil Report of the Military Governor.* 15 vols. Havana: Government Printing Office, 1901–2.

———. *Report of Military Governor of Cuba on Civil Affairs.* 5 vols. Washington, D.C.: Government Printing Office, 1900.

First Annual Report of the Public Schools of the Island of Cuba for September, October, November, December. Havana: n.p., 1900.

First Annual Report of the Commissioner of Public Schools together with the Annual Reports of the Provincial Superintendents and Others: 1900–1901. Havana: n.p., 1902.

Informe sobre el censo de Cuba, 1899. Washington, D.C.: Government Printing Office, 1900.

Newspapers, Magazines, and Bulletins

La Aurora (Consolación del Sur)
El Bobo (Camagüey)
El Ciudadano (San Antonio de los Baños)
El Cubano (Havana)
Cuba Pedagógica (Havana)
Cuba y América (Havana)
La Democracia (Havana)
Diario de la Marina (Havana)

La Discusión (Havana)
Donahue's Magazine (Boston)
La Escuela Cubana (Havana)
La Escuela de Verano (Cienfuegos)
La Escuela Moderna (Havana)
La Estrella Cubana (Havana)
La Estrella Solitaria (Havana)
El Fígaro (Havana)

Gaceta de La Habana
La Guásima (Marianao)
El Güireño (Güira de Melena)
Harvard Graduates Magazine
Harvard Illustrated Magazine
La Independencia (Havana)
Independent (Cambridge, Mass.?)
El Independiente (Havana)
La Libertad (Havana)
La Lucha (Havana)
La Luz del Hogar (Güines)
La Nación (Havana)
New York Herald

New York Tribune
El Nuevo País (Havana)
El Occidente (Guanajay)
Patria (Havana)
Patria (New York)
El Porvenir (Santiago de Cuba)
El Reconcentrado (Havana)
Revista de Instrucción Pública (Havana)
Revista Pedagógica Cubana (Havana)
La Solución (Surgidero de Batabanó)
El Telégrafo (Trinidad)
El Vigilante (Guanajay)

Other Works

Abad, Diana. *De la Guerra Grande al Partido Revolucionaro Cubano*. Havana: Ciencias Sociales, 1995.

Adas, Michael. *"High" Imperialism and the "New" History. Essays in Global and Comparative History*. Washington, D.C.: American Historical Association, 1993.

Aguirre, Sergio, "El cincuentenario de un gran crimen." In *Eco de Caminos*, edited by Sergio Aguirre, 337–53. Nuestra Historia. Havana: Ciencias Sociales/Instituto Cubano del Libro, 1974.

Alcover y Beltrán, Antonio. *Historia de la villa de Sagua la Grande y su jurisdicción*. Sagua la Grande: Imprentas Unidas La Historia y El Correo Español, 1905.

Almanaque Baillo-Bailliere para el año 1899. Madrid: Baillo-Bailliere e Hijos, 1898.

Almanaque del maestro cubano para el año 1901. Havana: Propagandista, 1901.

Almanaque del maestro para el año de 1883. Havana: Nueva Principal, 1883.

Almodóvar, Carmen. *Antología crítica de la historiografía cubana (Período neocolonial)*. Havana: Pueblo y Educación, 1989.

———. "La escuela primaria cubana en el período de ocupación." In *La nación soñada: Cuba, Puerto Rico y Filipinas ante el 98*, edited by Consuelo Naranjo, Miguel Ángel Puig-Samper, and Luis Miguel García Mora, 467–77. Aranjuez: Doce Calles, 1996.

Alonso, Rogelio M. *Cartilla histórico-descriptiva de Macuriges*. Havana: Propagandista, 1901.

Alsina Neto, Arturo. *Última bandera que cobijó al soldado español en América*. Madrid: Patronato de Huérfanos de la Administración Militar, 1908.

Álvarez Curbelo, Silvia. "La batalla de los signos: 1898 y la vida cotidiana." *Diálogos* [San Juan, P.R.], May 1997.

———. "Las fiestas públicas de Ponce: Políticas de la memoria y cultura cívica." In *Los arcos de la Memoria: El 98 de los pueblos puertorriqueños*, edited by Silvia Álvarez Curbelo, Mary Frances Gallart, and Carmen Raffucci de García, 208–31. San Juan: Universidad de Puerto Rico, 1998.

Álvarez Estévez, Rolando. *Azúcar e inmigración, 1900–1940*. Havana: Ciencias Sociales, 1988.

Anderson, Benedict. *Imagined Communities: Reflections on the Origin and Spread of Nationalism*. London: Verso, 1994.

Antonio Maceo: Vida y hechos gloriosos de este heroico general cubano—Novela histórica. Havana: Moderna Poesía, 1900.

Appadurai, Arjun, ed. *The Social Life of Things*. Cambridge: Cambridge University Press, 1988.

Arendt, Hannah. *On Revolution*. New York: Viking, 1967 [1963].

Armas, Juan Ignacio de. *Orígenes del lenguaje criollo*. Havana: Viuda de Soler, 1882.

Armas, Ramón de. "Esquema para un análisis de los partidos políticos burgueses en Cuba: Antecedentes, surgimiento y principales características (1899–1925)." In *Los partidos políticos burgueses en Cuba neocolonial, 1899–1952*, edited by Ramón de Armas, Francisco López Segrera, and Germán Sánchez Otero, 1–87. Havana: Ciencias Sociales, 1985.

———. *La revolución pospuesta: Contenido y alcance de la revolución martiana por la independencia*. Havana: Ciencias Sociales, 1975.

Arredondo, Alberto. *El negro en Cuba*. Havana: Alfa, 1939.

Asociación Monumentos "Martí-Céspedes." *Reseña de los trabajos realizados por la Comisión Ejecutiva de la Asociación Monumentos "Martí-Céspedes" hasta el acto de Inaugurar la estatua ilustre: José Martí en el Parque Central de La Habana (24 de febrero de 1905), seguida de una relación rigurosamente histórica de la expedición en que se trasladó a Cuba el insigne patriota y sus heroicos compañeros hasta su gloriosa muerte en Dos Ríos, el 19 de mayo de 1958; copiada de su diario de operaciones por el invicto mayor general Máximo Gómez*. Havana: Avisador Comercial, 1905.

Atkins, Edwin F. *Sixty Years in Cuba*. Cambridge, Mass.: Riverside, 1926.

Bacardí y Moreau, Emilio. *Crónicas de Santiago de Cuba*. 10 vols. Santiago de Cuba: Arroyo Hermanos, 1923–25.

Backzo, Bronislaw. "Le calendrier républicain: Décréter l'éternité." In *Les lieux de mémoire*, vol. 1: *La République*, edited by Pierre Nora, 67–108. Paris: Gallimard, 1997.

Barceló y Pérez, Miguel, Miguel A. Barceló y Reyes, and Fernando G. de Peralta, comps. *Recuerdo literario del Día de la Patria*. Gibara: "La República" de M. Bin, 1902.

Barcia, María del Carmen. "Los deportados de la guerra: Cuba 1895–1898." In *La nación soñada: Cuba, Puerto Rico y Filipinas ante el 98*, edited by Consuelo Naranjo, Miguel Ángel Puig, and Luis Miguel García, 635–46. Aranjuez: Doce Calles, 1996.

———. *Elites y grupos de presión: Cuba, 1868–1898*. Havana: Ciencias Sociales, 1998.

———. "La historia profunda: La sociedad civil del 98." *Temas*, nos. 12–13 (1998).

———. "El 98 en La Habana: Sociedad y vida cotidiana." *Revista de Indias* 58, no. 212 (January–April 1998).

———. *Una sociedad en crisis: La Habana a finales del siglo XIX*. Havana: Ciencias Sociales, 2000.

Bartra, Roger. *La jaula de la melancolía: Identidad y metamorfosis del mexicano*. Mexico City: Grijalbo, 1987.

Batrell y Oviedo, Ricardo. *Para la historia: Apuntes autobiográficos*. Havana: Seoane y Álvarez, 1912.

Bellah, Robert. "Civil Religion in America." In *Culture and Society: Contemporary*

Debates, edited by Alexander Jeffrey and Steven Seidman, 262–72. Cambridge: Cambridge University Press, 1993.

Benítez Rojo, Antonio. "Música y nación: El rol de la música negra y mulata en la construcción de la nación cubana moderna." *Encuentro de la Cultura Cubana*, nos. 8–9 (Spring–Summer 1998).

Biosca Comellas, Luis. *Nociones de historia de Cuba*. Havana: Propagandista, 1901.

Boyer, M. Ch. *Dreaming the Rational City: The Myth of American City Planning*. Cambridge, Mass.: MIT Press, 1983.

Bronfman, Alejandra. "Reading Maceo's Skull (Or the Paradoxes of Race in Cuba)." [Program in Latin American Studies, Princeton University] *Boletín* (Fall 1998).

———. "Unsettled and Nomadic: Law, Anthropology, and Race in Early Twentieth-Century Cuba." University of Maryland Latin American Studies Center Working Papers Series, 2002, no. 9.

Brooke, John. *Civil Orders, 1899*. Washington, D.C.: Government Printing Office, 1899.

Burke, Peter. *Varieties of Cultural History*. Ithaca, N.Y.: Cornell University Press, 1997.

Calendario 1900, obsequio de la droguería y farmacia La Reunión. Havana: Imprenta La Habana, 1900.

Calendario del Obispado de La Habana para el año 1861. Havana: B. May, 1860.

Calendario del Obispado de La Habana para el año 1867. Havana: B. May, 1866.

Calendario del Obispado de La Habana para el año 1893. Havana: P. Fernández, 1892.

Calendario del Obispado de La Habana para el año 1899. Havana: P. Fernández, 1898.

Calendario del Obispado de La Habana para el año 1900. Havana: P. Fernández, 1899.

Calendario del Obispado de La Habana para el año 1901. Havana: P. Fernández, 1900.

Calendario del Obispado de La Habana para el año 1902. Havana: P. Fernández, 1901.

Cantón Navarro, José, et al. *Historia de Cuba: La neocolonia—Organización y crisis desde 1899 hasta 1940*. Havana: Instituto de Historia de Cuba/Editora Política, 1998.

Carrión, Miguel de. "El desenvolvimiento social de Cuba en los últimos años." *Cuba Contemporánea*, no. 27 (September 1921).

Castañeda, Digna. "El Caribe colonial en 1898: Ruptura y continuidad." *Temas* nos. 12–13 (1998).

Castellanos, Isabel. *La brujería y el águismo en Cuba desde el punto de vista médico-legal*. Havana: Lloredo, 1916.

Castillo y Zúñiga, José Rogelio. *Autobiografía del general José Rogelio Castillo*. Havana: Ciencias Sociales/Instituto Cubano del Libro, 1973.

Certeau, Michel de. *The Practice of Everyday Life*. Berkeley: University of California Press, 1984.

Céspedes, José María. *La intervención*. Havana: Rambla y Bouza, 1901.

Chailloux Cardona, Juan M. *Síntesis histórica de la vivienda popular: Los horrores del solar habanero*. Havana: Jesús Montero, 1945.

Chapman, Charles E. A. *History of the Cuban Republic: A Study in Hispanic American Politics*. New York: Macmillan, 1927.

Chartier, Roger. "De la historia social de la cultura a la historia cultural de lo social." *Historia Social* [Valencia, Spain], no. 17 (Fall 1993).

———. "El mundo como representación." *Historia Social* [Valencia, Spain], no. 10 (Spring–Summer 1991).

———. "Texts, Printing, Readings." In *The New Cultural History*, edited by Lynn Hunt, 154–75. Studies on the History of Society and Culture, 6. Berkeley: University of California Press, 1989.

Chatterjee, Partha. *The Nation and Its Fragments: Colonial and Postcolonial Histories.* Princeton Studies in Culture/Power/History. Princeton, N.J.: Princeton University Press, 1993.

———. *Nationalist Thought and the Colonial World: A Derivative Discourse?* Third World Studies. Minneapolis: University of Minnesota Press, 1986.

Collazo, Enrique. *Los americanos en Cuba.* 2 vols. Havana: C. Martínez, 1905.

Cordoví Núñez, Yoel. "*La Independencia* en su laberinto hacia el conservadurismo, 1880–1904." Unpublished paper. 2001.

Corvisón, Segundo. *En la guerra y en la paz: Episodios históricos de la Revolución por la Independencia y consideraciones acerca de la República cordial.* Havana: Cultural, 1939.

"The Cuban Summer School." *Harvard Graduates Magazine*, September 1900.

Cuevas Zequeira, Sergio. *En la contienda.* Havana: Fígaro, 1901.

Deschamps Chapeaux, Pedro. *Rafael Serra y Montalvo, obrero incansable de nuestra independencia.* Havana: UNEAC, 1975.

Domosh, M. *Invented Cities: The Creation of Landscape in Nineteenth-Century New York and Boston.* New Haven, Conn.: Yale University Press, 1996.

Duke, Cathy. "The Idea of Race: The Cultural Impact of American Intervention in Cuba, 1898–1912." In *Politics, Society, and Culture in the Caribbean: Selected Papers of the XIV Conference of Caribbean Historians*, edited by Blanca G. Silvestrini. San Juan: Universidad de Puerto Rico, 1983.

Dumoulin, John. "El primer desarrollo del movimiento obrero y la formación del proletariado en el sector azucarero: Cruces, 1886–1902." *Islas* [Villa Clara, Cuba], no. 48 (May–August 1974): 3–66.

Duque, Francisco M., and Julio G. Bellever, eds. *Jurisprudencia en materia de policía urbana: Decretos, acuerdos y otras resoluciones sobre dicha materia, dictados para el Municipio de La Habana.* Havana: Moderna Poesía, 1924.

El tiple cubano, décimas criollas; cantos del pueblo de Cuba, amorosos, descriptivos, patrióticos, compuestos por los más célebres poetas y recogidos en los campos para cantar al son del tiple campesino. Havana: Moderna Poesía, 1901.

Estévez y Romero, Luis. *Desde el Zanjón hasta Baire; datos para la historia política de Cuba.* Havana: Propaganda Literaria, 1899.

Fernández Muñiz, Aurea Matilde. "Desastre, realidad, regeneracionismo: España y el 98." *Temas*, nos. 12–13 (1998).

Fernández Robaina, Tomás. *El negro en Cuba, 1902–1958: Apuntes para la historia de la lucha contra la discriminación racial.* Havana: Ciencias Sociales, 1990.

Ferraroti, Franco. *La historia y lo cotidiano.* Barcelona: Península, 1991.

Ferrer, Ada. "Esclavitud, ciudadanía y los límites de la nacionalidad cubana: La Guerra de los Diez Años, 1868–1878." *Historia Social* [Valencia, Spain] no. 22 (1995).

———. *Insurgent Cuba: Race, Nation, and Revolution, 1868–1898.* Chapel Hill: University of North Carolina Press, 1999.

———. "Rustic Men, Civilized Nation: Race, Culture, and Contention on the Eve of

Cuban Independence." Paper presented at the Taller de Historia, Archivo Provincial, Cienfuegos, Cuba, March 1998.

―――. "Social Aspects of Cuban Nationalism: Race, Slavery and the Guerra Chiquita, 1879–1880." *Cuban Studies* 21 (1991): 37–56.

Figueras, Francisco. *Cuba y su evolución colonial.* Havana: Avisador Comercial, 1907.

Foner, S. Philip. *La guerra hispano-cubano-norteamericana y el surgimiento del imperialismo yanqui.* Havana: Ciencias Sociales, 1978.

―――. *El orden del discurso.* Barcelona: Tusquet, 1980.

Foucault, Michel. *La microfísica del poder.* Barcelona: Piqueta, 1993.

Fuente, Alejandro de la. "Negros y electores: Desigualdad y políticas raciales en Cuba, 1900–1930." In *La nación soñada: Cuba, Puerto Rico y Filipinas ante el 98*, edited by Consuelo Naranjo, Miguel Ángel Puig-Samper, and Luis Miguel García Mora, 163–77. Aranjuez: Doce Calles, 1996.

Frye, Alexis A. *Manual para maestros: Aprobado por los superintendentes asociados Esteban Borrero Echevarria y Lincoln de Zayas.* Havana, n.p., 1900.

García Álvarez, Alejandro. "Estructuras de una economía colonial en transición." In *La nación soñada: Cuba, Puerto Rico y Filipinas ante el 98*, edited by Consuelo Naranjo, Miguel Ángel Puig-Samper, and Luis Miguel García Mora, 195–209. Aranjuez: Doce Calles, 1996.

―――. *La gran burguesía comercial en Cuba, 1899–1920.* Havana: Ciencias Sociales, 1990.

García Álvarez, Alejandro, and Consuelo Naranjo. "Cubanos y españoles después del 98." *Revista de Indias* 58, no. 212 (January–April 1998).

Geertz, Clifford. "Después de la revolución: El destino del nacionalismo en los nuevos estados." In *La interpretación de las culturas.* Madrid: Gedisa, 1992.

Gellner, Ernest. *Nations and Nationalism.* Oxford: Basil Blackwell, 1983.

González Hechvarría, Roberto. "Literatura, baile y béisbol en el (último) fin de siglo cubano." *Encuentro de la Cultura Cubana*, no. 8/9 (Spring–Summer 1998).

Guerra, Lillian. "Esculpir a Martí: Memorias y monumentos en la primera República Cubana." *Revista de Ciencias Sociales* [San Juan, P.R.], January 2000.

―――. *The Myth of José Martí: Conflicting Nationalisms in Early Twentieth-Century Cuba.* Envisioning Cuba. Chapel Hill: University of North Carolina Press, 2005.

Guerra, Ramiro. *Azúcar y población en las Antillas.* Havana: Lex, 1961.

―――. "Difusión y afirmación del sentimiento nacional." *Social* [Havana] (November 1924).

―――. *En el camino de la independencia.* Havana: Ciencias Sociales, 1974.

―――. *La expansión territorial de los Estados Unidos.* Havana: Ciencias Sociales, 1975.

―――. *Historia de la nación cubana.* 10 vols. Havana: Historia de la Nación Cubana, 1952.

―――. *Mudos testigos.* Havana: Ciencias Sociales, 1974.

―――. *Por las veredas del pasado, 1880–1902.* Havana: Lex, 1957.

Habermas, Jürgen. *Historia y crítica de la opinión pública. La transformación estructural de la vida pública.* Translated by Antoni Domènech, with the collaboration of Rafael Grasa. Barcelona: Gustavo Gili, 1981.

———. *La inclusión del otro: Estudios de teoría política*. Translated by Juan Carlos Velasco Arroyo and Gerard Vilar Roca. Barcelona: Paidós, 1999.

Harroun, H. K. "The Cuban Educational Association of the United States." *American Monthly Review of Reviews* 20, no. 3 (September 1899): 334–35.

Harvard University. Cuban Summer School. *La Escuela de Verano para los maestros cubanos*. Cambridge, Mass. *Cuban Summer School, 1900*. Cambridge, Mass.: Eduard W. Wheeler, 1900.

Helg, Aline. *Our Rightful Share: The Afro-Cuban Struggle for Equality, 1886–1912*. Chapel Hill: University of North Carolina Press, 1995.

Heller, Agnes. *Sociología de la vida cotidiana*. Barcelona: Península, 1987.

Hernández, José Joaquín. "Santiago de Cuba en 1898: Memorias de un bloqueado." In *Crónicas de Santiago de Cuba*, compiled and edited by Emilio Barcardí y Moreau and Manuel A. Barrera García, 363–64. Santiago de Cuba: Arroyo Hermanos, 1923–25.

Hernández Millares, Enrique. Vol. 2 of *Obras completas*. Havana: Avisador Comercial, 1916.

Herzfeld, Michael. *Cultural Intimacy: Social Poetics in the Nation-State*. New York: Routledge, 1997.

Hevia Lanier, Oilda. *El directorio central de las sociedades negras de Cuba, 1886–1894*. Havana: Ciencias Sociales, 1996.

Hobsbawm, E. J. *Nations and Nationalism since 1789: Programme, Myth, Reality*. Cambridge: Cambridge University Press, 1990.

Hobsbawm, E. J., and Terence Ranger, eds. *The Invention of Tradition*. Cambridge: Cambridge University Press, 1993.

Ibarra, Jorge. *Cuba, 1898–1921: Partidos políticos y clases sociales*. Havana: Ciencias Sociales, 1992.

———. "Cultura e identidad nacional en el Caribe hispánico: El caso puertorriqueño y el cubano." In *La nación soñada: Cuba, Puerto Rico y Filipinas ante el 98*, edited by Consuelo Naranjo, Miguel Ángel Puig-Samper, and Luis Miguel García Mora, 85–95. Aranjuez: Doce Calles, 1996.

———. *Ideología mambisa*. Havana: Ciencias Sociales, 1967.

———. "Máximo Gómez entre Escila y Caribdis." *Revista Bimestre Cubana*, no. 7, 3d ser. (July–December 1997).

———. *Máximo Gómez frente al imperio, 1898–1905*. Havana: Ciencias Sociales, 2000.

Iglesias, Fe. "La reconstrucción de la economía cubana, 1898–1915." In *Cien años de sociedad: Los 98 del Gran Caribe*, edited by Antonio Gaztambide Géigel, Juan González-Mendoza, and Mario R. Cancel, 59–73. San Juan, P.R.: Callejón, 2000.

Iglesias, Marial. "José Martí: Mito, legitimación y símbolo—La génesis del mito martiano y la emergencia del nacionalismo republicano." In *Diez nuevas miradas a la Historia de Cuba*, edited by José A. Piqueras Arenas, 201–26. Collecció Espai i Història, 2. Castelló de la Plana [Spain]: Universitat Jaime I, 1998.

Instituto de Historia del Movimiento Comunista y de la Revolución Socialista de Cuba. *Historia del movimiento obrero cubano, 1865–1958*. Havana: Política, 1985.

Iraizoz, Antonio. *Sensaciones del momento (Artículos de actualidad)*. Havana: "Siglo XX," 1919.

James, Ariel. *Banes: Imperialismo y nación en una plantación azucarera*. Havana: Ciencias Sociales, 1976.

Jenks, Leland H. *Nuestra colonia de Cuba*. Foreword by Gregorio Selser, translated by Ignacio López Valencia. Havana: Revolucionaria, 1966.

Kaplan, Amy, and Donald Pease, eds. *Cultures of United States Imperialism*. New Americanists. Durham, N.C.: Duke University Press, 1993.

Knight, W. Franklin. "Cuba, Puerto Rico, las Antillas y los imperios en la Guerra del 98." In *Cien años de sociedad: Los 98 del Gran Caribe*, edited by Antonio Gaztambide Géigel, Juan González-Mendoza, and Mario R. Cancel, 43–55. San Juan, P.R.: Callejón, 2000.

Kutzinski, Vera M. *Sugar's Secrets: Race and the Erotics of Cuban Nationalism*. Charlottesville: University Press of Virginia, 1993.

La nueva lira criolla: Guarachas, canciones y décimas y canciones de la guerra por un vueltabajero. 5th ed. Havana: Moderna Poesía, 1903.

Leal, Rine. *Teatro bufo, siglo XIX: Antología*. 2 vols. Biblioteca Básica de Literatura Cubana. Havana: Arte y Literatura, 1975.

León, Argeliers. "La fiesta del carnaval." *Temas* (Havana), no. 6 [n.d.].

Le Riverend, Julio. *Historia económica de Cuba*. Havana: Instituto Cubano del Libro, 1967.

López, Alejandro M. *Historia de Cuba en breve compendio*. Havana: Propagandista, 1900.

López, Sergio, and Marial Iglesias. "José Martí: El origen del símbolo fundacional del nacionalismo en Cuba." *L'Avenc, revista d'Historia* [Barcelona], no. 217 (September 1997): 38–43.

López Segrera, Francisco. *Raíces históricas de la Revolución cubana (1868–1959): Introducción al estudio de las clases sociales en Cuba en sus relaciones con la política y la economía*. Havana: Unión, 1978.

Lorini, Alexandra. *Rituals of Race: American Public Culture and the Search for Racial Democracy*. Charlottesville: University Press of Virginia, 1999.

Loyola, Oscar. "La alternativa histórica de un 98 no consumado." *Temas* [Havana], nos. 12–13 (1998).

Lubián, Silvia. *El Club revolucionario "Juan Bruno Zayas."* Santa Clara, Cuba: Dirección de Publicaciones de la Universidad Central de Las Villas, 1961.

Mallon, Florencia E. *Peasant and Nation: The Making of Postcolonial Mexico and Peru*. Berkeley: University of California Press, 1995.

Maluquer de Motes, Jordi. "La inmigración española en Cuba: Elementos de un debate histórico." In *Cuba, la perla de las Antillas: Actas de las I Jornadas sobre "Cuba y su Historia,"* edited by Consuelo Naranjo Orovio and Tomás Mallo Gutiérrez, 137–47. Aranjuez: Doce Calles; Madrid: Consejo Superior de Investigaciones Científicas, 1994.

Manual o guía para los exámenes de los maestros cubanos conforme al programa oficial acordado por la Junta de Superintendentes de escuelas públicas de la Isla de Cuba: Segundo grado. Edited by Carlos de la Torre, preface by Eusebio Borrero. Havana: Moderna Poesía, 1902.

Márquez Sterling, Manuel. *Doctrina de la República*. Havana: Dirección de Cultura, 1967.

Martí, José. *Obras escogidas*. 3 vols. Havana: Ciencias Sociales, 1992.

Martí: Novela histórica por un patriota. Havana: Cultural, 1901.

Martínez Arango, Felipe. *Cronología crítica de la guerra hispano-cubano-americana*. Cuadernos de Historia Habanera, 43. Havana: Municipio, 1950.

Martínez-Fortún y Foyo, José A. Vol. 5 of *Anales y efemérides de San Juan de los Remedios y su jurisdicción (1899–1919)*. Havana: Pérez Sierra, 1919.

———. *Apuntes históricos de Caibarién*. Caibarién, Cuba: Eudaldo Valdés e Hijos, 1940.

Martínez-Fortún y Foyo, José A., and José Ramón Rodríguez Arce. *Monografías históricos de Placetas: Con noticias de las actas del ayuntamiento, las anécdotas placenteras de Rodríguez Arce y 60 fotograbados en el texto*. Remedios: "El Popular Cubano," 1944.

Martínez Ortiz, Rafael. *Cuba: Los primeros años de la independencia*. 2 vols. Paris: Artistique Lux, 1921.

Martínez Peláez, Severo. *La patria del criollo: Ensayo de interpretación de la realidad guatemalteca*. San José, Costa Rica: Editorial Universitaria Centroamericana, 1985.

McClintock, Anne. *Imperial Leather: Race, Gender and Sexuality in the Colonial Contest*. New York: Routledge, 1995.

McQuire, Scott. "Immaterial Architectures: Urban Space and Electric Light." *Space and Culture* 8, no. 2 (May 2005): 126–40.

Montalvo, José R., Carlos de la Torre, and Luis Montané. *El cráneo de Antonio Maceo (Estudio antropológico)*. Havana: Imprenta Militar, 1900.

Montori, Arturo. "La educación: Fragmentos de una reseña histórico-crítica." In *El libro de Cuba*. Habana: n.p., 1925.

Moore, Robin D. *Nationalizing Blackness: Afrocubanismo and Artistic Revolution in Havana, 1920–1940*. Pittsburgh: University of Pittsburgh Press, 1997.

Morales y Morales, Vidal. *Iniciadores y primeros mártires de la Revolución cubana*. Havana: Avisador Comercial, 1901.

Musgrave, George C. *Under Three Flags in Cuba*. Boston: Little, Brown, 1899.

Naranjo Orovio, Consuelo. "Análisis histórico de la emigración española a Cuba, 1900–1959." *Revista de Indias*, no. 174 (1984).

Olmsted, Frederick Law, and S. B. Sutton, eds. *Civilizing American Cities: A Selection of Frederick Law Olmsted's Writings on City Landscape*. Cambridge, Mass.: MIT Press, 1979.

Ortiz, Fernando. "La crisis política cubana: Sus causas y remedios." *Revista Bimestre Cubana*, no. 14 (1919).

———. *La decadencia cubana*. Havana: Universal, 1924.

———. *La Virgen de la Caridad del Cobre: Historia y etnografía*. Compiled and edited, with a prologue, by José A. Matos Arévalo. Havana: Fundación Fernando Ortiz, 2008.

Pepper, Charles M. *To-morrow in Cuba*. New York: Harper & Brothers, 1899.

Pérez, Louis, Jr. "Between Baseball and Bullfighting: The Quest for a Nationality in Cuba, 1868–1898." *Journal of American History* 81, no. 2 (September 1994): 493–517.

———. *Cuba and the United States: Ties of Singular Intimacy.* Athens: University of Georgia Press, 1990.

———. *Cuba between Empires, 1878–1902.* Pittsburgh: University of Pittsburgh Press, 1983.

———. *Cuba: Between Reform and Revolution.* New York: Oxford University Press, 1988.

———. *Cuba under the Platt Amendment.* Pittsburgh: University of Pittsburgh Press, 1986.

———. "El diseño imperial: Política y pedagogía en el período de la ocupación de Cuba, 1899–1902." *Estudios Cubanos* 12, no. 2 (July 1982): 35–55.

———. "Identidad y nacionalidad: Las raíces del separatismo cubano, 1868–1898." *Revista del Centro de Investigaciones Históricas,* no. 9 (1997).

———. "The Imperial Design: Politics and Pedagogy in Occupied Cuba, 1899–1902." In *Essays on Cuban History,* edited by Louis Pérez Jr. Gainesville: University Press of Florida, 1995.

———. "Intervention and Collaboration: The Politics of Cuban Independence, 1898–1899." In *Essays on Cuban History,* edited by Louis Pérez Jr. Gainesville: University Press of Florida, 1995.

———. *On Becoming Cuban: Identity, Nationality, and Culture.* Chapel Hill: University of North Carolina Press, 1999.

———. *The War of 1898: The United States and Cuba in History and Historiography.* Chapel Hill: University of North Carolina Press, 1998.

Pérez de la Riva, Juan. *El barracón y otros ensayos.* Havana: Ciencias Sociales, 1975.

———. "Los recursos humanos de Cuba al comenzar el siglo: Inmigración, economía y nacionalidad (1899–1906)." *Anuario de Estudios Cubanos,* no. 1 (1975).

Pérez Guzmán, Francisco. *Herida profunda.* Havana: Unión, 1998.

Pérez Rivero, Manuel F. *Historia local de Pinar del Río.* Mimeograph, n.d.

Pichardo, Hortensia, ed. *Documentos para la historia de Cuba.* 4 vols. Havana: Ciencias Sociales, 1969.

Picó, Fernando. *Cada guaragüo: Galería de oficiales norteamericanos en Puerto Rico (1898–1899).* Río Piedras, P.R.: Huracán, 1998.

———. "Gente del 98." *Diálogo* [San Juan, P.R.], February 1997.

———. *La guerra después de la guerra.* Río Piedras, P.R.: Huracán, 1987.

Piedra Martel, Manuel. *Memorias de un mambí.* Havana: Editora del Consejo Nacional de Cultura, 1966.

Pino Santos, Oscar. "El acá y los otros 98: Un enfoque global." *Temas* [Havana], nos. 12–13 (1998).

———. *El asalto a Cuba por la oligarquía financiera yanqui.* Havana: Casa de las Américas, 1973.

Plana, Víctor. *Recuerdos del pasado (1898).* Havana: n.p., 1899.

Ponte y Domínguez, Francisco J. *Matanzas: Biografía de una provincia.* Havana: Academia de la Historia de Cuba/Siglo XX, 1959.

Portell Vilá, Herminio. *Los Estados Unidos contra Cuba libre.* Havana: Oficina del Historiador de la Ciudad, 1959.

————. *Historia de Cuba en sus relaciones con los Estados Unidos y España*. 4 vols. Havana: Jesús Montero, 1938–41.

————. "El superintendente Frye, creador de la escuela cubana." In *Los Estados Unidos contra Cuba libre*. Havana: Oficina del Historiador de la Ciudad, 1959.

Portuondo Zúñiga, Olga. "Marcos Maceo, el santiaguero." In *Visión múltiple de Antonio Maceo*, edited by Efraín Nadereau et al., 19–37. Santiago de Cuba: Oriente, 1998.

————. *La Virgen de la Caridad del Cobre: Símbolo de cubanía*. Santiago de Cuba: Oriente, 1995.

Poumier, María. *Apuntes sobre la vida cotidiana en Cuba en 1898*. Havana: Ciencias Sociales, 1975.

Poyo, Gerald E. *"With All, and for the Good of All": The Emergence of Popular Nationalism in the Cuban Communities of the United States, 1848–1898*. Durham, N.C.: Duke University Press, 1989.

Quintero Rivera, Ángel G. "Los modales y el cuerpo: 'El Carreño' y el análisis de la emergencia del orden civil en el Caribe." *Nómada* [San Juan, P.R.], no. 2 (1995).

————. *Patricios y plebeyos: Burgueses, hacendados, artesanos y obreros—Las relaciones de clase en el Puerto Rico del cambio de siglo*. San Juan, P.R.: Huracán, 1988.

————. *Salsa, sabor y control: Sociología de la música tropical*. Mexico City: Siglo XXI, 1998.

Rafael, Vicente L. "White Love: Surveillance and Nationalist Resistance in the U.S. Colonization of the Philippines." In *Cultures of United States Imperialism*, edited by Amy Kaplan and Donald Pease, 185–218. Durham, N.C.: Duke University Press, 1993.

Rama, Ángel. *La ciudad letrada*. Hanover, N.H.: Del Norte, 1984.

Ramos y Ramos, Facundo, and Carlos A. Martínez-Fortún y Foyo. *Cosas de Remedios*. Remedios: Luz, 1932.

Riaño San Marful, Pablo. *Gallos y toros en Cuba*. Colección Fuente Viva, 21. Havana: Fundación Fernando Ortiz, 2002.

Ricoeur, Paul. *Ideología utopía*. Compiled by George H. Taylor. Barcelona: Gedisa, 1993.

Riera, Mario. *Cuba política, 1899–1955*. Havana: Modelo, 1955.

Risquet, Juan Felipe. *Rectificaciones: La cuestión político-social en la Isla de Cuba*. Havana: América, 1900.

Robinson, Albert G. *Cuba and the Intervention*. New York: Longmans, Green, 1905.

Rodríguez, José Ignacio. *Estudio histórico sobre el origin, desenvolvimiento y manifestaciones prácticas de la idea de la anexión de la Isla de Cuba á los Estados Unidos de América*. Havana: Propaganda Literaria, 1900.

Rodríguez, Pedro Pablo. "Modernidad y 98 en Cuba: Alternativas y contradicciones." *Temas* [Havana], nos. 12–13 (1998).

Rodríguez, Rolando. *Cuba: La forja de una nación*. 2 vols. Havana: Ciencias Sociales, 1998.

Roig de Leuchsenring, Emilio. "Aventuras y peripecias de las estatuas de Isabel II que existieron en el Parque Central." *Arquitectura*, no. 108 (July 1942): 257.

————. *El libro de Cuba: Obra de propaganda nacional*. Havana: n.p., 1925.

————. *Los Estados Unidos contra Cuba republicana*. Havana: Oficina del Historiador de la Ciudad de La Habana, 1960.

———. *Historia de la Enmienda Platt: Una interpretación de la realidad cubana.* 2 vols. Havana: Oficina del Historiador de la Ciudad de La Habana, 1961.

———. *La lucha cubana por la República, contra la anexión y la Enmienda Platt, 1899–.* Colección Histórica Cubana y Americana, 8. Havana: Oficina del Historiador de la Ciudad de La Habana, 1952.

———. *Tradición antimperialista de nuestra historia.* Havana: Ciencias Sociales, 1977.

Rousseau, Pablo L., and Pablo Díaz de Villegas. *Memoria descriptiva, histórica y biográfica de Cienfuegos y de las fiestas del primer centenario de la fundación de la ciudad.* Havana: Siglo XX, 1920.

Ryan, Mary. "The American Parade: Representations of the Nineteenth-Century Social Order." In *The New Cultural History,* edited by Lynn Hunt, 131–54. Berkeley: University of California Press, 1989.

———. *Civil Wars: Democracy and Public Life in the American City during the Nineteenth Century.* Berkeley: University of California Press, 1997.

Said, Edward W. *Culture and Imperialism.* New York: Knopf, 1993.

Sánchez de Fuentes, Eduardo. Vol. 1 of *Cuba monumentaria estatuaria y epígrafica.* Havana: Solana, 1916.

Sanguily, Manuel. *Discursos y conferencias.* Havana: Rambla y Bouza, 1918.

———. "José de la Luz y Caballero." *Revista Pedagógica Cubana* 1, no. 2 (June 1900): 31.

Sanjenís, Avelino. *Memorias de la Revolución de 1895 por la independencia de Cuba.* Havana: Rambla y Bouza, 1913.

Sarachaga, Ignacio. *¡Arriba con el Himno! Revista política, joco-seria y bailable en un acto, cinco cuadros y apoteosis final.* In *Teatro bufo, siglo XIX: Antología,* edited by Rine Leal, 2:230. Havana: Editorial Arte y Literatura, 1975.

Scott, Rebecca J. *Degrees of Freedom: Louisiana and Cuba after Slavery.* Cambridge, Mass.: Belknap Press of Harvard University Press, 2005.

———. *La emancipación de los esclavos en Cuba: La transición al trabajo libre, 1860–1899.* Mexico City: Fondo de Cultura Económica, 1989.

———. "Reclamando la mula de Gregoria Quesada: El significado de la libertad en los valles de Arimao y del Caunao." *Islas e Imperios* [Cienfuegos, Cuba], no. 2 (Spring 1999).

———. "Relaciones de clase e ideologías raciales: Acción rural colectiva en Louisiana y Cuba, 1865–1912." *Historia Social* [Valencia, Spain], no. 22 (1995).

Souza, Benigno. *El generalísimo.* Havana: Trópico, 1936.

Stoler, Ann L., and Frederick Cooper. "Between Metropole and Colony: Rethinking a Research Agenda." In *Tensions of Empire: Colonial Culture in a Bourgeois World,* edited by Ann L. Stoler and Frederick Cooper, 1–58. Berkeley: University of California Press, 1997.

Stoner, K. Lynn. *From the House to the Streets: The Cuban Woman's Movement for Legal Reform, 1898–1940.* Durham, N.C.: Duke University Press, 1991.

Tamayo, Diego. "La vivienda en procomún (Casa de vecindad)." In *Tercera Conferencia Nacional de Beneficiencia y Corrección,* 23–31. Havana: Moderna Poesía, 1904.

Tejera, Diego Vicente. *Blancos y negros.* Havana: Patria, 1900.

Thompson, E. P. *The Making of the English Working Class.* London: V. Gollancz, 1963.

Universidad de La Habana. *Memoria anuario correspondiente al curso académico de 1900 a 1901*. Havana: M. Ruiz, 1900.

Universidad de La Habana, Escuela de Historia, Sección de Investigadores. *United Fruit Company: Un caso de dominio imperialista en Cuba*. Havana: Ciencias Sociales, 1976.

Vega Suñol, José. "La colonización norteamericana en el territorio nororiental de Cuba: 1898–1933." *Anales del Caribe* [Santiago de Cuba], no. 10 (1990).

Venegas Fornias, Carlos. "La arquitectura de la intervención (1889–1902)." In *Espacios, silencios y los sentidos de la libertad: Cuba entre 1878 y 1912*, edited by Fernando Martínez Heredia, Rebecca J. Scott, and Orlando F. García Martínez, 53–72. Havana: Unión, 2001.

Venegas Fornias, Carlos, Narciso G. Menocal, and Edward Shaw. "Havana between Two Centuries." *Journal of Decorative and Propaganda Arts* 22 (1996): 12–35.

Villanueva, Pelayo. *Colón: Hechos, personas y cosas de este pueblo que no deben ser olvidados al escribirse su historia*. 3 vols. Colón: Paltenghi, 1934.

Wade, Peter. *Blackness and Race Mixture: The Dynamics of Race Identity in Colombia*. Baltimore: John Hopkins University Press, 1993.

Waldstreicher, David. "Rites of Rebellion, Rites of Assent: Celebrations, Print Culture, and the Origins of American Nationalism." *Journal of American History* 82, no. 1 (June 1995): 36–61.

Williams, Joseph Roger. "Boston's Cuban Guests." *Donahue's Magazine*, August 1900, 137–38.

Yglesia, Teresita. *Cuba: Primera república, segunda ocupación*. Havana: Ciencias Sociales, 1976.

———. *El segundo ensayo de república*. Havana: Ciencias Sociales, 1980.

Zanetti, Oscar. *Comercio y poder: Relaciones hispano-norteamericanas en torno a 1898*. Havana: Casa de las Américas, 1998.

Zeuske, Michael. "1898: Cuba y el problema de la 'transición pactada'—Prolegómenos a una historia de la cultura política en Cuba (1880–1920)." In *La nación soñada: Cuba, Puerto Rico y Filipinas ante el 98*, edited by Consuelo Naranjo, Miguel Ángel Puig-Samper, and Luis Miguel García Mora, 131–47. Aranjuez: Doce Calles, 1996.

———. "Clientelas regionales, alianzas interraciales y poder nacional en torno a la 'Guerrita de agosto.'" *Islas e Imperios* [Barcelona], no. 2 (Spring 1999).

INDEX

Abakuá secret religious society, 138
Abreu, Eulogio, 162 (n. 81)
Abreu, Marta, 93–94
Academy of Sciences, 18
Acosta, Emilio, 52
Advertisements: of consumer goods from United States, 25; endorsements of products in, by independence leaders, 120; in English language, 9, 56, 66, 69, 163 (n. 2); for flags, 108, 119–20; government regulations on, 155 (n. 39); for hotels and restaurants, 95–96; illustrations for, 15; for patriotic objects, 119–20
Afro-Cuban culture: and Abakuá secret religious society, 138; and *danzón*, 4, 56–60, 62, 161 (n. 74); and drumming, 53, 59–60, 62, 138, 162 (nn. 79, 81); and Santería, 158 (n. 31), 159 (n. 45). *See also* Blacks
Aguilera, Francisco Vicente, 117
Alfonso XII (king of Spain), portrait of, 14
Almanacs, 29–33, 42–43
Alquízar, 89
Alsina Neto, Arturo, 152 (n. 7)
Álvarez Curbelo, Silvia, 34
American Book Company, 72–73
American Humane Association, 164–65 (n. 20)
Americanization of Cuba: and changes in place names, 87–99, 169 (n. 24); and conflicts of identity, 10–13, 25–26, 83–86; and consumer goods, 2, 5, 24–25; and English language, 1–2, 6, 65–83, 163 (nn. 1–2), 164 (n. 6); and modernization generally, 2–3, 5–6, 8–9, 11, 12; nongovernmental or philanthropic organizations influencing, 164–65 (n. 20); overview of, 1–2, 5; and public hygiene, 22–25; and schools, 16, 69–86; and separation of church and state, 37–38, 42;

and significance of everyday activities, 3–4, 9; and Statue of Liberty, 26, 27, 28; tension between Cuban nationalism and, 2–4, 8–9, 11, 77–78; and urban development, 2, 5, 18–22, 153 (n. 22); and U.S. celebrations, 33–36. *See also* United States; U.S. military occupation of Cuba
American Monthly Review of Reviews, 70
American Revolutionary War, 81
Amerindian tradition, 116–17
Anderson, Benedict, 7, 44, 128, 158–59 (n. 42)
Animals, 22–23
Appadurai, Arjun, 118
Appleton, Ginn, and Company, 72
Aragonés, Pedro, 81
Archibald, James F. J., 161 (n. 74)
Archives, Cuban, 17, 114
Archivo General de la Isla, 17
Arendt, Hannah, 150
Arimao, 107
Armas, Juan Ignacio de, 163 (n. 1)
Arredondo, Antonio, 143
Asociación de Maestros, Maestras y Manates de la Niñez Cubana (Association of Teachers and Supporters of Cuban Children), 76
Automobiles, 21, 24, 25

Bacardí y Moreau, Emilio, 116, 131
Banderas, Quintín, 109, 120, 121, 129, 130
Baptism, 42–44, 120
Bárbara, Santa, 159 (n. 45)
Barcia, María del Carmen, 170 (n. 15)
Barnada, Archbishop Francisco de Paula, 125
Barracks. *See* Military buildings
Barton, Clara, 76, 91, 98
Bartra, Roger, 104

133–34, 174 (n. 21); drumming, 53, 59–60, 62, 138, 162 (nn. 79, 81); and *guarachas*, 110, 133–34; and "Holguinero," 109; national anthem, 162–63 (n. 91); *son* and rumba, 60; and tension between Cuban nationalism and Americanization of Cuba generally, 9; on transfer of sovereignty to United States, 133–34; *zapateo*, 38. *See also* Dance

Mustelier, Father Luis, 144

La Nación, 61–62

Names of streets and businesses. *See* Place names

National anthem. *See* "Bayamesa"

National consciousness, 170 (n. 16)

National holidays (10 October and 24 February): celebration of, in Havana, 45, 47–48; celebration of, in Santiago de Cuba, 45; demonstrations and meetings for, 6; and local governments, 38, 46–47, 49–50, 52; and schools, 47–48, 111–12; struggle for, during U.S. military occupation, 38, 44–50, 52–53; and Wood, 46, 48, 49, 159 (n. 49)

Nationalism in Cuba: and Bartra on Mexican national identity, 104; and "Bayamesa," 1, 19, 44, 50, 55, 60–62, 80, 101, 109, 111–13, 125; beginnings of, 104–5; celebrations of, 5, 6, 7, 36–42, 44–50, 52–55, 62–63, 111–12, 127–38; and conflict over signs in Havana, 94–99; and conflicts of identity, 10–13, 25–26, 83–86; and construction of pantheon of heroes and martyrs, 20, 49, 125–26, 138–45; and *cubanía*, 3, 8, 41, 44, 64, 76, 82, 93, 99, 102, 128–29; of Cuban teachers in Harvard summer program, 80–83; in final months of colonial rule, 100–103; and "homogenization" trend, 141–42; and "imagined community of the nation," 7, 44, 64, 105, 128; information sources on, 8; and intellectual and political elites, 6–7, 98, 104–8; and monuments and plaques, 20, 25–28, 88, 127–29, 139, 141, 142, 143, 145–50; and museums, 14, 114–18; official version

of, 149–50; and oral tradition, 107–8; overview of, 3–9; and patriotic literature during U.S. military occupation, 108–13; and patriotic place names, 5, 89–94, 168 (n. 14), 168–69 (n. 20); and proposed new calendar following War of Independence, 31–32; and public ceremonies, 5, 6, 7; and public culture, 127–50; and sacred relics and patriotic merchandise, 118–26; and schools, 47–48, 111–12; and significance of everyday activities, 3–4, 9; and Spanish language, 83–86; and symbolic legacy of the wars, 104–8; and symbols, 6–7, 9, 100–126; tension between Americanization and, 2–4, 8–9, 11, 77–78; and transfer-of-sovereignty ceremony, 131–38; and underground newspapers, 95, 101–2, 108–9; and *Viva Cuba Libra*, 89, 101–3. *See also* National Party

National Library, 17

National Party, 38, 39, 47, 62, 83, 144

"National sentiment," 104

National University, 16

Navarrete, Florentino, 52

Negrito, 154 (n. 32)

Newspapers. *See* Underground newspapers; *and specific newspapers*

New York Herald, 77

New York Times, 66

New York Tribune, 72

Nuevitas, 76

El Nuevo País, 120

Núñez, Emilio, 13

Oberto y Zaldivar, Pancho, 39, 55

El Occidente, 67

Ochún, 158 (n. 31)

Oral tradition, 107–8

Oriente, 92

Our Lady of Charity of El Cobre, 40–42, 158 (nn. 31, 34)

Our Lady of Montserrat, 41

Pact of Zanjón, 106

Palacio de los Capitanes Generales, 17

Parades, 37, 45–46, 53, 55, 59–60, 62, 63, 64

literature and national identity, 108–13; and patriotic place names, 87–99; and sacred relics and patriotic merchandise, 118–26; socialization of, representing idea of country, 100–126; of star, 1, 36, 81, 102, 103, 106, 108, 109, 119, 132, 135, 136, 152 (n. 7); and symbolic legacy of the wars, 104–8; and *Viva Cuba Libra*, 89, 101–3

War of Independence. *See* Cuban War of
   Independence
Washington, George, 26, 35, 82, 113, 156
   (n. 15)
Weapons, 114–15, 116
Wedding ceremonies, 42–43, 62
Weyler, Valeriano, 61, 94, 168 (n. 13)
Wheeler, Joseph, 71
Williams, Joseph Roger, 80
Wilson, James H., 72, 156 (n. 15)
Women: clothing of, 121, 135–36;
   employment of, 2; and funeral rites
   for casualties of War of Independence,
   145; in Liberation Army, 167–68
   (n. 12); literacy of, 107; and patriotic
   celebrations, 134–36; as prostitutes,
101, 103; silver star worn by, 102; streets
   renamed for, 93–94; wife-mother image
   of, 93–94
Wood, Leonard: cartoon on, 24;
   correspondence of, 152 (n. 9); and
   funeral rites for Maceo, 129–31; and
   museums, 116, 117; and national
   holidays, 46, 48, 49, 159 (n. 49); and
   schools in Cuba, 74, 78, 112; street
   named for, 98; and teaching English in
   Cuban schools, 74, 78
Working class, 19, 20, 46, 100–103

Yoruba, 158 (n. 31), 159 (n. 45)

Zapateo music, 38